BECOMING FIERCE

Teen Stories IRL

FOREWORD BY SUSIN NIELSEN

Fierce Ink Press

Becoming Fierce: Teen Stories IRL

Published by Fierce Ink Press Co-op Ltd.
www.fierceinkpress.com

First edition, 2014

Library and Archives Canada Cataloguing in Publication information is available upon request.

ISBN-13: 978-1-927746-61-5 (paperback)

Foreword by Susin Nielsen
Edited by Allister Thompson
Cover design by Emma Dolan

Partial proceeds will be donated to:

KidsHelpPhone.ca
1800 668 6868

Kids Help Phone

TABLE OF CONTENTS

FOREWORD

There is no way around it. Sometimes being a teenager sucks, and sucks hard. You're going through so many changes, discovering yourself — all while often being mercilessly judged by your peers. Who, by the way, are going through the "same shit, different colour" — but that doesn't curb the cruelty of some.

I must come clean here: Sometimes I was on the receiving end of that cruelty. A few times, I doled it out. Doling it out felt better, but not by much. I still live with the shame of having periodically done hurtful things to people who, in that moment at least, seemed like an easy target — even though I had been, and would be again, the one with the bull's eye on my back. Maybe that's why I write for tweens and teens; maybe I am, in some small way, making amends for some past less than stellar behaviour.

The thing is, when you're in the thick of it, it's hard to imagine that things will get better. And yet the cross my heart, hope to die, stick a needle in my eye truth is: It does.

But don't take my word for it. Read the wonderful, heart-wrenching, devastating and sometimes laugh-out-loud funny stories in this anthology, written by Canadian authors of all backgrounds, about their own experiences growing up. The topics run the gamut, from bullying and self-image to sexuality and suicide. But while their circumstances vary, their stories prove that the trials and tribulations of growing up are universal. Read them knowing that each and every one of them came out the other end, and heck, look at them now — all successful published writers.

Read them and know that you are not alone.

The publishers are donating 20% of all sales of this book to a charity, and they kindly asked me to choose one. I've chosen Kids Help Phone, because there is always someone there to lend an ear at 1-800-668-6868, twenty-four/seven.

Now curl up in your favourite chair and enjoy the read. You'll laugh; you'll cry. And if you feel, as I sometimes did, that you are trapped in darkness, it's my hope that by reading these tales you'll catch a glimmer of the light at the end of the tunnel.

Susin Nielsen

SAY IT'S OKAY

by Benjamin Boudreau

"Do you hear them? Do you hear the wolves coming to get us?"

The words cut through the pitch-black basement, freezing my feet in place on the cold concrete floor.

"Ben? Do you hear them with the howlin' and the teeth that go like this?"

I didn't have to see him to know he was making a chomping motion in the dark. His hands would be clamped in front of his face, fingers interlocking like a piranha hand puppet. I had seen it many times before but it was far worse as my imagination filled in the details.

"Ben? Say it! Say, 'The wolves with the howlin' and the teeth that go like this!'"

Not good. Not good. Not good. Be calm. Stay calm. You're in charge.

"Pete? Where are you, buddy? Can you come to the sound of my voice?"

An underlying panic lingered in the air after every word. If there are people out there who can keep their cool while stuck in dark rooms with no exit strategy, I am certainly not one of them.

I felt seven years old again, paralyzed by fear at the top of the stairs leading up from my grandfather's basement, wishing my brother would stop holding the door shut from the other side. But this time I didn't know in what direction I'd even find the stairs, and I had to contend with a missing thirteen-year-old whispering about wolves.

The Baby-sitters Club did not prepare me for this.

* * *

My night with Pete had started like all the others.

As always, I crossed paths with his mom at the front door around six. She was on her way out to teach fitness classes. She told me she'd be back in a couple of hours and reminded me that her cell number was on the fridge. As always, the door made its usual *beep-beep* when it opened, and the same *beep-beep* as it closed.

As always, I dropped my backpack by the futon in the living room off the main hall and chatted with Pete's younger brother, Josh. He acted extra irritated at the interruption of his digital quest for global domination, so I acted extra irritating because I knew it bugged him, pointing all over the screen while he was trying to shoot aliens.

"What game are you playing? Are you winning? Who's that guy? Did you just die?"

As always, I tucked into some riveting required reading for my university classes and after a couple pages of *Writing Theory and Technique* waited to hear from the man himself.

"Beeeehhhn?"

He had a way of making my name stretch out over multiple syllables. Depending on his mood, it would come out sounding like a toddler lost in a museum at night: *Hellloooooo?* or a drill sergeant demanding to know why I was late for basic training. Either way, it was always music to my ears.

"Hey, Pete. What's new?"

"Say, 'It's okay.'"

"It's okay, Pete."

He'd respond with a goofy laugh and the signature drumline he always tapped with his open palm on his chest, and I'd listen as it grew fainter as he made his way back down the hallway. While I got through my reading, Pete would keep a busy schedule of spinning a yellow Duplo block on top of a purple Crayola marker as a makeshift axle.

Most nights Pete would breeze past the futon, pull a vintage wooden desk right in front of the television and watch the same two-minute clip of *Scooby-Doo 2: Monsters Unleashed* over and over. It was always the bit where the Scooby gang is falling apart before a triumphant victory. He'd watch, rewind, watch, rewind, and then start asking questions. It was as close to a game as we had.

"Is Freddie sad? Is Freddie going to scream and yell?"

"Freddie looks sad to me, Pete. I don't think he's going to scream or yell, though."

"Noooooo. Freddie is sad and is going to scream and yell. Say it."

"It doesn't look like it, buddy."

"'Freddie is sad with the screamin' and the yellin'.' Say it."

"We've been over this. No screamin', no yellin'."

He'd shoot me a confused look before changing the line of questioning.

"What does Shaggy say?"

"Come on, Scoob!"

While I could never master the vocal performance required for a convincing Shaggy — or Scooby, for that matter — Pete never minded. *Come on, Scoob* would instantly become the phrase of the night. He'd repeat it in between giggles, saying it along with the four-second clip until he got hungry.

"Does Ben want some soup?"

"Do you want soup, Pete?"

"Yes."

"What do you say?"

"I want some soup, PLEASE."

"Okay. Come on, Scoob," I'd say, trying to get a last laugh before we made our way to the kitchen. Even though the *please* was usually barked, I took it as emphasis rather than attitude.

By the time his soup was finished, his mom would be pulling in the driveway and I'd be singing along with Ashlee Simpson in the car on my way home.

But on this night our routine never got off the ground. The Scooby gang never fell apart, and they certainly never got their triumphant victory.

Before I even saw Pete, the house went dark. Looking out the living room window, I could see that the whole neighbourhood had lost power. The only light was the moon casting shadows of the trees between properties on the frosted road.

That meant no computer games for Josh, no Scooby-Doo or soup for Pete, and no reading light for me. One of those inconveniences worried me far more than the others.

"BEN!"

I could hear him thud down the stairs from his second-floor bedroom.

"It's okay, Pete!"

"Does Ben want the lights on?"

He was closer now. I could hear him frantically flipping light switches as he worked his way toward the living room. I tossed my book on the couch and jumped into the hall to block him at the front door. I could handle a power outage or a runner tonight, not both.

"Say, 'Pete, turn the lights on NOW.'"

There was enough light flooding in for me to see that his face was pressed up against the wall as he spoke. His fingers slowly moved the switches up and down as a moan began to form in the back of his throat.

"I know you want the lights on, Pete. We're just going to have to wait it out. They'll come on soon. It's okay."

"Ohhhhhhhhh no. The lights are gone. They're gone forever." He drew out the last word of his sentences before dropping down to a whisper, like he was telling the switches an important secret.

"The lights are not coming back. Ohhhh no. They're gone forever. Ben? Say, 'The lights are never coming back.' Say it. Say, 'Never coming back, gone forever!'"

I knew this didn't bode well for me. I was in for a long night. Pete was more upset than I had ever seen him. And the only words of comfort I could think of?

Ruh-roh...

* * *

I met Pete when he was seven, in my first days as a summer camp volunteer.

I was in junior high, uncomfortable in my own skin and already intimidated by the cool kid counsellors that I'd be working with for the next eight weeks.

The idea was to log hours at camps of all kinds — science, theatre, all the dreaded sports — and somehow come out on the other end as a *leader*, which I mistakenly took to mean I'd be like these high school jocks and teenaged dreams that all the campers worshipped like gods.

Instead, I spent my days being grilled by six- and seven-year-olds on why there were red dots all over my face, why my voice was so high, why I was so bad at soccer and why I didn't have a girlfriend. The real camp counsellors were Zac Efrons, and I was more of a bit part in an anti-bullying public service announcement.

Our camps were hosted out of a decrepit farmhouse. The white paint was cracked and peeling, the veranda was creaky with railings threatening to give out at the slightest pressure and the floor plan came complete with a *Blair Witch* basement.

The house overlooked an uneven field, a questionable swing set and red tube slide, a cracked tennis court without a net and a small sandy beach that met the lake.

The view of the water was what held the whole scene together. As parents dropped off their kids at 7:30 a.m., they'd look out from the sign-in sheet on the veranda and catch a final glimpse of the sun pulling up from the horizon. They probably thought about how lucky we were to spend our days there instead of being chained to cubicles, boardrooms and order counters.

Of course, we were subject to a different landscape.

The lawn was a minefield of divots perfectly sized to snag feet during a game of tag, the veranda would dole out splinters at an alarming rate, the tennis court was immediately deemed 'out of bounds' each day until we had the chance to remove unsavoury leave-behinds of the previous night's guests, and entering the lake was not recommended due to a generous population of surprisingly aggressive leeches.

The whole summer was just one big accident report but it never felt anything less than perfect.

As a teen, I wasn't the type to have a summer calendar filled with parties or road trips or beach dates. If left to make my own plans, the season would have been a haze of computer games and handheld pizza products. Even though I came home most days with fresh battle scars, it was nice to have something to come home from. So what if a lot of it was spent being simultaneously out-cooled both by people five years younger and older than me?

From week to week I sat in duck-duck-goose circles on the lawn, peered out from under the slide during hide-and-seek, fumbled a glue gun and got to know some pretty great kids. Each Monday we'd greet a mix of familiar faces and new arrivals, but there were only four or five campers who were there as consistently as the staff. One of those kids was Pete.

It didn't take long to notice him. He was always trotting around the grounds like a puppy that hadn't quite tamed all of its limbs, his legs and arms reverberating with each bounce. He was slight, with a blond bowl cut that spun back and forth in perfect formation as he gently shook his head from side to side.

Pete rarely interacted with the main group of kids and never joined in on planned activities. Instead, he'd parade around in what looked like a perfect mix of victory lap and scout mission.

"Who's that?"

"Oh. That's Pete," answered Trent, one of the counsellors. He had three seven-year-olds hanging off his arms as if he were a human jungle gym. "He's different. He kind of does his own thing. Stinky Pete — c'mere!"

Pete's head shot around in the distance, pausing for a moment before returning his focus to slicing through a patch of tall grass with a stick. Trent frowned. He never wanted to look anything less than a commanding authority figure in front of the group.

"Uh-oh, Pete. Is that a dog?" He turned to me and winked as the boy started running toward us. "He's afraid of dogs. It's the easiest way to get him to come when you need him."

"Ohhhhh, NO," I could hear the boy yell to himself as he flailed in distress. "You better run, Pete! He will bite you! Yes, he will bite you! Run, Pete, ruuuuun!"

He delivered these lines like they were rehearsed from a cheesy nineties movie, like he was just playing along with the gag. But as he got closer, there was real fear in his eyes. He cowered behind us, out of breath, and crouched low to the ground.

Trent put an arm over his shoulder and I could see the kid flinch at the touch.

"Do your numbers, buddy," he said, giving Pete little shake.

"onetwothreefourfivesixseveneightnineten." Pete rattled them off like one long word, keeping his gaze focused on the tall grass.

"And French?"

"undeuxtroisquatrescinqsixsepthuitneufdix."

"See? He's actually really smart." Trent turned his attention back to the other campers but Pete's head kept swivelling as he whispered reassurances to himself and stomped toward the house.

"Don't be afraid. It can't hurt you. It can't. You need to stop it. Grow up, Pete. Grow. Up."

Trent was already lining up the next challenge of Olympics Week, but I couldn't pull my gaze from the house, where Pete's face was pressed up against the windows on high alert.

* * *

Outside of on-demand counting performances, Pete only joined the rest of us for snack time.

He'd blow past the campers and counsellors eating on the veranda, ignoring high-five requests along the way, and rush into the house to find his bag. He'd emerge seconds later, shoving an entire Ziploc bag of Goldfish crackers into his mouth at once before tossing the empty plastic at Jane, his dedicated counsellor.

Jane was a good ten years older than the in-crowd camp leaders and was matched with Pete because of her experience working with special needs students throughout the year. As he wandered the property, she'd never be far behind, walking with a slight limp, symptomatic of a leg that didn't seem to be as long or bendy as the other.

Together, they didn't fit in with the rest of us. But more importantly, it was clear that 'fitting in' wasn't one of their priorities. They were a dynamic duo that seemed no more concerned with the rest of the campers than two blue jays soaring overhead. For this junior high misfit, their freedom was intoxicating.

The few times I'd see the two in conversation, it seemed like a secret code. I'd understand the words but never the meaning.

Most of the time, Pete would speak to no one in particular, shaking his hands for emphasis or sticking a finger in the air when making an important point. But a few times each hour, he'd freeze and call out, "Jane? Say, 'It's okay,'" and Jane would respond on cue with a simple, "It's okay, Pete."

When he wasn't speaking, I could hear him humming a constant beat, matching it with gentle taps on his chest. The kid had his own soundtrack; he actually did march to the beat of his own drum.

* * *

"Jane? Say, 'It's okay!'"

"Ben, can you run ahead and see what he's up to?"

Jane's lack of mobility sometimes kept her from matching Pete's pace around camp. This became my opportunity to spend more time learning about her work instead of embarrassing myself at basketball challenges or showcasing my inability to master even the simplest of crafts.

I jogged over to the bushes bordering the beach to report back and found him ankle deep in a pile of dirt. The black jeans, black T-shirt and black sneakers he wore every day were now a hazy shade of beige.

"Uhhhh ... he's kicking up sand clouds," I called out. "He looks like Pig-Pen from *Peanuts*..."

"PETE!"

Instantly, he stopped and turned to face me with a huge, toothy smile I had never seen before. Suppressing a returned grin was impossible. After weeks of looking through me, he had let me in on the joke and I couldn't help but laugh as Jane made it to the scene.

"Pete, you're filthy." She knocked some of the dust off the back of his shirt as he wriggled his arm free of her grip. "What am I going to do with you now?"

Stepping so close to me that our toes were practically touching, he looked toward my face with his head cocked and that devious smile. Eye contact wasn't part of Pete's repertoire but with a slight squint, I could tell he was trying to fake it for my benefit.

"Beeeehhhn? Saaaaaay … Itsokay." He spat out the last two words in a quick whisper, placing his hand on my arm and freezing in place as he waited for a response.

I had no idea he knew my name. I wasn't even sure he knew I existed.

There was no way I was squashing this breakthrough.

"It's okay, Pete!"

His smile doubled in size and his signature hum and tap started up again. He kept his hand on my arm and bounced up and down to the beat for a few notes before taking off again, leaving behind a cloud of dust like the roadrunner in a *Looney Tunes* cartoon.

"Nice one, kid. Have fun trying to cleaning him up before his mom gets here," Jane sighed, already turning in pursuit.

"Wait, what?"

"He played you." She chuckled a bit as she pulled me back from my delusions. "You just gave him the get-out-of-jail-free card."

"But you say *it's okay* all the time. I don't get it."

"When he's just doing his own thing — you know, just being Pete — *it's okay* is his way of checking in. When he's up to something, he's trying to get out of trouble. That's why you have to know what you're agreeing to before you go and say things that you shouldn't."

Perfect, I thought as I jogged a few steps to catch up to Jane. *Stellar volunteering, idiot.*

"Well, at least he likes you," she said.

We had caught up to him sitting in a swing. He was twirling the chains as tight as they'd go before releasing into a spin and shouting a cartoon-ish, "*Whoooaaaaaaaa!*"

"But this means we've got to get you up to speed before he has you wrapped around his finger." She grabbed the chains of his swing in between spins to keep him from getting too dizzy. "Pete, go grab your snack."

He took off, stumbling and laughing with every fall.

"So, what do you know about autism?"

* * *

"Does Ben want just this one on? Just this one? Say it!"

Even in the dark I could see Pete pointing at the light just over my shoulder as I stood with my back up against the front door. He was pressing his body into the corner, where the wall met the glass panel looking out over the step, careful to avoid touching me as I stood guard.

It was killing me that he thought I had the power to fix our problem and wouldn't after having been without electricity for half an hour. Worse still, as Pete got more and more frustrated, his bargaining turned to threats.

Finally, retreating from bolting distance of the door, he stormed into the living room and grabbed his brother by the arm.

"Does Pete hit Josh like this?" he said, faking a swat with his free hand. "Ohhhhh yes! Oh yes he will!"

"No, Pete. Let your brother go. Right now."

I tried to sound commanding, but nerves were starting to get to me. We were only thirty minutes into our stand-off and he was wearing me down.

"Does Pete punch a hole like this?" he asked, trading his grip on his brother for a closed fist that started thudding against the wall. "Ohhhhh yes! Oh yes he will!"

"Pete. Stop it." I tried getting into his personal space, hoping counter-intimidation might even the playing field. "I can't get the lights on for us. You're going to have to wait."

When his tactics failed, he shoved me aside and took off. Thankfully. Even with five years between us, we were about the same size and he was far stronger.

I heard the basement door slam, his feet hitting each of the steps on the way down, and then nothing. Thanks to the moonlight spilling in through the living room window, I spotted the silhouette of Josh still sitting comfortably in the computer chair.

"Josh? Are you okay?"

"Yeah. I'm fine." Josh seemed unfazed, clearly more experienced than I with this side of Pete. "He wasn't going to hit me anyway. I wasn't that afraid."

"Okay, good. You're such a trooper. Do you have a flashlight anywhere? I have to go after him and I won't be able to see a thing down there."

"None of them work anymore. He just turns them on and off until the batteries die."

"Perfect. Of course he does. Uhhhhhh ... new plan: you stay here and I'll be back."

"That's what people say in the scary movies before they get killed."

"That's very helpful, Josh. Thank you for being a constant source of support."

* * *

As I evolved from uncomfortable junior high kid to 'uncomfortable in new and completely unexpected ways' high school kid, I kept returning to spend my summers on the lake. A handful of us did. Together we went from youth volunteers to certified camp counsellors running the farm like our own rustic reality show family.

Summer Camp: The Next Generation, if you will.

We lived in a world that ran parallel to our school years, a loose spin-off that worried far less about whether I would turn out to be gay, that put far less value on the boys that did or didn't ask out my wonderful and beautiful co-counsellors, and that let us feel like it was okay to be good at the things we were good at doing.

Katie was incredible at building compassion among even the youngest campers, helping them understand each other's feelings and what it meant to be respectful. Leslie was a fearless role model as she showed kids it's okay to be confident in your own personal flavour of weird. And Zane, well, he was great at being a seven-foot-tall gladiator who kept the little jocks-to-be from going all *Lord of the Flies* on us. As for me? Well, in year two and three I was no better at the dreaded sports camps but it didn't matter as much when eight-year-old boys laughed as I scored on my own net. On year three and four, I was no better at making macaroni and glitter art but I *was* more comfortable declaring that my creations turned out precisely as I had intended.

But there was one thing I could do better than before, and better than all the other counsellors: I could work with Pete.

Each summer I would spend as much time as I could learning from Jane. I paid close attention to how she spoke to him, how she interpreted his key phrases and what separated them from having a good day or a really bad day. Both of which I had seen in abundance.

But more important than any research, I just felt more comfortable learning how to connect with one camper, even if he was a little more complicated, than I did building up the confidence to perform in front of dozens.

Through trial and error, his way of communicating slowly started making sense to me. The puzzle pieces were falling into place.

When he'd ask if *I* wanted to go outside, I knew he wanted me to give *him* permission to go outside. When he'd ask me about the *screamin' and the yellin'*, I knew he was making a joke about another camper who used to shriek — a phenomenon that Pete never failed to find hilarious. And when he'd say *don't let the bedbugs bite*, I knew we'd soon be desperate for end of day pick-up.

I knew Pete didn't appreciate these minor breakthroughs the way I did. But that was okay. I needed them more. We all need to feel good at something. We all need to feel like what we do matters. And from the time I was fifteen right up until twenty, Pete gave me enough to go on.

Every time he asked, *Ben? Say, it's okay*, I really believed my answer:

"It's okay, Pete."

* * *

"Pete? It's okay. Do you hear me? It's okay, okay?"

I spun my arms around me, trying to place myself in what I knew of the basement, but my eyes weren't adjusting. My sense of direction was shot after rushing into the darkness and my only reference point was the sound of Pete's voice as he let out a rising "Nooooooo" in response.

I had only been down there once in the year I had been spending a weekly evening with Pete. He had been upset that day too. A VHS tape he had replayed over and over had finally given up after years of suffering through the same ninety seconds. His mom had warned me when I arrived that it might be a tough visit, and she wasn't kidding.

"It's gone forever." He mourned his way through the house for hours. "Say it, Ben. Say, 'It's gone forever.'"

And maybe I shouldn't have, but I did say it. I said it because it *was* gone forever and there was no sense pretending otherwise. But that hadn't kept Pete from shutting the door of his bedroom and refusing to come out for most of the night until he opened the door, walked down to the basement and called my name.

I had sat halfway down the backless stairs as Pete pushed a plastic Fisher-Price tricycle around on the concrete floor. He stared at the circles the pedals made, keeping the pace slow at first before going as fast as possible. When he ran out of breath, he had turned the trike on its side and lay down next to it on the cool floor, using his hand to keep the pedals spinning.

It had taken time, but eventually he felt okay again. The wheels stopped spinning, his signature beat returned to his chest and he picked himself up.

But this time was different, and not just because of the power outage. Pete wasn't afraid of the lights being out, the basement or even the wolves he promised were coming to get us. He was frustrated. He was angry. He was trying to tell me something and I just wasn't getting it.

After five years of learning his code, I was completely in the dark.

"...the teeth that go like this, Ben? With the howlin' and the teeth that go like this? Say it. Please! Why won't you just say it?"

I knew I was letting him down. He saved *Why won't you just say it* for precisely those occasions. Our years of progress suddenly meant nothing and I was just a kid who had been winning on *Autism: Easy Mode* this whole time.

With no other ideas, I did what Pete would do. I got down on the cold concrete and waited for the wheels to stop spinning.

* * *

When I was eighteen, my family moved out of the home I grew up in, far away from the lake. I went from high school to university and decided that instead of spending another summer at camp I'd run off to Europe, as far as I could get from any lingering insecurities carried past graduation.

Within weeks I became immune to high school nostalgia. Within months, I started losing touch with best friends forever. Within a year, I was a completely different person. Except when I was with Pete.

Amid classes and midterms and job interviews, our routine — *Scooby-Doo* and all — was as much my comfort blanket as it was his, and through her sudden evolution into a single parent, it was an important relief for Pete's mom.

His dad and I were never close but it hurt that he left while I was away. It hurt because I knew Pete, Josh and their mom were hurting, because I wasn't there when they needed me and because there was nothing I could do to fix it. Like the lost VHS tape, all I could offer was help weathering the storm.

As we all got back into the swing of my visits, Pete's mom was incredible. She was working, smiling, strong and happy. Sure, I only saw her eight or ten hours out of the week, but let's face it, the fact that she could be so solid for even that was impressive.

Pete was still Pete. Spinning, tapping, soup-slurping, Scooby-watching Pete. He just didn't ask me to say *It's okay* as much anymore. Maybe he didn't want me to lie.

*   *   *

"Dad?"

"No, Pete. It's me. It's Ben."

He had been whispering about wolves in the darkness for so long that he must have forgotten I was there. It was hard to tell how much time we had spent in that basement together, but it must have been coming up on two hours.

"Is he coming back?"

"Who, Pete?"

"Is he gone forever?"

"Who?"

"Dad…" His whisper was little more than an exhale but the message was loud and clear.

"Do you miss your dad, Pete?"

"Yes."

"I'm sorry, buddy. Hopefully you'll get to see him soon though, right?"

"Does Ben want to see Dad? Does Ben want to go for a drive with Dad?"

"Soon, Pete. He's not gone forever. He's coming back."

Even Pete was quiet now. No more wolves, no more howling, no more teeth.

The spin of the tricycle pedal broke the silence and we sat there for a while longer.

*   *   *

As the house lurched with the sudden surge of electricity, my first sight was Pete barrelling up the stairs to the main floor.

I followed as soon as my eyes adjusted to the light, happy to be out of the basement, but happier to see Pete feeling better, to have made it past the barriers he put up that night.

Until I heard the *beep-beep* of the security system. He had bolted out the front door.

"Bennnnnn! Pete left."

"Yup. Got it. On it. Thanks, Josh." I sped past him, assuming he was okay given that he was already back on the computer.

Blowing through the open door, I crashed into Pete on the front step. He was staring at the illuminated light overhead with his right hand reaching slightly toward it. It was freezing. Pete was in his bare feet, I was in ankle socks.

"Ben? Say, 'He's coming back.'"

"He's coming back, Pete. Don't worry."

"Does Ben want this light to stay on forever?"

"Okay, Pete. We can leave the light on. It's okay."

"Say, 'It's okay.' Say, 'It's okay, we can leave the light on forever.'"

"It's okay, Pete, we can leave the light on forever. He'll know that you're home."

Pete turned to look at me, his hand still in the air. His eyes were tired and he had small concrete bits on his cheek from where his head had been resting on the floor. He mouthed a few words that I couldn't make out.

"What was that?"

"Ben?"

"Yeah, buddy?"

"Do you want soup?"

"I really, really do, Pete. Are you going to make it for me?"

"Nooooooo. Does Ben want soup? Say it."

"Do you want soup, Pete?"

"Yes."

"Alright. Come on, Scoob."

LOVE YOU LIKE SUICIDE

by Jo Treggiari

How should I write this?

In third person so it becomes just a story?

In second so that you can pretend you were there too?

In first, so that I can drown in a tidal wave of sorrow, sink under the weight of it, remember what it feels like to be utterly lost?

First person it is.

* * *

We cross the street to the corner store. As soon as we walk in, we are under the spotlight of her yellow glare. Even after all this time, it still makes me jumpy. I try and watch her without letting on. Most of the time she is as immobile as a great brown toad but I know she sees me seeing her. She draws my eyes as surely as the buzzing flies are drawn to the scrolls of sticky yellow paper that hang from the ceiling like gruesome Xmas decorations.

Today she wears a turban of bright floral cloth and a tight, stretchy mustard dress. Her immense bosom overflows from it, jutting from her skinny-legged frame and overflowing onto the counter in front of her like a sleeping cat. The guys around here are mesmerized by the sheer tonnage of her boobs, but that's not why all the white punks call her "Mama Jugs." She earned that neighbourhood nickname by being owner and booze nazi of Jugs Liquors. It's the only store of any kind for blocks around, sitting at the junction of San Pablo and Adeline, which separates the long, thin wedge of Emeryville from West Oakland. Our warehouse lies on the border between the two towns, and I like to joke that my bedroom loft is evenly divided. I can straddle Dogtown, so-called because of the packs of feral dogs that roam the streets (mostly trashed pit bulls or small ragged bait dogs that have escaped the fights somehow), and E-ville, aka Emeryville.

We hit the liquor store as soon as it opens at 8 a.m. for cheap beer and smokes. Mama Jugs sells single cigarettes for a dime, but you have to get in early or she'll have nothing left but menthols. Holly and I like the malt liquor that only the winos drink. Mama Jugs used to give us credit when we first moved in, let us settle up at the end of the week, but she got stiffed too many times. Now her fingers tap the counter until we slap the money down and then she counts it with a grimace as if we're trying to pull a scam. She never cards us, though, not like the other slightly classier liquor store up towards Berkeley. I have a fake ID that says I'm Donna Flores from San Leandro, age thirty-six, but thankfully I've never had to use it. Up close Mama Jugs smells of pot resin and her tongue is furred with mucus. She smokes fat joints rolled in cigar leaves. Her broad, deep-brown face is constructed of wide, doughy planes and her pupils are pinpricks in the bilious yellows of her eyes.

There aren't many white people around here, just us kids. Seventeen, eighteen years old and flushed with freedom, we don't care about fitting or blending in. We all speak loudly without saying a word. We are a tribe with our dyed hair and rags and big boots, and we think ourselves impervious to everything. The local folks must think we're crazy or lazy or both.

This is an old black neighbourhood going back for generations, founded on the shoulders of ship workers who came to work the Oakland docks. Miz Taylor, the old lady who lives over the fence in a tiny cottage, is one hundred years old and still has all her teeth. She proudly showed me the birthday card she received from President Reagan. On the other side of the chain-link, there's Henry. He comes over sometimes with his guitar and harmonica and smokes coke on funnels of aluminum foil with my housemates. Afterwards he plays the blues, music so dirty, so painful, it sounds like punk to me. I like him but I wouldn't be surprised if he robbed us if he ever got the chance. He always has something shady going on. Once it was a trunk full of cameras; another time, orange leather platform shoes.

I try to walk around without being noticed but I can't help attracting attention with my pink mohawk, black clothes and steel toes, and often I'm with Holly and we're both tall and arrogant. I struggle with wanting to observe from a distance and get in people's faces. It's an uneasy contradiction. Some days I feel as if I'm living under a magnifying glass with all my insides exposed.

The other girls in the punk scene drink sweet wine until they pass out on the street. For some reason this summer they've all taken to wearing short slips that show their tits and asses, with fishnet stockings and clunky, knee-high skinhead boots. They bum cigarettes from the vagrants outside the liquor store and get pissed off when the men call them cock-teases. No wonder the local pimp, Sweetmeat, actively tries to recruit us all. "Babycakes," he says, like he wants to eat us up. He exudes the acrid fumes of port wine and whiskey and leers and stands too close. He buys us cigarettes, flanked all the while by one of his sullen, bruised hookers, who's not so different from us, although she looks weary and grey.

We already have a 'pimp,' the older punk rocker who gave us free lines of meth until we were hooked and now keeps us short-leashed to him forever. He wants our devotion, not our bodies, and he has it. Since we started using regularly, Holly's skin is almost translucent and all my zits have cleared. My hips make a cage for my flat belly, which I admire when I lie down, and my legs look five feet long. We line up rails on a broken piece of mirror and drink vodka and OJ to calm the racing of our hearts. We hang out all night on the warehouse roof where we can spit on the johns who, on their way home from work, pick up the tranny hustlers, pulling the car over for a quick blowjob. Or we watch the college kids from Berkeley who come over to score weed and end up getting mugged. Up here in our castle in the sky.

* * *

Once, not long before the bad shit happened, Holly tossed a piece of masonry out her second-storey bedroom window at Sweetmeat's plush Cadillac parked on the road below and narrowly missed braining him. He chased us through the warren of winding, blind corridors until we lost him on top of the billboard scaffolding, which climbed high above the roof and extended over the freeway. She was always doing stupid things like that, but she was everything to me.

Up on the narrow planks, which spanned the space between both sides of the billboard, we could look out over the mudflats or up San Pablo Avenue towards West Berkeley or down the other way to Dogtown. I felt free up on the walkway. We could feel the scaffolding shudder and sway as if we were sailing across the sky on a great, groaning ship, and the air seemed cleaner up there, away from the grimy streets, which were tacky under the soles of our boots.

Our warehouse was called New Method because of the laundry it had once housed. The roof was still crowned with a large white and red-lettered plastic sign, though the company had gone out of business years before. New Method. New Meth. Pretty funny.

Sometimes we'd walk around the block past the chain-link lock-up for impounded cars, and I'd try and find a bit of nature — a live bug, a strip of grass free of cigarette butts. There weren't even trees embedded in circles of concrete here. The only relief was the sky above the uneven sagging rooftops and the concrete jumble of connecting freeway overpasses and underpasses looming over it all like a giant jungle gym. Frequently I'd find a discarded high-heeled pump or some other cheap plastic shoe, or a hank of thick wavy black hair. There was so much violence implied in these two things, especially paired as they often were. The hair was fake, at least — a crappy weave torn loose during some sex act. But the shoes. *How did she lose just the one shoe?* I always wondered and it made me sadder than anything else.

* * *

On a bike is the safest way to navigate around the neighbourhood, even though the two fat twin hookers down the block sometimes try to grab me as I cruise by. They wear matching outfits of cut-out Lycra that barely contain them. On a bike I can pretty much outrace anything or anyone — crackhead, hooker, cop, pimp, jock, dealer, thug, college boy. But not a pickup truck hurtling off the freeway ramp. Nope, not that.

* * *

It's so quiet I wonder if I've lost my hearing. When the cops show up I'm trying to jimmy my bike out from the hissing radiator of the truck, but I don't recall getting to my feet. My stockings are ripped and I can feel a trickle of blood running down my left leg from my knee to my ankle. I think the back of my head is bleeding too but I can't bring myself to touch it.

One of the cops leads me to the seat in the back of his squad car. "You hit the ground three times," he says, muffled as if speaking through a scarf. His hand slowly describes three circles, and I follow the motion with my eyes, feeling dizzy and sick. "Head over heels. Coulda died. Shoulda been wearing a helmet."

I had wondered how I ended up on my back about thirty feet down the road with my toes pointed towards the truck.

"The ambulance is on its way," he says.

I also wonder if he should have moved me but my tongue is too thick in my mouth to make words, and my ears still feel as if they're stuffed with cotton wool. An old black man sits in the back seat too. His pant leg is rolled up and he moans while massaging his knee. It takes me a while to realize this is the guy who ran the stop sign and ploughed into the truck. I feel a spurt of anger that they put us together in the same car. He wails and cries about being hurt but I can't see a scratch on him.

Outside, the Latino truck driver is repeating over and over again that it wasn't his fault. No one has asked me how I'm feeling, which is sick to my stomach and as if all the tendons in my body have been stretched to ten times their normal length. The blood from the cut on my leg is pooling inside my boot. I leave a wet smear on the brown Naugahyde seat, and when I feel the back of my thigh where my thick, black tights have torn my fingers come away red.

The paramedic has brawny arms covered in red hair. I think he has a Scottish accent. There's a lilt to his voice and he calls me lass. This calms me. He braces my neck, straps me onto a gurney, wraps my leg and tells me I have a slight head wound but no apparent concussion. He says I'm lucky.

"What's your name? Where do you live? Phone number?"

For some reason all I can remember is the address of my work and my name.

And Alejo. I'm worried about him, about letting him down. This was the day I was going to tell him that we could be together after all. I think about his toffee-coloured skin and beautiful face: short upper lip like a pillow and soft brown eyes. He has a mouth I want to feed on. He tastes of burnt sugar.

I answer the paramedic. I also ask him not to take me to Eastmont Hospital, which is where they automatically go, especially if they think you don't have health insurance. Eastmont is in East Oakland. I went there once after I knelt on an upholstery nail that had pushed out from the arm of a chair. I was so drunk I didn't notice until I pulled away and the blood spurted like a broken fountain pen. I had to stick my little finger in the hole until it clotted, like that little Dutch boy with the dam. The waiting room at the hospital was full of bleeding people, mostly gunshot wounds and stabbings, some domestic violence. Patients writhed and moaned on gurneys lining the walls.

All the colours, white mostly and red, seemed like extra-vivid splashes. Like someone with a paint can had gone crazy in there. I remember a gangly teenager wrapped in a torn sheet, his arm savaged by a pit bull. It looked more like a shark attack. "Hit that damn dog with a shovel at least twenty times before it would stay down," his mother said in an almost conversational tone. Another guy had his head turbaned in a blood-soaked towel. When he unwound it I saw a crown of glass shards embedded in his scalp and cheek.

"Kaiser Hospital, then?" the paramedic asks.

I nod and under the brace my neck screams as if the metal and straps are all that's keeping my head attached.

Kaiser is close by, up the same street my work is on. I have no insurance but I don't care. I can't bear the thought of lying immobile for hours at Eastmont surrounded by death and dying. There's death at Kaiser too but it's behind the doors of private rooms, and they're quicker with the painkillers.

I think of Alejo waiting for me to show up, believing I don't love him after all.

I spend hours at Kaiser being wheeled from corridor to corridor. No one really tells me anything. Someone comes and asks me for my personal information. I can remember most details now, enough to satisfy them. A police officer takes a statement, tells me that what remains of my bike is at the fire station. A nurse manipulates my neck and arms and legs, cuts away my tights, dresses the long wounds, and dabs an antibacterial ointment on the back of my scalp.

Nothing is broken. I was boneless when I flew through the air like a big black bird, and I feel boneless now. They give me two tablets of Vicodin and a paper cup of lukewarm water, and I stare at the fluorescent lights above my head. One flickers and eventually fizzles out. The long glass rod is clouded and smudged with black.

They move me from the gurney to a wheelchair and an orderly waits while I fill a prescription for sixty Vicodin and then again while I phone home (no answer) and then work. Mr. Harris, one of my record store customers, comes to get me in his old Cadillac. He is soft-spoken, well-dressed and paternal with a thin worm of a moustache. He hugs me and I sob quietly on the shoulder of his tweedy jacket. He smells of oranges.

I'm embarrassed when he insists on seeing me inside the front door of New Meth. It's been hot and sunny recently so the mould and mushrooms have dried up, but still the place smells dank and the fibreboard walls are stained with the remains of black spores and water damage. No one has taken the trash out for weeks. Instead it's heaped with the bikes under the stairs.

My boyfriend Billy Nitro isn't home, though I don't expect him to be. We argue all the time now — vicious physical fights. Lately he's been crashing at the band's rehearsal space. I try not to care but I still do a little bit. That old love needs to be carved out of me so that I can love Alejo completely.

When I first met Billy I thought about sucking his eyes right out of their sockets. They're like turquoise gum drops, too large for his face and too pretty for a boy. The only reason he doesn't look like a wimp is because they're offset by a square jaw.

Normally I don't date guys in bands. They're all cheaters, but I didn't know that then. Billy seemed different, though in hindsight I remember that he always had a girl or two in tow. He could carry on a conversation without talking to my chest and he kissed slow, but that wasn't what decided me. I made up my mind after I ended up crashing at his space in the warehouse. He fixed me up a bed on the floor, just a squashy pillow and a pile of mouldy-smelling blankets, and then he told me bedtime stories until I fell asleep.

I glance up the stairs, listening for any sound of movement. There is nothing. Marek must have crashed. Lately he's only up at night, when the sun can't hurt his speed-sensitive eyes.

Mr. Harris gives me another careful hug. He would stay but I mumble something and push him out the door. My body feels as if it's balanced on top of wooden legs. The room smells of unwashed laundry and stale air with rumpled sheets piled on the edge of the mattress where I left them. The phone sits close by on the floor. I've kept it next to the bed since the Holly argument, hoping she'll call. She hasn't and it's been months. I hear that she's been hanging out with Connie, but still I hope. In an ironic twist, Connie is the one my boyfriend is screwing on the side. Oh yeah, we are an incestuous bunch.

If Holly is hanging out with her, it's a much bigger betrayal than what Billy is doing. Holly doesn't usually like other girls, and she always said she hated Connie. It was always me and her, a tribe of two.

* * *

We first met outside a punk show we were having at New Meth. People around town had buzzed about her for a couple of weeks at least. *Oh, she's so cool, so tall, she's from somewhere down south, she wears leather gauntlets and rings with big chunky unpolished stones.* Blah, blah, blah. Consequently, she was the last person I wanted to meet.

We were like two strange dogs approaching one another. Sideways. No eye contact. Lips slightly curled back over our teeth. I tracked her coming from across the street by the liquor store. Watched her loose-limbed gait as she walked in front of a car, ignored the honking horn and squeal of brakes with that perfect lack of concern I aspired to. I was leaning against the fence, and as she got closer, I shifted my gaze to the ground as if there was something fascinating concealed among the butts and empty baggies.

She walked straight up to me. "Want a beer?" she said, pulling one from the bag she held under her jacket. I looked her in the face. She had round green eyes and a generous mouth, heavy, straight brows, long nose, every feature large and strong. It shouldn't have worked together but somehow it did, beautifully. Her hair was dark, buzzed short except for long bangs, and covered with a bandana. And she was wearing a beaten-up leather jacket just a little too big across the shoulders with no band names on it and no decoration save for a single row of metal studs along the bottom hem.

I reached my hand out and grabbed the beer. "Sure. Want a cigarette?"

After that day we were inseparable, but then she picked a fight over something stupid and I didn't back down, didn't apologize, didn't show up on her doorstep. Now so much time has gone by, I think we'll never fix it. It's like losing a limb.

Only one thing could fill a hole that big.

Let me tell you about the thing I love second only to Holly. Seriously.

Peanut butter, glass, sour apple, ice, stink-finger. So many flavours and I've had them all over the last two years and never shared my wealth with anyone until Holly. That's how much I loved her.

Let me tell you about my dealer Ted, and Holly's debut at the altar of speed.

Holly was hunched over the table, her mouth slightly open, green eyes glazed. I knew that expression well, had seen it reflected back at me when I leaned over my own mirror to cut lines. Ted tapped the razor across the glass surface of the table. Small shards of crystal shattered and spun, catching the light from partially blacked-out windows.

I drew my tongue over dry lips. Holly's breath hitched. I was a total fiend but pretended to be civilized, to be patient even though my gut was tied in knots and cramps ran up and down my calves. I leaned back, crossing my legs and admiring the thick soles of my new twenty-hole Doc Martens. I lit a cigarette. My hand didn't even shake, although my whole body felt as if a current ran through it. It was almost orgasmic.

Holly motioned for a smoke without moving her gaze. It was the first time she'd been let in through the door instead of having to wait for me outside, and she didn't know the ritual of it all. Didn't know that Ted would drag this out until I was screaming inside, until the sores in my nose broke open and bled, they wanted the drug so bad.

I chewed the inside of my cheek and the flesh felt raw. I'd seen Ted change his mind before, close up shop, kick everybody out just because someone looked at him wrong or had an annoying twitch, and I wouldn't risk that. I kicked Holly under the table, steel cap against fine shinbone, and her body barely jerked in response, she was so intent. Like a cat with a mouse.

My eyes drifted over the product on the table. It was glass —

Ted's own formula of crystal meth — brittle and sharp like tiny pronged daggers. He tweaked the recipe sometimes, added less of this pharmaceutical compound, more of that one. Each batch had its own nuances and flavours. He'd told me all the chemical formulas before but I couldn't care less. It was the end product I was interested in.

He was talking now — base temperatures and molecular structure. I nodded. I was willing to listen to his ramblings just as long as he didn't ask me to remember or contribute to the dialogue.

I'd been dropping by Ted's for over a year, and before that he was the shadowy figure behind the slightly more expensive prices I had been paying to his Hell's Angels dealers. First a flail-swinging biker guy who had been built like a brick wall and barely reached my shoulder. He'd ended up in a stand-off against a phalanx of FBI who'd finally got him after a few days' siege. Then a dippy hippie chick who'd weighed less than ninety pounds and could snort more than anyone I'd ever met, without losing her vague and effete dreaminess. I'd been forced to listen to the Grateful Dead and Jefferson Airplane without throttling her. Finally I'd been okayed through some lengthy and convoluted system of vetting and allowed to buy directly from Ted — a connoisseur, a gourmand.

He pushed the mirror in Holly's direction. "It doesn't mean anything if it doesn't hurt," she said, a massive smile curving her lips. A rail four inches long and as sinuous as an earthworm disappeared up her nose. I could see the tiny capillaries explode and flush at the edge of her eyeballs.

I took my turn. Glass wasn't my favourite — it tore up my nose and had too much chemical tang. But I preferred it to his stink-finger variety, which smelled musty and sour like rotten cheese and was so wet it clumped in the straw. This went down easily, almost too smooth until it reached the membranes of the throat where the ammoniac punch was so pungent it made me gag.

It's not like I ever turned it down. We'd take anything he had for us because he cooked it himself and he didn't add the filler some of the trailer park chemists did, anything that was lying around, it seemed. I'd heard some of the kids in Hunter's Point were using formaldehyde in all their drugs.

Ted's shit was as pure poison as you could get. You only had to look at him. He was the Keith Richards of crank: fifty-six, fifty-seven, with a craggy face like a sallow mudslide covered in six days of stubble, a mouthful of broken teeth and doleful eyes. His hands were always grimy with engine oil, and his front door was barricaded with engine parts from motorcycles and tiny sports cars, all Italian models, nothing but.

To get in you had to call first, then hope that if Ted answered and said "Okay" in his low-key grumble, he'd still remember issuing the invitation twenty minutes later — the time it took to scamper across town to the industrial wasteland he called home. There was a heavy steel door bolted at the first floor level of the concrete tower he lived in, no intercom, and the only way to get in was to throw pebbles up against the third-floor window until he heard you and sent his wraith-like girlfriend down to unbolt the door. She never said a word, though her eyes always looked hungry, and he never spoke to her either, though he was almost garrulous with me. I wondered if she was afraid of annoying him, losing her connection. She just sat there, arms wrapped around her spidery legs, and sucked up whatever he occasionally tossed in her direction. Often I'd be there for hours, shooting the shit with him, before I realized she was one of the indistinct shadows in the corner wedged up against the columns of textbooks and manuals.

So we'd take whatever, the heavy chemical stuff, the wet stuff, a variety that had brown crystal clusters in it and a faint scent of peanuts, another that smelled sour like green apple bubblegum, and the cheesy one that dripped down your throat for hours after you snorted it. We accepted it all and we were grateful because it was the best.

* * *

I rummage in the top dresser drawer for my razor and straw, clumsy in my painfully disjointed body. Most of a bottle of Captain Morgan spiced rum sits on top so I grab that too. It's hard getting onto the bed even though the mattress rests on a low platform on the floor. I half fall, bracing myself for the pain of impact, but once I'm horizontal it's all right. The mattress is lumpy but soft, and I immediately swig straight from the bottle, letting the juniper-flavoured alcohol wash over my tongue.

Then I take inventory: Vicodin, a little booze, half a smushed pack of cigarettes, four grams of very glassy, dry speed and an eighth of the stink-finger. I put everything within easy reach. I'm not sure how the speed will go down but I'm already feeling antsy from not having done any for over twelve hours. I snort up two clumpy lines, which arrow straight to my heart, then lie back feeling like my whole body is made up of wires and pain centres. Eventually the Vicodin and the rum get together and I lapse into a foggy sleep.

I dream that my limbs are heavy, swollen, the flesh ballooning out until I cannot move, as if I'm bound in rubber bands and can barely breathe. It's a recurring nightmare. Then I dream that Holly and I are bombing down the freeway in her old Dodge Dart.

The windows are down and it's a blazing hot day. We're drunk on Bacardi 151 washed down with warm Coke and I'm trying to cut lines on the worn cover of a hardcover book while she zigzags down the road, trying not to puke as the rum and Coke works its way back up my throat, trying not to lose the speed. I wake up breathless and sweaty, in acute pain from head to toe, missing her so much and hating her at the same time for being a stubborn selfish bitch who can't just pick up the phone and call me.

Getting to the bathroom is my biggest problem. I can totter to the sink but I can't haul myself up high enough to perch on the edge and pee. I pee in cans and empty them when the smell grows too ripe. The concrete sink is filmy yellow around the drain and no amount of bleach will remove the stain now. Shitting means having to get up the stairs and over to the other side of the warehouse. The first time I try it takes an hour and I'm trembling and sweating by the end of it. I come back down the stairs on my butt like a toddler and have to stop for multiple cigarettes until my hands and legs quit their shaking.

On other days I bump into Gunther, the tall, golden, German exchange student, an anomaly in this warehouse full of young punks and old drug addicts. He's visiting for the summer and staying with Ruth, a quiet, bespectacled art student who keeps to herself. Everyone wonders if they're having sex, if he's gay.

He insists on sunbathing up on the tar-paper roof, usually wearing tiny red Speedos. And he insists on carrying me up the stairs to the toilets. He smells of coconut oil and his shoulders are spotted with moles. His hair is so sun-bronzed it's almost green. I attempt not to look at the bulge in his swimming trunks but it's right there, pressed against my thigh.

I try to shit as little as possible. Luckily, a bonus side effect of speed is constipation.

Marek brings me booze and cigarettes and sits on the edge of the mattress smoking his stinky roll-ups that always leave flakes of tobacco on his lips. We talk about death a lot. He thinks our old housemate Paul went to the desert to drop acid and die, and he's probably right, but still I dream that Paul's coming back any day now, his dyed black dreadlocks snaking around his face like he's some kind of Greek god.

These are my days and they blend into each other. I try to stay in an altered state for as long as I can while my body mends itself. I sell Marek some of the stink-finger at a profit so he can keep me in hard alcohol and cigarettes. He feeds me cereal and artificially flavoured fruit juice, and brings me the small television from upstairs. After Vicodin and more rum, it doesn't matter what's on. I can stare at the snowstorm when the channels have gone off-air for hours, until those dancing white dots have imprinted on my eyeballs and they're all I see.

Eventually I make it upstairs to our kitchen. I eat a hot meal. I call into work. Kenny picks up. He's one of the inventory workers, the guy who trained me on the receiving dock. Sometimes I ride with him in his Beamer when we have to pick up lunch or something. He slouches, the seat reclined almost all the way back, one arm dangling negligently out the window, the other resting on the steering wheel. He steers with two fingers. He's got four huge speakers in the trunk and the souped-up stereo has the whole car vibrating and bouncing.

I'm the first and only woman to work in restocking and at the start the gangsta rap-loving guys from East Oakland couldn't handle it. They looked at my mohawk and my chains, my leopard-spotted mini-skirts and shit-kicking boots, and said, "Hell no." But Kenny, who likes Rick James and Prince too, talked them round.

He's large, with fat overlaying slabs of muscle, and meaty hands that can carry twenty cassette tapes at a time. In the heat of the summer, he wears cotton pyjamas and handkerchiefs knotted around his close-shaved head. John, our boss, started calling him 'The Sheik' and it stuck, but I always call him by his real name.

Kenny doesn't talk a whole lot but he sees everything and he can keep a secret. I tell him a little bit about my life and the rest he sniffs out like a German shepherd. Even he doesn't know about the drug habit, though. Hasn't noticed how many visits I pay to the bathroom, or the perpetual sniffles, or how I can stay up all night doing inventory and still be the first one there the next morning. Or how skinny I am becoming.

"You all right?" he asks. His deep voice is muffled as if he's covering the receiver.

"Yeah. I'm not coming back for a couple more weeks, though."

"I have to tell you something. It's bad."

"Oh yeah? Is John being an asshole?"

"Naw, no more than usual." He pauses. "The day after you got hit by the truck, someone shot and killed Alejo."

Execution-style: two bullets at close range to the back of the head. Only witness: his four-year-old nephew. There were whispers of mistaken identity. His older brother Eric, who helped him run the record shop, was rumoured to have been involved with a gang leader's wife.

There should be hot tears, like when my dog was hit by a car. I can feel them flooding into my pores, weighing me down, filling every inch of my body — which is so cold — but I can't get them out. Instead, they solidify into crystals like knives, killing me slowly from the inside.

The thing that remains with me is that in the space of twenty-four hours, Alejo died and I lived.

* * *

I think I've always had it in mind to kill myself. Eight years old: in eastern Canada where we used to live, I buried myself in a snowdrift and went to sleep. Ten years old: I concocted a brew of water and oleander flowers picked from the bushes growing all around my nana's house. It was so bitter I only managed a mouthful, which made me vomit for hours. Twelve years old: I sliced my wrists in the bathtub using my father's old-fashioned razor. I wasn't old enough to know I should be cutting along the length of the vein. Fifteen: I swallowed a bottle of Aspirin and had to have my stomach pumped after my roommate discovered me passed out on the bed. I'd been having such a lovely dream. My sixteenth birthday: I injected air into my arm using a hypodermic needle, but nothing happened, and later the same day to celebrate being one year older, I went on a drug binge that lasted a week.

But after Alejo's murder I don't try and kill myself. Instead I move out, dump Billy once and for all, and get my own apartment.

* * *

The new apartment is tiny. But it has hardwood floors and lots of shelves and Victorian-looking dark wood built-ins with latticed panes of glass. The bed tucks away during the day and rolls out on casters at night. I just love that.

I have hardly any furniture: a futon mattress, a trunk with all my record albums but no stereo, and a small coffee table. I'm used to eating standing up, anyway. The kitchen is small, with a sliver of counter-space, mini refrigerator and irregular walls that I hit my head on, but I'm on the third floor, up in the trees and level with the freeway to Berkeley. It's familiar like home to hear the constant whisper of cars and feel the breeze that comes down from the hills. There's a laundry room downstairs and a fenced backyard with straggly grass and concrete steps that smell of animal piss.

I bring my cats with me. There are four: Mama, Mars, Tuffy and Ralph. Two tabbies and two black. I tell the landlord that I only have two and count on not getting my deposit back. I also lie about my age and have Mr. Harris sign the reference letters.

The other tenants are a mix of students and artistic types. They all seem much older than me. Like they have purpose. They move in and move out regularly, leaving abandoned possessions in the dumpster outside or piled against the brick walls. I score a silky pink upholstered armchair that turns out to be infested with fleas, a small black and white television and the first three albums by NY punk pioneers The Dictators.

The neighbourhood is up and coming. There's a liquor store around the corner, an Eritrean restaurant (run by the same family as the store) that offers big plates of eggs and toast on Saturday mornings, along with spicy vegetarian stews and spongy pan breads, and an occult store where I pick up the Catholic candles I'm so fond of. I especially like Santa Barbara, who offers protection from the evil people who dwell in the shadows. I know a lot of those kinds of people.

The clerk is a surly man with a greasy ponytail, an array of silver rings on his thick fingers mostly incorporating a pentagram into the design, and a liking for really tight jeans. Jeans so tight he can't sit down, so he just perches on the edge of his stool. I figure he's into Crowley and sex-magic, like most warlocks trying to get laid. I know he belongs to OTO (the local witchy group) because my next-door neighbour, who goes by Lilith, told me that a lot of the members live in the building and the neighbourhood. She's sweet but kind of dumb, has wide-spaced brown eyes and jet black hair that appears to be natural. She always wears flowing red clothing and is usually clutching a chalice of doctored wine no matter what time of day. Recently the chalice was full of poppies and some kind of black paste. She let me have a sip. There was a weird medicinal aftertaste that wouldn't disappear until I had brushed my teeth three times. I sincerely hope she's not screwing the old guy from the occult shop.

I don't see anyone from New Method except for Marek. He comes over and we eat pizza and drink red wine, sitting on the floor. I give him a couple of quarter bags. It's a new variety: icy, sharp and it smells like rubbing alcohol. I don't like it much.

Marek's moved back to Hayward — a depressing collection of modular homes and strip malls — to live with his older brother. It's pretty miserable and the state is threatening to cut his SSI checks, which he gets monthly ever since he proved he's emotionally and psychologically incapable of holding down a job. Fucking Reagan.

"Have you seen her?" I ask Marek. 'Her' is always Holly. It hurts too much to say her name. I can't believe that someone I saw every day for three years has vanished so completely from my life. Not only that but we don't run into each other at shows, and none of the people we mutually know ever mention her. It's as if she's hiding from me.

He shakes his head.

* * *

Her boyfriend Shawn arrives on the front doorstep one sunny day soon after I move. I hear indecipherable shouting, then my name, and I heave up the window and lean out. He's standing wild-eyed on the front step. I don't want to buzz him up so I yell that I'm coming down.

It's only been three weeks since my accident and my bones feel less battered, but my legs are still black and purple from blood pooling under the skin. I'm wearing shorts, and when I get down all three flights of stairs and out the heavy front door, letting it latch behind me, Shawn stares at my injuries, his mouth working as if he doesn't have enough saliva to form words. "I didn't do that to you," he says finally, his voice thick with phlegm.

He's tweaking hard, I can tell. Paranoid and seeing webs of cause and effect everywhere, himself in the middle of them. Speed is a very selfish habit.

"What do you want?"

He mutters something dumb about wanting to see how I'm doing and then says, "It's dry out there. You holding anything?"

I ignore the request. "How's Holly?"

"We split up." He's hopping from foot to foot. His lips are chapped and it looks like he's been picking at them. "Bitch."

My hands curl into fists and I force them to relax. Shawn used to be a skinhead and just because he's sporting a couple of inches of hair now doesn't mean he's changed deep down. I've seen him and his boys jump a suburban weekend punk and grind the poor kid into the pavement.

"Try the Manor House," I say. I don't want to talk to him anymore.

The Manor House is the punk house across the street. It's pretty much trashed now and flanked by apartment buildings on one side and the arch of the freeway on the other, but it was once a rich person's home. It has a long ivy-covered porch and a big overgrown backyard with twenty-foot high persimmon trees that splatter soft fruit on the ground.

There are lots of these punk houses scattered around Oakland, vast brick Victorians with rotting foundations and mouldy carpeting, their porches filled with empty beer cans. There's always at least one party going on, kids skateboarding on homemade ramps or bands playing in the backyards and idiots drunk on Boone's Farm strawberry wine. The Manor House punks are always holding, though they don't use any of the dealers I know.

Sometimes I go over and watch bad sitcoms in their messy light-filled sitting room with its sloppy, sagging couches. If you look, there are cigarette burns like braille on everything.

*   *   *

I don't go back to work for a few weeks, long after my body has ceased its constant aching and creaking. Truth be told, I've been drunk for pretty much the whole time. It's booze I've turned to rather than my trusty standby. I'm trying to fog my brain, not tweak it. Drugs make me think too much. I'm going for an enveloping stupor, and most days I achieve it, but all good things come to an end.

I've been thinking about the random way things happen. How things change for no apparent reason. How everything is uncertain. The terrible weight of Billy gone. Holly as good as gone. Alejo dead. I'm alone for the first time in my life.

And for the first time I want some kind of a life.

I quit using speed. Easy to say, harder to do. Time blunts the stomach-twisting pain of getting clean, the memory of my hair falling out and my skin dulling, my teeth loose in my gums. The small wound in my nostril where I'd picked a raw scab and how long that took to heal. My fear that my septum was gnawed through by the drug, and the constant runny noses. The twitchiness, the nerves strung so tight I felt like screaming.

I flush my drugs and the plastic bags, pulling them from drawers, from inside rolled-up socks, taped underneath the mattress, inside the secret hidey-hole in the base of an Indonesian wooden cat, and the sugar can in the kitchen. I toss my razor, my mirror, my specially made straws — a length of Bic pen with the ink tube removed, heated with a pocket lighter and twirled until one end flared out like a trumpet — and I don't even feel a flicker of regret. I do have countless dreams for months afterward that I've missed one of my hiding places and stumble across a monster bag filled with white crystals sparkling like new-laid snow, but none of these dreams comes true, so I'm not tested.

I think of my drug dealer Ted and his morose eyes, long lantern-jawed face and oil-stained fingers. Cutting him loose after all this time is almost harder than letting the drugs go. I had courted and nurtured him for years, and I'm surprised to find out he considered me a friend. Marek brings little notes from him, covered in careful lines of chemical formulas as if Ted is sending me love letters in code. Finally, after a week, he stops calling and leaving sad messages begging me to come back. Maybe he's given up or has misplaced my number in one of his piles of papers, or maybe the memory of me has slipped from his Swiss cheese brain.

I miss Holly. I drive by her new place, the blue house above the liquor store, hoping to catch a glimpse of her. I never do but there's graffiti up around her neighbourhood and I recognize her scrawl and her rage.

* * *

Sometimes I sit on the floor in front of my windows and watch the street below. Yesterday it was the scrappy kids from down the block who normally hang out in front of the liquor store and give me sideways glances and occasionally spit on the ground an inch from my boots. They were beating a dead possum with sticks, kicking at it with their Air Jordans. It was long dead, its body just a piece of twisted leather and its face frozen in that piteous perplexed expression that roadkill often wears. Teeth locked in a grimace.

Sometimes I open the windows in the kitchen and let the air billow around the room. I listen to the cars whizzing past and remember how she and I used to sit fifty feet up on the billboard with cherry bombs and bottle rockets. How we lit the fuses and aimed them out over the freeway, half hoping and half fearing that we'd hit our targets, hear that gut-wrenching sound of metal impacting metal. Once, my rocket went through an open car window and another time Billy tossed one that hit my leg, leaving a bruise the size of a grapefruit on my calf.

Sometimes I watch the woman across the street. Her apartment windows look out onto mine. She never draws the curtains, although mine are often closed all day long. I'm always surprised at how people think they have privacy merely because they're perched forty feet off the ground. When I walk on the street my eyes are either directed upwards or downwards. I used to bump into telephone poles and trees frequently as a kid. This always angered my father and he would haul me off and hit me across the head with his forearm, as if I'd embarrassed him. But nothing of interest to me happens at eye level. I love to watch the birds free-wheeling. I lean backwards until I feel the weight of the sky, heavy but comforting against my body like a good, thick blanket.

I spy on the woman, not in a pervy way but because I find her fascinating. She practices a crazy kind of martial arts with a sword, and not some willowy fencing foil but a large sword with a wicked curved blade and a guard that extends over her wrist and arm. There's no furniture that I can see in the room and she uses the entire floor, moving from one side to the other, changing direction suddenly, holding dancer-like poses for long seconds, swinging that big sword around in graceful arcs.

I'm watching her and wondering if I should take up karate or boxing, something where I could learn to hit hard without breaking my bones, when someone knocks on my door. No one ever knocks on my door. Marek always calls from the BART station down the street and we usually meet on the front steps or at the liquor store. I'm reluctant to answer, but whoever it is pounds again, harder this time.

I look through the peephole. In the hallway is a young guy I don't know with a wide blue mohawk like a deep shag rug. Next to him is a girl I don't recognize at first, until with an intake of breath, which is so deep and so sharp that it hurts my chest, I realize it's Holly.

I open the door and she folds herself into my arms. She's shaved her head again, down to a quarter-inch of bleached blonde fuzz. Across the sharp ridges of skull above her temples the hair looks more like a shadow against the bone. Although she is my height, she tucks herself under my chin like a child and lets me draw her to the futon. The guy hangs around the doorway looking uncomfortable.

"I asked where she wanted to go and she said here, to you," he says.

"That's Pete," Holly whispers. He pulls a crumpled pack of smokes from his pocket, looks at me inquiringly, lights a match with a flick of his thumbnail, then moves out into the hallway.

"He's nice," she says.

She starts crying quietly.

I pat her, clumsily, stroking her hand. It's cold and clenched in mine. She is painfully thin. Her shoulders rise in spiny peaks.

"Baby," I murmur, "it's going to be okay." My fingers rub her like she's a cat. Her skin is dry and yellowed, like old paper, and her nostrils look raw, but her eyes are the same — moss green and shiny as wet stones—and her quivery smile too, the way her lip hitches on one side on the snaggle-tooth at the left edge of her mouth.

She tells me that she's been so depressed she borrowed a car the day before, drove it out to the Berkeley Marina, hooked up a rubber hose to the exhaust and left the motor running. Someone had called the cops and they'd taken her to the psychiatric hospital.

"Jimmy's gonna kill me. I left his car out there."

I make comforting noises. Mixed in with the horror of seeing how bad it has gotten is joy. I am so happy to have her with me again. I feel the holes filling in.

"And they just let you go?"

"I told them I didn't mean to do it."

"What are you going to do now? You can stay with me."

She shakes her head, reaches for my Marlboros on the coffee table, lights two and hands one to me as if it is a gift. She sucks hard on the cigarette. Her hand is still in mine. My fingers feel the knobs on her knuckles. Her hand is warmer now, the bluish tinge less pronounced.

I wait to hear what she will say.

"I have to get out of Oakland. Away from Shawn and Jimmy. My dealer, you know…" Her voice trails away and she takes another long drag. "I was thinking of going to stay with some old friends of my mom's near Santa Cruz. Old hippies."

She turns her head towards me, shifting so the bones of her spine ripple against my hand. I remember how after my abortion she'd stroked my back for hours and brought me socks for my freezing feet and a hot compress for my aching belly.

"I could come and visit you," I say, wanting to comfort her in some way but not knowing how. I'm lacking the mother gene she has. Whatever it is that makes her adopt every stray cat in the neighbourhood.

"Yes. Yes, you could."

Pete pokes his head in. "Gotta go to work," he mumbles. "Sorry."

Holly stands up. "I need to get my stuff out before Shawn gets back. He's been in Seattle visiting his mom." She squeezes my hand and smiles again. I don't want to let her hand go but I do.

"See you soon," she says, and they leave.

I watch them out the window. Pete's car is a beat-up Datsun in a virulent shade of green. Like the car I used to have before Billy smashed it up. Hell, maybe it's the same car. The passenger side door is dented and jammed. He puts his shoulder against it, works the handle and then holds it open while Holly gets in. I hear a clicking as the engine turns over before it finally catches. Pete has to rev the accelerator for a good five minutes before pulling away from the curb.

The exhaust fumes hang in the air for a long time.

* * *

We took a trip together once. Before she got hooked and when I could still pretend I didn't need it all the time.

It felt like an escape. We 'borrowed' Billy's car, a mammoth light blue station wagon, which barrelled down the road at seventy miles per hour propelled by its own mass.

Even though the sky was inky black and a stiff wind blew, we had all the windows down. I drove with my right hand wrapped in dirty Ace bandages. In the midst of a drunken fight with Billy after I'd found out that he was still banging Connie, I'd fallen into the tangle of bicycles under the stairs and Holly had fallen on top of me. I had two broken bones near the knuckles, weird bumps that twinged when I moved my hand.

Our friend Dolores hung out the window and whooped.

Marek had lent us a musty tent and two coolers all for the price of half a gram. We were on our way up the coast with no specific destination in mind, but I liked the idea of the sea. I used to go out to the Cliff House in San Francisco whenever I needed some time to myself, even though it involved a confusing series of buses and a lot of walking at the end of it. I'd perch on the edge of the old stone wall just above the height of the salty whip of the spray and look down into the tumult of blue-green water and foam. I'd watch the mewling gulls swoop low for scraps, the raccoons digging in the parking lot garbage cans and the gay men cruising the ruins of the old Sutro Baths.

We had twelve hits of acid with Tweety Bird printed on them, two cases of beer, some bananas and granola bars, and a good supply of Ted's prime stuff. Also three mildewed sleeping bags and a blanket.

Halfway across the Richmond-San Rafael Bridge the rain started pelting down. Dolores was soaked in seconds, her dark curls plastered against the strong bones of her skull. Holly took over the wheel because I couldn't see a thing and the big car was fishtailing all over the road. She wasn't scared of losing control, maybe because she was more used to driving, maybe because she had no fear, maybe because she was already drunk. I weighed another DUI for Holly against my anxiety and moved over on the seat to make room for her.

It was pitch black and there was fog behind the sheets of rain, but somehow she found her way. I knew we were there — wherever *there* was — when I felt the tires sink into sand and the car came to a halt with a weird groaning sigh.

It was all impenetrable darkness and silence beyond the windows, except for an occasional soft thump of wind, which shook the car frame.

Dolores climbed into the front seat and wedged herself in between us. She held six beer bottles between her fingers like a barmaid. We drank with the sleeping bags tucked around our legs, watching lightning flash and disappear into the black, starless sky.

We crashed in the back of the station wagon and in the morning woke to the smell of overripe bananas and salt, and the sound of the surf crashing just over the dunes. The storm had blown out, leaving the sky a pale, pearly grey. It was almost unbearably hot in the car from the heat of our bodies.

It took two hours to get the damn tent up. By the end Dolores was stumbling around, tripping over the guy ropes and drunk off her ass. One side of the hexagonal tent hung limply and I was left holding an extra bamboo cane and some anchors, but it looked steady enough.

We dropped acid, washing the hits — two apiece — down with more lukewarm beer.

The beach was light brown, like raw sugar or unprocessed speed, strewn with huge pieces of driftwood. Sand-smoothed logs lay scattered around like dinosaur bones, gigantic fossilized femurs, or bleached and battered church pews. I suddenly understood how someone could believe in God if they were on acid and looking at this great cathedral of sky and sea.

I kicked off my Converse high-tops. Dolores had taken off her boots. We were both wearing cut-off jeans. I wore a tank top and she had on some kind of fishnet number over a dingy white bra. We ran down to the ocean and went in up to our knees. We felt the sand slough away at our feet and the head-spinning drag of the tide. Small polished stones rolled between our toes as another wave picked us up and dropped us gently down.

"Come on," I shouted to Holly. She shook her head.

When the acid came on, it was in the best sense of the drug: slow and mellow without any of the strychnine kick. I felt warm in my skin.

Dolores splashed in the waves, spattered acid trails from the ends of her fingers. She had eyes like in those kitschy velvet paintings of children or like Disney animals — all iris and lashes. Her flesh was crème caramel. The water beaded on her smooth skin. I could see her huge aureoles like griddle cakes, and her nipples poked through the fishnet.

"Shit, your nipples are big," I said or maybe I just thought it. My brain jumped around like a frog. She started laughing, so maybe I had said it out loud or maybe she could read my mind. She looked more like a fertility goddess made out of cocoa now. We splashed each other, bobbed around like corks. A whiskery seal with melted chocolate eyes swam with us. I wasn't sure if it was really there or part of my trip. Last time we were up in Mono Lake, on hallucinogens, I talked for hours with a brontosaurus that turned out to be a stick poking out of the water.

"Come and swim with us," I yelled back to shore.

"Where there are seals there are sharks," Holly said. The acid didn't seem to be affecting her the same way. She was huddled up on one of the logs with a blanket around her shoulders. Dolores and I didn't feel the cold. The sea boiled and foamed and the smell was as fresh as lime juice, none of that sour, seaweedy tang.

We stumbled from the waves on unsteady legs. The suck, swallow, regurgitation of the sea was stronger, or I was weaker with my muscles drained away. I plopped down on the sand next to Holly, ran my fingers through the sand and admired the way it turned my hands into diamond-crusted gloves. I buried my feet in the warm sand and shivered with delight. My toes looked like cinnamon donut holes. Dolores skipped off down the beach, turning cartwheels and singing the Dead Kennedys at the top of her lungs.

I looked away from her and back to Holly. Her features were so still, she wasn't familiar to me. There were lines on her forehead and sloping down from the corners of her nose. I got a sudden image of how she would look when she was old.

"Hey," I said to her, wanting to see expression, movement, "what's going on with you?"

"Nothing. Nothing is going on. It's a wasted life." There was nothing light in her inflection, although this was an old joke of ours.

"Got drugs, got beer, got sun. What else is there?"

"Is that it?"

I thought of the holes that drugs didn't quite fill anymore but didn't say anything to her because I wasn't sure where she was going with it. My stuttering brain couldn't follow her.

"Besides, you also have your paintings and your poetry," she said.

"They're pretty shitty." I felt embarrassed. My paintings were brushed onto found wood and scraps of metal with house paint and melted wax, the colours subdued and dark. I'd been pretty drunk when I showed her my poetry, sentimental crap about death and silence and being lost. I could never find the right words. I could feel them burrowing into my organs like bugs, but they hid from me.

"But you have them. To get the poisons out."

She brushed her fingers against her chest. Sand rubbed off and glittered there like a gold collar around her neck.

"Well, you have stuff too." The acid robbed words from my mouth. My voice echoed in my ears and the light kept splintering.

She shook her head, leaving trails in the air that dizzied me. "Just you."

I wished I had more to give her.

Holly looked like she was carved from fine white wood. She watched the dunlins in their ivory and buff plumage as they twinkled over the sand in the wake of the waves, hunting for food. And I watched her, trying to find my friend in the statue she had become.

I have a photo of her from then — she was wearing a beret, a pair of cut-offs over long underwear. Her arms were clasped around her chest, knees tucked under her chin. Who knew what she was thinking about?

I asked her.

"I'm thinking what's the point?" Holly said. She laughed a little but it sounded wrong, like canned laughter on a sitcom. "God, I'm such a stereotype."

"Really?" I said. I was feeling exhilarated. I reminded her of the stash in the tent.

"Do a line?" I suggested. She shook her head.

"I'm tired. Bored. Empty." Her palm pressed against her chest as if she was trying to feel her heartbeat. I noticed thin silver lines on her wrists, strands of a spider's web. I'd never seen them before. How had I never seen them before?

"Um, yeah," I said, feeling helpless. The words were stuck somewhere under my ribcage. Used to be we'd feel the same about everything, but it crossed my mind that I didn't get what she was talking about.

"My brain is mush," I mumbled. "Wait until I come down."

She smiled at me, her crooked, sweet, sad smile where it looked like her lip was snagged on her tooth. There was a wealth of something in her eyes that I could not identify. It was beyond the physical. It had nothing to do with time and place or us or pain or boredom or drugs or anything else I could understand.

* * *

You know how sometimes you'll catch sight of a number from the corner of your eye, like your birth date on a digital clock or a license plate, or your grocery bill will add up to $6.66 or $13.33 or some other cool series of numbers? I always got a kick out of $6.66 — it kind of underscored my belief that I was evil.

The alarm clock by the side of my bed reads 7:44 a.m. And afterwards I remember thinking, wow, 7:44 a.m. on July fourth, well I'm sure as hell never going to forget that. I am actually asleep when the phone rings. Okay, not exactly asleep, more like passed out. I'd felt really lonely the night before so I watched an old Katherine Hepburn movie and drank a bottle of wine by myself. I'm pretty groggy when I answer the phone and when I glance at the digital alarm clock and see that it isn't even eight a.m., yet I am also kind of pissed off.

"What?" My voice has that gravelly before-the-first-cigarette-of-the-day quality.

I half expect a wrong number. No one I know gets up before noon unless they work, in which case they'd be on their way to their job and not calling me.

"Who the hell is this?" I rasp. I can hear breathing on the other end.

"Peter."

"Peter who?"

"I came over with Holly that time…" His voice kind of makes a hitching sound. I hear the popping strike of a match and then he inhales and exhales deeply a few times as if he is sucking really hard on his cigarette. I lean up on my elbow, more awake now.

"The guy with the blue mohawk?" I remember the way he lit his match with his thumbnail.

"Yeah."

I fumble a smoke out of the pack next to the bed.

"What?" I say again, but in a quieter voice.

"She's gone."

Immediately I know he means Holly. But what is he talking about?

"Gone where?" Christ, it's like pulling teeth.

"Gone."

And suddenly I know he means dead.

* * *

I guess she decided to do it that way because she was in an old A-frame house with exposed beams. Easy enough to sling a rope over one.

I lose my hearing for six months. Six months where I feel completely trapped in my own head. Years later I still won't be able to say her name without my throat closing up as if a hand is gripping it or a rope is pulled tight around it, won't be able say out loud, '*She hung herself.*'

* * *

I pour a bag of cat food into my cats' dishes, fill a big bowl of water and then close the kitchen door on them. I can't stand the thought of anyone or anything touching me. I can't go to work so I don't go. I tell Kenny that something bad has happened and I don't know when or if I'll be back. He tells me not to sweat it. He asks me no questions. I don't think I could force the words past the swelling in my throat anyway. Instead the words, all those words, like a storm, thunder inside my skull until I think I'll go crazy.

I drink and I smoke but I don't go out and score. I don't know why. Maybe it's just because I don't have the hook-up anymore. Maybe it's because speed sharpens everything, brings it into focus and makes you dwell on things. Tiny details, inconsequential events, stupid tedious projects — like when I covered the walls and the ceiling of a corner of my warehouse space with hundreds of sheets of tinfoil and then couldn't remember why I'd thought it was such a cool idea.

I'm terrified that this, the fact that Holly is really and truly gone forever, would be magnified with drugs to such a degree that it would encompass everything. It would swallow me and the apartment whole.

This horror I feel. This sticky black web that chokes me and wraps itself around my head so that I'm suffocating, and even though I can still see out of my eyes, I feel like I'm trapped and nobody on the outside notices a goddamn thing. No one sees that everything has changed now, and nothing matters. Nothing.

And I obsess. I think about our last conversations. When she sounded so optimistic. When she talked about going back to school. When she talked about breaking up with Shawn for good. When we talked about me coming down to visit her soon and she laughed at the thought of me staying in a hippie house with her mother's crazy Deadhead friends, eating granola and working in the vegetable garden.

She wasn't lying. I know it. I try to get into her head and figure out what changed. What made her phone Shawn and tell him to listen to her while she died?

Punks are unhappy and nihilistic and cynical and fucked-up and sometimes we are abused and sometimes we abuse others, but we rarely kill ourselves. Not outright. We do drugs and drink to excess and for me at least that was a slow form of suicide, but when you get right down to it, none of us really wants to die.

So Holly's successful suicide is a first. We never knew if Paul had managed to pull off his desert death, since all the cops did was list him as a missing person, and after we all left New Method his parents had no way of reaching us. I prefer to believe that he just had enough of the bullshit and disappeared off the grid and he's out there somewhere. Happy, even.

I can't talk about it. I can't talk about her but I need to be around people who knew her and remember us together. Part of the fear consuming me is the fear of forgetting. I need to remember everything about her. Everything she did, every expression, the things that only I knew about her and the things that others knew. Even those I need to steal and remake into my own memories so that then maybe it'll feel like she didn't die.

I go to punk parties and they seem really stupid to me. I sit and drink and stare at people with hate and contempt. Shawn, Marek, John, Dolores and even Billy stand nearby and keep everyone away. I overhear a girl talking about Holly and how sad she is now that she's gone. I've never seen her before. Shawn has to restrain me from ripping her head from her shoulders. Mohawk Mica whispers in her ear, and the girl looks at me with her mouth open, and I can't stand the pity in her eyes. People are whispering and it drives me crazy to think that Holly is gossip, that people who aren't good enough to have her name in their mouths talk about her, that she has been reduced to a vicarious thrill. It makes me want to kill.

Instead I throw my bottle against the wall and let the glass hit me as it ricochets back. I want to be sliced to pieces, but it just spatters against my skin. I pick up a piece and rip at my palm. This hardly makes a stir. I can still hear the words echoing in my ears.

They're talking about what kind of a friend would let her best friend die, and what kind of a person could drink a twelve pack of malt liquor, call her ex-boyfriend, then climb on a chair with a rope around her neck and step off. How could she be so wasted but so cruelly methodical at the same time? I'd like to believe she died quickly but I know she thrashed and panicked and she died scared and alone.

I don't ever hate her. I know she was desperate but I don't know why she did this to me. Left me to face the rest of my life without her.

* * *

I love Piedmont Cemetery. Holly used to tease me about how much time I spent there. I tried to take her once but she laughed and said I was too morbid hanging out with dead people.

It doesn't seem that way to me, though. I call it the safest park in Oakland. No pushers, no winos, no hookers, no scary gangbangers. It's empty of anyone and I can walk there from my apartment. Occasionally, I'll catch a glimpse of a gardener tending a flowerbed or hear the rumble of a truck, but mostly I have it all to myself: the winding paths, the views to the hills or the bay with the city wreathed in mist like some kind of fairy-tale kingdom. The rolling green — it's so green up here, it soothes my eyes.

There's a gigantic granite monument I climb up the hill to reach, out of breath, but I'm trying to quit smoking. And I sit up there and just gaze out, not focusing on anything, and sometimes, yes, I will have a quiet smoke because it's the perfect place for it and sometimes I'll have a little nip of whiskey. This is about the only place I can drink hard liquor. It just feels right after clambering up the steep steps. I've scratched our initials in the wall surrounding the plinth, using my penknife to etch the letters in over and over again as if we were lovers.

In the spring the algae that covers the pond is so thick it looks like an emerald carpet. There are painted turtles piggybacked on the old dock where they sunbathe. I come to the pond via the new part of the cemetery, past the mausoleums containing the bodies of Oakland's first families, past the huge magnolia dropping its brown tissue paper blossoms, and through the overgrown section of woodland where smooth old tombstones lie tumbled like loose teeth. Cherubs are missing their heads, their arms.

Holly is not buried here. She was cremated, her ashes blown over the ocean far to the south by a bunch of hippies in white robes, but I need a place to visit her.

There's a children's cemetery with the plastic pinwheels, balloons and sodden teddy bears, and the Chinese section where they burn hell bank notes and incense for the protection of the soul. I find smouldering scraps of the fake bills with the suave picture of the Devil sometimes and keep them for luck. There's my favourite wistful angel who sits with her wings curled behind her, head leaning on one hand. She looks like a real girl, like someone I could be friends with.

I adopt the gravesite and headstone of a kid who died two weeks before Holly. He was twenty years old, and his photograph is etched into the stone marker. He has laughing eyes, a mop of curls and a smiling mouth. Looks like a good guide for her. I figure she hadn't meant to do it. I can't believe that she would leave me on purpose. I think maybe this guy, who'd been killed in a hiking accident on Mount Fuji, will ease the way. Bring her to peace.

I have my favourite route. Up along the back path, behind the row of family tombs. We — Marek, Billy, this fanzine kid Rick from

Sacramento and I — broke into one of them once. Not really broke in, since someone had been there before us and smashed the half-circle window at the top of the door. We climbed in using the doorknob to get a foot up and then jumped down to a dusty marble floor.

There were four coffins, big slabs of polished rock balanced on more rock, and others shelved in the walls like books. One had a glass top, smeared with dust. It was hard to see inside it and I was actually beginning to feel spooked but the boys teased me until I took a look.

The body inside had hair like matted wool and skin like leather. The flesh around the mouth had pulled back over the teeth, showing the incisors, and around the eye sockets and cheekbones the yellowed skin looked melted and waxy. I thought it was a woman. It was wearing a dress and had a delicate gold ring on one shrunken, black-nailed finger. Billy and Rick joked around, talked of stealing the ring, kidding me about vampires and zombies. They argued in loud voices and slapped each other on the arms as boys do when they're nervous.

My flashlight beam bobbed around, picking out the years of dusty cobwebs, cigarette butts and some empty beer cans. When we finally climbed out, they tried to make me go last, even though I needed a boost up, there being no doorknob on the inside. For one heart-stopping moment I thought they would leave me trapped but Marek talked them out of it and laced his fingers together so I could make the jump up to the edge of the window.

* * *

I find I like being alone. I come here a few times a week, follow the familiar paths. I enjoy the sameness of it and how slowly my darkly clustered thoughts stop yammering at me. I begin to feel some sense of ownership almost, or maybe I start to feel as if I belong here.

My angel is always here, always looking off into the distance, the views not changing much from season to season. Spring and summer green mellow to russet and gold, fog rolls down from the Berkeley Hills, my turtles pile higgledy-piggledy by the pond. And there's my hawk. For a few months I've seen the same red-tailed hawk flying ahead of me along the woodland path. It stays close by, twenty yards or so ahead, and at the risk of sounding like some zonked-out hippie,

I am sure it is Holly. It is a certainty I feel in my gut or wherever such instinctual feelings dwell. I don't try and rationalize it or understand it, I just know it, and it gives me back the connection I feared was broken forever.

I'm happy. I kiss my angel on her smooth cheek, run my fingers along her polished stone shoulders. My hawk travels with me on the long winding loop back down to the row of mausoleums I call Dead Man's Curve. After that I lose sight of her, but I know she is somewhere close by, perched in one of the needle-straight pines.

I hear the growling before I see the dogs. Dogs aren't allowed in the cemetery but I'd met plenty of dog walkers early in the morning so I don't pay much attention. The low grumble continues, though, so I scan around and eventually find them — two muscular, short-haired dogs on the roof of one of the tombs.

They look like pit bulls but I figure they are tied up and their owner is nearby. I alter my course slightly, not wanting to piss them off any further, and cut across a lawn that takes me about thirty yards away from where they stand, motionless like gargoyles.

The moment I realize they aren't tied up is the moment they begin to run towards me, mouths open, teeth bared, fur bristling along the ridges of their spines. I hear a shout from somewhere below me, hear the honking of a car horn. A man yells, "Don't run! Don't run!"

My legs feel frozen in place. I look behind me for a tree to climb. Nothing close enough, nothing higher than a gravestone nearby. No heavy sticks lie on the ground. I am weaponless and the dogs are covering ground frighteningly fast. To my right I can see a worker's truck coming up the road, but there is no quick and direct route to where I stand, almost fainting with fear.

The truck has to wind its way slowly towards me. I can still hear the man yelling, still hear the horn blaring, but all my attention is on the dogs, now close enough for me to see their yellow eyes, the black lips pulled back from sharp teeth, the fur so short it is almost like coloured skin — one brindled, the other reddish gold — and the bundles of muscle propelling those compact bodies towards me.

They are coming at me at the same time, one slightly to the left, one slightly to the right, working as a team to bring me down. The horn blasts again but the man is still too far away. I see the dogs' leg muscles bunch as they leap at my face, jaws agape, teeth like small ivory daggers. I swear I can feel hot breath and the lash of steaming saliva against my cheeks, and then I shut my eyes.

The tearing pain does not come. When I crack my eyes open again the dogs are past where I stand rooted, hands limp, completely defenseless. I didn't even try to protect myself, but for some reason they had changed direction in mid-air, landing to each side of me and continuing down the hill. When the truck gets to me, the driver is sweaty and pale. He pushes me into the passenger seat with shaking hands. "Goddamn killers. Someone just dumped them here," he says.

He drives me down to the entrance gate. I wait in the truck while he goes into the office and calls animal control and the cops. Then he takes me a couple of blocks down Piedmont Avenue to where the coffee shops and boutiques begin and lets me out in front of the liquor store. I have just enough money on me for a small bottle of Jack.

"What'll happen to the dogs?" I ask.

"They'll probably shoot them," he says.

"But they didn't actually hurt me."

"Dogs like that, no one wants them. Better they should die now than later."

I stare at him, and it's as if Holly is suddenly there beside me. She would have risen to her full height, her eyes flashing like green fire, a crazy smile on her face and both middle fingers extended.

I straighten my back, square my shoulders, widen my stance. My lips curl away from my teeth, bared like the dogs' were.

How should I end this?

Not with a whimper.

CUISVE

by Chris Benjamin

My coordinator at Canadian Crossroads International warned me about what would happen next, but the wave of tropical heat overwhelmed me anyway. It was like the heat of a blanket when you have a fever, comforting at first, until the fever breaks, then suffocating. I staggered down the aircraft steps onto the steaming tarmac, my ears a ringing ache from the landings in Toronto then St. Lucia, my eyes still teary from my goodbye to Heather in Halifax.

"What a state you're in," Heather had said, her arm slipping around my waist and her shoulder supporting my armpit. This was our final goodbye. I didn't want her touch to feel so comfortable. I wanted her to shove me onto the plane, maybe spit at it as it took off, if she could reach that far. It would have been easier to leave that way.

But she wasn't mean, and cruelty never came naturally to her. Don't get me wrong — she took guff from no one. But she was a defender, not an aggressor. She perhaps saw no reason to hurt me, but it would have saved me several months of wishing I was back in icy Halifax with her instead of floating on my back in the Caribbean Sea with a beer resting on my belly.

There in the airport, all that had gone right and wrong with Heather and I seeped into the cracks between our bodies, and I reached the unspoken conclusion she had drawn months before: our relationship wouldn't survive these three months apart. We had been merely pretending it would. And since she was too kind to be cruel, that left me the job of creating an unpleasant departure. If indeed this was it, perhaps a little nastiness could minimize the longing for something we couldn't have anymore.

I had squinted down at her, wondering what a leading man from one of those old black-and-white movies might say to send his woman into an angered frenzy without quite making her hate him. I needed a line like that, but I couldn't think of one. I was too distracted by the way she looked — not her beauty, but her differences from the people around us.

Friends and family of other passengers had dressed in their Sunday best, perhaps wanting to leave behind the most flattering images of themselves in the minds of departing loved ones. Heather hadn't bothered, and I wouldn't have wanted her to. She wore black tear-away track pants with white stripes down the side. They were popular then and she'd fallen in love with the style, form-fitting yet comfortable, easy, quick and fun to rip off using the snaps on the sides. She always got lingering looks from the guys on campus, whatever she wore; her long, auburn hair had certainly drawn my eye to her face and over her shoulders and everywhere. Or maybe it was the curves of her body. But the campus guys had no idea they were looking at the daughter of a Bacchus biker outlaw, a girl who had withstood frequent punches from her mother and the rape attempt of an obese first cousin, had gone on to be her high school valedictorian, and could beat most guys in an arm wrestling match despite her thin arms. I'd dated her for two years before I realized she could probably kick my ass if I pissed her off enough.

And when the time for my trip to St. Lucia had finally arrived, she took me to the airport to say goodbye, and I had to make her angry without overdoing it. "I'm a distant kind of person," I said. It was the best shoving-off sentence I could think of at the time. They weren't mean words, exactly, but they did the job. The alternative would have been to break down completely and blubber like a fool. That was no way to start an adventure — my first foray into exotic, distant lands.

Heather shrugged and let go. I picked up my carry-on and headed to my gate, and she didn't bother to follow. After clearing security, I took a final look back and found no satisfaction in seeing tears mar her face.

* * *

Now I was in St. Lucia. My counterpart, Ben, smiled and bit his lower lip and strutted across the sweltering tarmac. "Danny DeVito coming," he said.

He meant his diminutive father, a cop named Mr. John who moved quickly toward us. He had a young, bright face, but unlike Ben, a tall and muscular twenty-one year old with his hair cut into a short fade, Mr. John was thin, wore dark-rimmed glasses and had a slight afro surrounding a little bald patch at the back. He reminded me more of the dad from *The Jeffersons* than Danny DeVito, and he and Ben had the same strut. Ben swore you could always identify a St. Lucian by that strut. An entourage of three beefy men — Ben's uncles — followed Mr. John. He came up to their shoulders. Mr. John reached up, shook Ben's hand and flashed a toothy grin. He then turned to me and shook my hand too, a competitive grip.

We followed him through customs and immigration. The customs officer took a cursory glance at our baggage and beamed at us before making an official proclamation on our fates. "On the good word of Mr. John, you may now enter our country," he said in the high English I would soon realize St. Lucians reserved for formalities and foreigners.

Ben had spent three months living with me near the subdivisions of Beaver Bank, my rural/suburban hometown of several thousand people, twenty minutes from Halifax. He'd been one of the only people there who wasn't white. He'd laughed when he told me that other black men in the sticks or in town would invariably give him a nod when they saw him. Whatever commonality they felt, Ben didn't reciprocate it. He nodded politely, but his brethren remained far away. He and I spent much of that summer hip-deep in the Sackville River, mildly electrocuting fish, stunning them long enough to tag them for a non-profit salmon conservation organization. Volunteer science.

Back home, Ben was a forester. We were counterparts in an environmental youth exchange paid for by the Government of Nova Scotia and Canadian Crossroads. I knew little about the environment and nothing about St. Lucia, but I was young and willing. In Nova Scotia Ben had paid his dues, becoming a "visible minority" for the first time in his life. Now it was my turn.

The exit from the immigration room led directly outside, and the heat enveloped me again. There was a welcoming party for Ben: old friends eager to update him on the previous three months, his niece Boom-Boom and nephew Hawk (they'd be in pre-school if they lived in Nova Scotia) climbing up his arms. He hoisted one up in each arm and spun them around until they squealed in fear and delight, then put them down and patted their bums. They shuffled off to their mother, Ben's sister, dizzy and satisfied. The men smiled and shared guttural laughs with him, taking turns shaking his hand. His mother was in the backseat of the car, an old white sedan. She reached up through the open window and hugged him.

Mr. John handed Ben a miniature bottle of Piton — St. Lucian lager — as Ben climbed into the car. I was given one as well.

Mr. John had just celebrated his twenty-fifth anniversary with a box of red wine and wasn't up for driving anymore. He told me to sit up front.

During Ben's time in Nova Scotia he had always sat in the back. Now he reached over the clutch with his Piton and we clinked bottles. "Welcome to St. Lucia," he said. "Where we're *really* free and no one starves, because every tree has its fruit."

* * *

When Ben arrived in Nova Scotia I'd asked him what he did for fun.

"Drink beer," he said.

The national profile that Canadian Crossroads had given me said Lucians weren't heavy drinkers. I'd also been told Lucians were deeply religious, but Ben hadn't set foot in a church in fourteen years. He was a father of two children by different mothers and was a lover of large women's bodies. He wanted to try everything he saw in Halifax stores and spent money freely — his own and mine. He ate everything he was given and more, and drank almost every day. His favourite topic of conversation was trees. We hit it off well. I had just quit a well-paying and somewhat enjoyable job in the city. I had left capitalism and all its rewards and follies behind and had a vague notion of healing Mother Earth. Ben, with all his love of material things, told me I'd made a good choice, that in St. Lucia I'd see how little money is needed to enjoy the good life.

In Beaver Bank, life was slow — save the noise of sewage installation on Beaver Bank Road and the steady ticking of my parents' cuckoo clock. But Ben never complained, even on the slowest nights when we rented movies my parents liked (and even though he had no interest in them because they lacked violence). He watched hours of television and played solitaire like a civil servant, tinkered on my brother's old piano and taught me the British-St. Lucian version of checkers, draughts, the rules of which kept shifting under my fingers. He went to bed early and woke up at 5 a.m. (We didn't work until nine thirty). On weekends we went driving, seeing the sights and listening to three cassettes: Paul Simon's *Graceland*, Tracy Chapman's *Crossroads* and *Bob Marley: Greatest Hits*. That was the extent of our overlapping musical tastes. Ben complained only about our work placement catching and tagging salmon and building structures to help them migrate. "Mad science," he called it. "Mad science" was Ben's catch-all phrase for human stupidity. What bothered him most about the work was that there was too much sitting around talking, making plans instead of being in the field, he said. He missed spending full days hiking through the rainforest.

His frustration turned to anger just once, when we almost got shot. We'd been surveying the river, which, if healthy, would change routes annually but always meander side to side. Sackville River runs straight through a military rifle range. That is, a rifle range had been constructed over it. Our supervisor had told us that they never fire in July. As a courtesy, we'd visited the chief of the range to tell him we'd be in the river.

"No worries," he said.

The moment we finished our survey one day, the distinct sound of gunfire echoed in our ears. We froze a moment before peeking up over the riverbank to see half a dozen young, armed riflemen. We crawled back upstream and climbed out, walked to the chief's office and asked what the hell was going on.

"Yuh, it was safe this morning," the chief said. "But it's not safe now."

"That's weird," our supervisor, Roger, said when we told him what had happened.

"It's fucking mad science!" Ben shouted, referring not to the military but rather to the whole process of mucking around in rivers getting shot at without a lot of planning — or at least not that they told us about. He'd had enough of Roger and his shoulder shrugging, as if a few bullets whizzing over our heads was no biggie.

Roger took a step back. "Easy," he said. "It's just a miscommunication."

"Tell that to my children when you send my corpse home."

* * *

Ben drove us from the airport, taking a brief detour through the countryside, where we stopped to visit his Uncle Dingo. In Dingo's yard, names were uttered at me at an unfathomable rate, and everyone but the veterinarian, Conrad, and Mr. John were named after animal species, or modified versions. Dog-face, Pussycat, Mutt, Python, Ratty. "Hello, they call me Ratty. It's a long story."

My head spun with the heat and the beer and my exhaustion from the flight and the emotional turmoil of leaving Heather and the speed with which new people shook my hand and disappeared back in the shadows. It was far from unpleasant. Canadian Crossroads had told us to expect a bout of euphoria on arrival, and it was hitting me hard. My ears buzzed and my fingertips tingled, but I hadn't no idea what to say to people. They looked at me expectantly, wanting clues about my homeland and my strange ways. Always one to resist categorization, I was afraid to speak, afraid to identify myself and equally afraid to offend.

Already I longed for Heather, who was merely a touch more extraverted than I but had a quiet charisma — she could hold a person's gaze and invite them beyond words to a place inside of her that was brave enough to be vulnerable. I tried not to think about her, instead focusing on smiling and nodding and laughing when everyone else did. I offered firm handshakes and high-fived the children. I wished we could stash the small talk and dance together, but I was a terrible dancer.

I noticed Ben's mother had a severe limp in both legs. She was a tall woman, a head taller than her husband despite being hunched over. Her posture and forced smile gave me the impression that she was in a great deal of pain, that whatever had hurt her legs left her in permanent shock and forced her to curl inward, a protective response. She wore a navy blue dress with white flowers on it. No one told me her name and she never spoke, but when I smiled at her she smiled back, with some effort it seemed, and ushered me into the house.

Dingo's house was small, Spanish style, with rounded plaster doorways. Wild cocks ran around the yard, chased by bone-rail skinny mutts as starved for attention as for food. Their eyes shone as if they had been crying and I wondered if they carried diseases that over-stimulated their canine tear ducts. I stank of them when I entered the house.

Dingo made a face. "You touch dem filthy mongrel, Chris?" He held an open Piton halfway toward me, hesitating as if afraid to spoil a good vintage. Boom-Boom and Hawk hid behind his legs, sneaking peeks and tucking their heads away as if my gaze might curse them if they were caught in it.

"I just gave a couple of them some scratches behind the ears."

"Don't do that. Dey mutts kill you soon as look you way."

I laughed, but he did not. "Sink is dere," he said, pointing to a vinyl curtain. "Come have beer when you clean."

I did as I was told, and when I emerged from the tiny bathroom for my prize, a cousin had arrived with a plastic half-jug of pale red liquid. He wore a ragged sleeveless shirt with the Lucian flag and near-evaporated shorts and spoke only in slurred patois. Every sentence he uttered inspired an explosion of laughter over the room, until he passed out on the floor.

Uncle Dingo kept the Pitons coming until he ran out about three hours later and then suggested we visit the rum shop. Ben and I joined him but Mr. and Mrs. John stayed behind with the kids, who looked asleep on their feet. So did the Johns, for that matter. We walked along the highway being serenaded by a double-forte insect symphony under stars that invaded my personal space beside a deep ditch. I fell in once, leaning away from a speeding car, and landed in a stream of foul black goop with my heart exploding in my chest. Surely Ben and Dingo had been smoked by the car and I'd be alone to find my way back and break the bad news to the rest of the family. But no, they were fine. They laughed and hauled me out. I exhaled and tried to make it sound like laughter to hide my terror at what they seemed to consider normal traffic. I caught my breath and walked on with them, my heart still pounding so hard I could hear it.

The rum shop was down a dirt road right off the highway, an open-faced shack with a bar and five stools. Two men sitting on the middle stools shoved over and stared at me. "A white man and two black men," one of the men said, laughing maniacally, half bemused and half annoyed, as if a pig had just flown over us and shat on the hood of someone's car.

George Jones' greatest hits blared from a small speaker, shaking it and distorting George's baritone. Dingo sat on the middle stool and ordered three rum and Cokes. Ben and I joined him at either side. The Coke was mere colouring. The rum's sweetness burned and singed the Piton already in my belly.

"Come visit me any time, Chris," Dingo said. "You friends and family must come to St. Lucia. What you tink of my country?"

I thought of Ben's thin family and Dingo's plaster home, the fowl and mutts and palm trees. "Different," I said.

Dingo looked taken aback for a moment and then laughed from the diaphragm, as if trained.

"It's beautiful here. Good beer," I added.

He nodded. "When you family come dey must stay with me, Chris."

I nodded: of course they would. After my head rolled forward on the initial nod, it seemed to gain its own momentum and I couldn't stop nodding, couldn't agree with this man emphatically enough.

"I love my country," he said.

"Wonderful," I said.

"But I tell you, at forty-eight, next year dey have to arrest me."

"Yes," I said. His words sank in then, and with all my focus I managed to stop nodding.

Dingo laughed. "From my sixteen birthday I work like a dog, until last year. I work up in dat factory, brewing Piton. Then I get sacked. So I go in business for me myself. I call de bastards at Social Insurance Policy and say to dem, 'I want keep making my payment so I get my money when I retire.' And the motherfuckers say no! So I never see no of my money and dey go put me in jail because I go Castries and take care those bastards."

I laughed but Dingo did not.

"In England, U.S., Canada. Dey have system take care of dey entrepreneurs. You pay in, you get benefits," he said.

I told him I had already paid thousands into Canada's system, working part-time and summer jobs, and didn't expect to get anything back. "Program'll be cut by the time *I'm* old," I said. And I told him about unemployment insurance, all the money pooled into it that never goes out.

Dingo nodded, apparently satisfied with international commiseration.

* * *

I became indestructible on the winding ride to Monier, in the north of the island. Cars headed toward hundred-click collisions and then mutually veered left a few metres away from one another. I closed my eyes the first couple dozen times until I finally realized the system worked reasonably well. I then watched in fascination as we approached each oncoming car with ferocious speed. Ben passed slower cars on the laneless road, the deep ditches ever-threatening, but never spoiling my good time.

The heat, the semi-cool breeze through high-speed windows, the alcohol, the banana, mango, plum and palm trees flying by. Those flirting stars. Mr. John's drunken chatter in the back and the country and western wailing from the tape deck convinced me I was safe from incidents like those we passed: the truck wrapped around a telephone pole and the four-car pile-up, the cops, Mr. John nodding and waving to his colleagues — them seeing his glazed eyes and nodding back as we passed, having slowed for a moment. That kind of accident couldn't happen to me. I didn't belong here, wasn't part of it. I was merely on a roller coaster ride at Canada's Wonderland, like last year with Heather, only more thrilling. She'd be glad to know I was having such fun, letting loose a little.

But it was more than that. It was gliding down a paved volcano, twenty steep hills adjoined by hairpin turns, toward a dancing array of lights and houses swirled into a small but bustling metropolis: Castries. The population wasn't much greater than Sackville, Nova Scotia, but it was dense, a maelstrom of people and buildings with cruise ships the size of skyscrapers looking on from the harbour. The bustle of cities always got me going, like a sweet madness was about to settle in on me, and I'd go wild with joy, kissing strangers and doing handstands in the street. It never quite happened that way, but that's why anticipation is such a beautiful prelude to disappointment. I was certain this time would be different. This city, in a new country, would be a chunk of paradise.

Ben's house was just beyond the city. It was small and sparkling clean. The inside was all white-tiled walls and linoleum floors. A framed picture of Mr. John with Nelson Mandela adorned the wall. Mandela had signed it. "Pops was guarding the prime minister when Mandela come," Ben said.

I was shown to a small room with cracked, peach-coloured concrete walls and no lights and told to make myself at home. There was no furniture other than a twin-sized bed with a wool bedspread that felt like a well-worn area rug. No bookshelves or bureau. I'd be living out of my suitcase. But there was a window with slatted, horizontal panes. The glass didn't close and the lizards and mosquitoes found their way in and out. I don't know what I expected, but I was surprised — and glad — there was no malaria in St. Lucia. Just the occasional mosquito startling me with its chainsaw buzz in my ear. My heart sank a little, though. I'd hoped Ben's family would have books. I hadn't brought many from home, not wanting the added weight.

Ben handed me a phone and said I should call home to tell them I was safe. I took it off the receiver with thoughts of calling Heather instead, but the line was dead, disconnected. Ben shrugged. "Might work tomorrow," he said.

I put the phone back in the cradle, already coming down from my initial Lucian high.

"Come, we ride," Ben said, as if to change the subject.

I forced my eyes to stay open and realized I was ravenous. Ben drove me around for a while, checking in with his people on the block, getting the story on a friend who stood accused of shooting a man to death. Every household gave me a bottle of beer, which I politely drank despite already feeling hung over and wanting only food. We picked up Ben's girlfriend, Jennie, and went to the Triangle, an outdoor bar and concert venue, to watch a soca band. Ben bought me fish, salad, rice, macaroni, potatoes and several things I didn't recognize. I washed it all down with another Piton.

"Come shoot pools," Ben said.

I looked up at the bright stars and wondered if they were permanent; if this night would last forever, in this place so unlike my home. We left the Triangle to hit another bar called Waves, which faced the sea and had no front wall. We drove, played pool, ate, danced, drank, swam, ate, drove, ate and drank. Every time I finished a miniature beer, another appeared in my hand.

"What time is it?" I asked eventually, knowing no one would answer.

Ben showed me his watch. It said 9 p.m., which was impossible. It had to be way past midnight. The second hand wasn't moving. "Your watch stopped," I said.

Ben shrugged, just as he had when the phone didn't work. "We go now back to Triangle," he said. "We see Canadians there."

Rain fell harmlessly on the pavilion while we danced. Somehow I wound up in a corner with the other Canadians, who were on six-month internships. They raved about the St. Lucian *joie de vivre*, the beauty of the island and the unsurpassed quality of its marijuana, and complained as enthusiastically about the lack of good coffee and the laziness and general disorganization of its people, the inefficiency of its systems. These were dangerous attitudes to encounter on my first night there. I needed an unbiased experience, or at leased one biased by Ben and his friends and family. These Canadians weren't my people anymore than the Africadians in Nova Scotia had been Ben's people. The euphoria I'd experienced on arrival — which Canadian Crossroads said usually lasts a week — had already been replaced by panic. I was utterly alone here, a stranger at a three-month party I couldn't leave.

All the Lucians were waving and smiling at the other Canadians and me, inviting us to Shamrock's for karaoke, where they sang "Let it Be" with half the words improvised: "shrieking her own wisdom, let it be."

* * *

At Ben's house there was a bathroom with a toilet, but no shower or sink. We washed at a tap attached to the outside of the house. The water came in brief, weak spurts. Back inside, wanting a shave, there were no mirrors in sight. How typical was this lack of amenities? I didn't ask, didn't want to offend a poor, if well-connected family. Regardless, I wished I could grow a real beard. In the absence of a shaving mirror I was either stuck with the sparse patches of hair scattered across my face or I could risk slicing a jugular vein. I went with the sparse patches.

I wondered if maybe these conditions were temporary. No one

had told me to expect them, despite my ample orientation on culture shock. I was warned about travellers' diarrhea. Inevitable, I was told. Avoid too much alcohol. Stick with home cooking and make sure the food isn't sitting around in the heat all day, the exchange package said. Well, I'd already failed to heed those warnings. But the package hadn't mentioned the lack of sinks and water, the inability to wash my hands after multiple bowel movements. Nor had it mentioned three-year-old Boom-Boom's fixation with me. I asked Ben why Boom-Boom didn't live with her parents, but after raving about St. Lucia his whole time in Nova Scotia he'd begun dismissing all my questions with the same pat answer. "That's St. Lucia." It made no sense to me, but regardless, Boom-Boom was a fixture and she loved snuggling with her grandmother and pestering Ben, climbing on him like a jungle gym whenever she saw him. I hadn't expected a toddler, still in diapers, following me around, watching me eat, watching me through the curtain — which served as a bathroom door — while I defecated. Had it not been for the creepy bathroom-watching, I would have loved her attention, would have tried tickling her or making funny faces at her. That's what I should have done, anyway, but I didn't have much experience with kids and whenever I *did* smile at her she ran away in terror.

They also didn't tell me about the tear-inducing fever. They said I'd be homesick. They said everybody gets homesick after the initial euphoria wears off, but I hadn't believed them. Being of an age when I still believed myself emotionally and physically indestructible, I couldn't wait to ramble around the world outside Nova Scotia, and this trip was to be the beginning. I'd heard plenty of songs about ramblers and gamblers and none of them ever got homesick until they lay down upon their deathbeds. How quickly dysentery knocked me from my horse so that I clung to my rough woollen blanket, scratching as it made me itch, wishing for Mommy.

I also wished for the strength of Heather. She'd always been good at knowing when I needed coddling and when I needed a swift kick in the ego to shake me from a funk. She was better with people than I was, too. And where I saw difference, she had a gift for finding commonalities. If only the phone worked I could get her advice on how to connect better with St. Lucians.

Only with the benefit of age do I see that if it hadn't been illness, something else would have sprung the tears. The people running the exchange program spoke the truth: everybody gets homesick after the initial euphoria wears off. But they weren't specific enough for a young fool like me. They didn't say that a virus would try to "drive white man back where he belong." They didn't mention the pain, the aches, cold chills, nausea, loss of appetite, lack of medicine, dependence on green tea, the depression.

No one had told me I'd be unable to rise for work at 6:30 a.m., sleep until my ride was long gone and be sweated out of bed by the unbearable heat of 8:30 a.m., then spend six regrettable hours bored by myself. I wasn't warned I'd have nothing to do but read my novel on 16th century Japan and that I'd actually feel relief knowing someone had it worse than I did over on the Pacific more than four hundred years earlier.

I had no idea I'd find myself praying that the lucky ones — people with the wealth and power to enjoy safe, secure and comfortable lives — would realize that their advantages in life come at the expense of others, and that the unlucky ones — without tap water let alone cash to spend on bottled spring water or disposable dishes, sugary cereals and diet pills — would persevere. Or that asking God to cure my diarrhea amidst an impoverished world would seem selfish. Or how I'd long for something familiar after a lifetime of longing for something different.

They didn't mention the lack of a phone — not hearing Heather's whisper in my ear again as if we still lay entwined like a singular body. I wanted so badly to hear that whisper, to allow myself the delusion that we could one day reunite. Nobody mentioned that there'd be no television distraction even, no understanding of what was going on as Ben's mother limped silently, cleaning, and he and his father disappeared for days at a time.

Eventually, Ben saved me from all that, took me into the forestry office where I would job shadow him to meet the boss, Mr. David. He was a mountainous man with a Rastafarian hat, nicknamed Jabba (but not to his face). Mr. David sat behind a large teak desk, a thing of beauty in the back corner of a mostly empty space. There were no chairs for guests, no bookshelves, no carpet over the cracked concrete floor with the occasional gecko scurrying across, just the desk with a phone and computer, and Mr. David. The pale brown walls were bare, save a poster of a parrot.

"You don't look well," Mr. David said, shaking my hand.

"Touch of dysentery," I said in a fake British accent he didn't pick up on. I was making a joke, but he nodded and told me to sit.

"Take notes, Ben," he said, but Ben had forgotten his pen. "You have a three-month vacation in Canada and you can't even bring back a damn pen?"

I laughed. Ben and Mr. David looked at me.

"I demand professionalism in my office," Mr. David said. He spoke in the high English, but I was never sure if it was for my benefit, or if it had to do with his position of authority. Maybe it was simply because of his generally reserved nature.

Regardless, he rolled his eyes up toward the ceiling so I couldn't tell if he was still lecturing Ben about the pen or had moved on to me and was annoyed by my inappropriate laughter. The orientation package had warned that while humour itself was universal, it didn't always translate from one culture to another. I cursed myself for consistently failing to heed the warnings of the orientation package. Trying to save my chance to make a good first impression, I promised Mr. David he could count on me to work hard and learn fast.

"Good," he said, shaking my hand again. "We need that." He took a form from the top drawer of his desk and handed it to Ben, who stood, nodded and left.

I looked at Mr. David and back at Ben as he left the room, then back to Mr. David. "Have a good day," he said.

I thanked him and hurried after Ben, who hopped into a Jeep with a St. Lucia Forestry Department logo. I ran to the passenger side and found him there at the wheel, starting it up. "Oh yeah, other side," I said.

We drove south along the west coast, my left arm hanging out the window getting burned, the soca music at top volume and hurting my ears a little, the smell of bananas and pesticides wafting through the windows from the forests to our right, Ben not saying a word, seeming happy in his element. I was hungry and yet didn't feel like eating. The air from the windows was a welcome relief from the heat wave that even St. Lucians had been complaining about.

I tried not to think about home, about pizza and video games and bar-hopping with the boys, and particularly not about Heather. Instead I focused on how quickly I'd progressed through the stages of culture shock. The worst of my depression had passed before my dysentery, but a deeper sense of displacement had set in. I could handle most of the things the orientation package had warned me about. The different sounds, smells and sights were a new experience, and that was what I had wanted. These things were mere adjustments, a process of finding new things to like and dislike about the world around me.

The much bigger challenge was my being transformed into a baby, one so completely clueless about the most basic realities and social norms: where to leave my shoes or knowing how to catch a bus or where was safe to travel at night. How to respond to being followed around the house by the ironically nicknamed and rather silent Boom-Boom. How to answer the stares when I left home, and the calls of "Hey Mike!" or "Hey Pinkie!" or "Hey White Man!" usually shouted in the hope of selling me something. And, more than anything else, how to handle standing out like a walking bag of foreign power and money, even though I didn't feel like one and only had a few dollars a week to spend.

Had Nova Scotia been this strange to Ben? I hadn't noticed. Maybe I'd been too caught up the drama of my crumbling relationship with Heather.

After an hour's drive down the coast without conversation, Ben and I stopped at a gas station, where he filled the tank and completed the form Mr. David had given him. He gave it to an attendant, who gave us sandwiches. Tuna. We ate, though I feared I'd regret it soon if there were no toilets around. We sat in the Jeep for a while listening to more soca, then drove back to town and popped in to see Ben's mother at her workplace, a cultural centre with a theatre inside where children learned to perform traditional dance. She gave Ben a beer and I declined, asking if there was a toilet. We hung out there a few hours and drove back to the house.

"Tomorrow we get you some boots for the forest," Ben said.

I nodded, thanked him and ran to the toilet. Luckily, Boom-Boom didn't seem to be around.

* * *

I was sick for a few weeks before Ben sent me to see a traditional doctor he knew, an herbalist faith healer in the south who could help me. I would stay with Uncle Dingo, who met my bus at the stop on the main road near his house. He took one look at me and said I needed to go to the rum shop with him for therapy.

"A black man and a white man together," the bartender said, smiling at me as if hers was a fresh observation rather than one I'd heard a few times already hanging around with Ben. I cringed every time I heard it. In Canada my race had never been an issue, and a couple of things were now dawning on me. One: when people scrutinize you because of how you look, you end up carrying a certain frustrated hurt around, a scream you're afraid to let out because of the inevitable backlash that will once again be attributed to your appearance. And two: maybe that's why Ben had been unmoved by the nods of black people in Nova Scotia. Maybe even being noticed for having the same skin colour felt artificial to him. I'd asked him about it, but Ben seemed like a 'colourblind' type of person. He always pooh-poohed the St. Lucians who brought up my skin colour, and I appreciated that a great deal. It seemed disrespectful then to pry about his feelings about Nova Scotian racial attitudes.

Dingo and I took our seats at the bar. It was mid-morning and we were the first customers. The bartender was a teenager, maybe a year or two younger than I was. Her smile animated most of her face and I felt like she was a cousin of mine, someone I might have played hide-and-seek with at a family reunion in another life. But when I saw her eyes, there was no actual joy in them. They looked weary, old beyond their years, and I couldn't decide whether to smile back or to put my hand on her shoulder like a sympathetic older brother.

"Two rum and Coke," Dingo said, waving his hand dismissively. "Be careful of her, she slutty as a hairdresser."

The bartender hit play on a tape deck. I couldn't believe it: George Jones. "She Thinks I Still Care."

She brought us our drinks. "Your friend awful cute, Dingo."

"He got a girl back home."

"So what?"

"He don' mess around behind her."

She pouted and went to work unloading a new box of rum. The brand was called 'Strong.'

"She's cute, though," I said.

"Mm. She special in her way. Born same day as my daughter. April 29, 1980. Seconds apart. Best friend for dey first four year, could not live without each other. But in 1984 my daughter die."

George Jones switched to "Hello, Darling," and in the brief silence between songs the bartender caught my eye and winked.

I pursed my lips, still unsure whether to smile back. In St. Lucia, my foreignness had made the simplest decisions difficult. I put a hand on Dingo's shoulder instead.

"She had a worm," he said, not moving, not reaching for his drink or looking up.

I swallowed and wondered why he was telling me his story and how I should respond. I was just a kid. I'd never known anyone who had lost a child. I was exhausted by the constant uncertainty of how to act. So I made a decision. Not about Dingo, but about the bartender. I gave her a smile. I wondered what her name was, and what Dingo's daughter's name had been and if they'd had nicknames. No one else in the family had mentioned his dead daughter.

"Come," Dingo said, standing up and grabbing his drink.

"Can we take these?" I asked.

He carried his down the dirt road so I took mine, smiled at the nameless former best friend of his dead daughter and followed him. He was almost power walking and I could barely keep up, my legs rubbery under me and my stomach turning. But the rum couldn't be any worse than this traditional doctor, could it?

At the end of the dirt road he turned onto the highway and I followed behind him, one eye on the ditch and the other on the traffic. Dingo took me to his house and pointed down at the front of the driveway. "Here," he said.

I looked down and then up at him, then over his head at the roof of his house. I pointed down. "Um … here?"

"She die in my arm right here." He was fighting tears telling me this, all these years later. "And Angel, de girl who work at de bar, she fall sick the exact same moment. Only her daddy own de rum shop so he can fly her to Cuba to see a good doctor."

I nodded, still not sure what to say, still feeling sick but suddenly more secure in the heartbreaking knowledge that while Dingo's daughter had died, I would somehow get well, traditional healer or not. I could do this not because I was young and indestructible, but because I was Canadian and white and richer than anyone I'd yet met in St. Lucia — my low cash flow was a temporary state. Was this what Dingo was really trying to teach me, with his earlier complaints about how he'd been ripped off by his country's Social Insurance

Policy and now this story about his lost daughter, dead because of what her father didn't have? Or was he just sharing his pain? Maybe it was his way of doing what I had failed to do in my state of cultural paralysis: establishing a connection between us, a former beer factory worker and a young student too far from home.

Regardless, I felt it. Deeper than my own sickness I felt his loss, or his pain at least, and I wanted to comfort him more than I wanted my health back. But even at eighteen I knew there was no comfort a visitor could give for the loss of a small child.

"So Angel, she live. But she never been de same again since. Those two had de *cuisvé*, the warm connection inside."

"Sorry," I said, my shoulders shaking.

He waved at me, the same dismissive hand he'd given Angel at the bar. His own tears had emerged only for a second or two, and a quick swipe of his hand had put an end to such nonsense. Sorrow was of no use to him. He was angry now. "I hate my country," he said.

I nodded, looked up at the stars. I was getting used to their closeness; they'd become a piece of splendour that followed me around at night, like they were a marching band and I was the head of the parade. I didn't want to be homesick anymore, or angry or sad. Time to end that nonsense. I had a marching band in the night sky, after all. "But you have the *cuisvé*," I said. "St. Lucia, I mean. I don't think we have any word like that in English. It's a great word."

Dingo laughed but I didn't understand why. I thought I was being deep. "Cheers," he said.

We clinked glasses and drank, me wincing at the burn, both of us feeling the warmth inside. We weren't drinking to a word but rather to a meaning, and to a resilient culture that embodied that meaning by surviving slavery and colonialism and neo-colonialism and all manner of things far beyond either of us standing in Dingo's driveway, because of the warm inner connection of its people.

"Tomorrow we get you healed," he said. "And when your family come down, dey stay with me."

THE LONG LAST YEAR

by Gerard Collins

(For Keisha, who has had her own long last year)

I don't have plans for the fall. I don't know where I'm going.

I've been walking away from my parents' house and towards town, trying to shake this crappy, soul-sucking feeling. I've strutted for forty-five minutes alongside a dark, narrow road with my legs numb and my mind racing with bad thoughts. Even though it's August the cool wind is stinging my eyes and making salty tears stream down my cheeks. When I swipe at them it only makes my vision worse and my eyes sting.

I can't feel anything but hurt, can't see anything but blur.

Times like this I don't know where to turn or who to talk to. Everyone thinks they know what it's like to be me. They assume I'm handling it, that I'm perfectly fine, that a good night's sleep or a good cry will take care of everything. But I don't sleep and I'm not much for crying. No one knows me at all. Sometimes I want to scream or tell everyone where to go but that's not the way I am.

I'm usually a stereotypical good boy. I respect my parents and do what they tell me. I don't let my mother down and I get good grades. I go to mass every week and confession once a month. I don't smoke or drink. I don't swear. I don't tell people where to go or what to do with themselves when they get there.

But today I feel like I could.

That's why I had to get out. Sometimes it all gets to be too much and I start walking and leave everything behind. Just never stop walking until I'm in a place where I don't recognize anything and can just lay down somewhere and go to sleep.

Two months ago I finished my last year of high school and that's part of what's bugging me. Everyone seems to know what they're doing this fall now that they've graduated. Everyone except me.

Right now I couldn't care less about school or grades or what I'm gonna do next year or anytime after that. There is no next year. There's not even a tomorrow.

The crescent moon is dull silver against the sky as I march past houses with their yellow-lit windows. I can't see much detail other than a few shrubs, buildings and telephone poles. But then that's about all there is to see anyway, even in the daytime.

There's not much business in my small hometown — a few stores here and there, a 'supermarket' where everyone buys groceries, a small convenience store that's really just the front part of someone's house, a drugstore where the old people get their medications and the young ones buy comic books and Popsicles. Right in the middle of it all is the big, white Sacred Heart Church, the tallest building in town. It has a steeple that points to the sky like it's showing the way to God, and a bell that rings throughout the town so everyone knows when Mass begins or when there's a funeral.

I don't know what keeps the place alive. The fishery, I suppose. But not everyone is doing that. Lots of people are leaving.

Most of my classmates are going to the city this fall. They've had plans all year. Some of them have been making regular appointments with the guidance counsellor to discuss their future. University. Marine Institute. Trade school.

We have a trade school in town but that's only good if you want a trade. A few of my friends are into carpentry but I can't drive a straight nail. I had to do a two-week woodworking course last year. When the instructor gave me a handsaw and told me to cut a piece of two-by-four in half, it took me forever to saw through it. The cut was so jagged it looked like I'd gnawed it apart.

Some of the boys are gonna do electronics or electrical, but if I can't be trusted to drive a nail or saw a piece of wood, why would anyone trust me to wire their house?

Three of my four brothers went to trade school. Cal, the oldest, did auto mechanics but works at boatbuilding. Ian, the next oldest, did electrical but he's working at construction in Labrador. Jimmy is in St. John's doing a tourism course and Patrick works at carpentry. My little sister is still in grade six but she hates school.

My father's the best mechanic around but he drives a snowplough with the department of highways for a living. He can fix anything that runs, but he never showed me how. Not that I have any interest in fixing cars — couldn't even fill a tank with gas if my life depended on it. Besides, showing an interest would mean putting expectations on him to teach and, worse, on me to learn. We're not close like that. One time when I was younger he was out in the meadow by the house working on a Volkswagen with the bonnet up and parts spread out on the ground. I asked what was wrong with it. "Transmission," he said without looking up. I asked him what the transmission did but he barely glanced at me, lit a cigarette and said, "I don't have time to explain it to you." Then he blew a cloud of smoke over my head. I never asked again.

No one's ever suggested I go to university but that's where nearly everyone else in my class is going — except for the few who will eventually end up in jail. When the guy and girl from the university came to talk to our class in February and asked, "How many of you know what you plan to do this fall?" everyone put up their hand, even me.

When they asked, "How many are going to university?" half the class put up their hands. I scrunched down in my desk, trying to make myself invisible. I could lie about having some kind of plan because that could mean nearly anything. But I couldn't lie about going to university. I was afraid they'd make me sign something. Sure enough, everyone who'd raised their hands had to fill out a form and take it home for their parents to read.

My parents wouldn't want to read that. Reading stuff like that means work. Even worse, it means money. And that's something my parents don't have.

* * *

I rush past the Esso station. It closes at six o'clock, same as everything else. There's a light on in the office but the place is empty.

The owners leave the lights on so the young crowd can see there's no money in the cash register, left open at night like a dog with its tongue hanging out. As I dart by the gas pump I wonder what it would be like to break into that office and wreck it — turn everything bottom up, fling a chair through a window — and run.

But I push those thoughts away and just keep moving. That's what it's all about in this hellhole. You don't do stuff that disturbs everyone's perfect little paradise. You don't mess things up and you don't ask questions. Everyone knows your business, but you don't talk about certain things and you shouldn't ask why things *have* to be the way they are. Just pretend it all matters, that everything's okay, that you give a shit about school and hanging out, getting drunk or stoned at the ball field Friday nights or standing on the drugstore steps smokin' and spittin', tellin' dirty jokes, leering at the girls that go in and out with their mothers and drive off with them too. Safe and sound.

It's easier for girls. They can do whatever they want and nobody cares. If they want to stay home Saturday night and watch some stupid show, nobody questions it. But 'da boys' got to be out all the time, gettin' into mischief and gettin' away with it. Drinking, smoking, cursing, snowmobiling, hunting, fishing. And screwing, or at least pretending you are so nobody thinks you're queer.

I read a lot of books so they all think I'm strange. I don't mind, though. It's easier to be left alone.

I don't belong to that crowd.

I don't belong to any crowd.

A car passes by, slows down as it goes. I recognize it as Rooster Dunphy's car. They call him Rooster because he's got red hair. I guess it was either that or "Red." It's not that anyone here has that kind of imagination, just that we already got a Red O'Reilly, a Red Pittman and a Red Pendergast. So we had our quota of Reds, and Dunphy got nicknamed Rooster. His girlfriend, Molly Corrigan, is in the car with him but I can't tell who's in the backseat. They broke up back in May just before graduation but now they're back together. On again, off again. That's just what they do.

I've always had a thing for Molly. Not that she knows it. I don't really know her, I suppose, but she's really pretty with long, dark brown hair and she's really slender and smarter than almost anybody in school. She always gets the big award every year for best marks in her grade and just last week she got a scholarship to go to MUN. If I could have her for my girlfriend, my troubles would be over. But I'm too shy to talk to her or to any girl.

Rooster blares his horn and then suddenly tears off, burning rubber and screeching his tires. Shivering from the tension and the cold, I sniffle and wipe my nose as I shake my head. I suddenly feel colder, so I shove my hands into my coat pockets again. It's bloody August, for cripes sake. "Capelin weather" they call it, when the fog and cold come in from the ocean in summer and bring the little fish with it by the thousands. It's supposed to be only in June that it happens but really it's most nights of summer. Now and then I have to rub my hands together and blow on them to warm them, then stick them back in my pockets.

I'm rubbing my palms together as I pass by the courthouse and see a rock the size of a softball right in the middle of the pavement like someone laid it there.

The courthouse is nearly a hundred years old and is almost as high as the church, except instead of a bell it's got a big, round clock at the top so that everyone knows exactly what time it is. We're all on courthouse clock and church bell time, all of us marching to the same rhythm, doing the same things at the same time. Every time I see that clock, I just want to smash its face in. When you look up at the second floor window you can see where they put people on trial. Pretty exciting place. But in the dead of night it just looks haunted. I've heard stories there are ghosts in the courthouse because of a couple of hangings that took place there a few decades ago. So every time I pass by there at night I look up and imagine I see a ghost in the window. But I don't tell anyone that.

No one knows where I am. I told Mom I was going for a walk and she asked, "Where to?"

"Out."

She went back to watching TV with Dad, but I could tell she was miffed. It's pretty unusual for me to go out at night and not tell her where I'm going. But what can she do about it? If she said not to go I'd go anyway and she'd lose control over me. Truth is, she doesn't own me. Most times I act like my parents, teachers, brothers and even my little sister have complete control over me — where I go, what I think, when I eat, pray and shit — but I pretty much want to tell them all to shove it. Just leave me alone and let me live my life. I won't do that because I'm too "good", but I want to.

Anyway, tonight I just had to get out.

I pick up that rock and consider throwing it through the courthouse window, the one where I've seen the ghosts. It's the same feeling I had when I passed the Esso station — I just want to destroy something. It's not the first time I've felt that way, but it's the first time I've come close to doing something that might land me in jail. But instead I shove the rock into my pocket with my fist wrapped around it and keep on walking. Throwing rocks through courthouse windows seems wrong, mostly because I like that old building. I even have some good memories of goofing around in there after school with a friend of mine whose father was the magistrate. But I'm not in the mood for good memories, so I keep going and tighten my grip on the rock in my pocket.

* * *

My father drinks a lot. Or used to. We don't have much money but he always finds some for that. And cigarettes. Two packs a day and at least a half dozen beer. If there wasn't money, he'd find, beg or borrow it.

He tries to be a good man, my father. He always makes sure we're fed and have a roof over our heads. There are six of us kids and it can't be easy on him, especially since he hardly ever has full-time work. It seems he's always either on employment insurance or starting a new job or waiting to get called in for a day of work with the department of highways.

He's a skinny man — not an ounce of fat on him — but he eats salt meat, cabbage and potatoes like they're candy. Or cod tongues and cod heads. Anything that's fried or salty, he eats by the bucketload. And before he had the stroke, he never got sick a day in his life, unless he needed a day off to work on the car or go to St. John's on personal business. Our cars are always broke down. I can't remember a time when we ever went for a drive and there wasn't some kind of racket between my parents because the car wouldn't start. Too many times to count, Mom's flooded the engine from turning the ignition and stomping too many times on the gas pedal. And it just makes him madder and madder. Lately everything seems to make him mad. I've always figured one day he was going to explode in a terrible way.

He's got a helluva temper and sometimes he takes it out on us. On me. He always says I deserve it, and sometimes I do. Most of the time it's for talking back or asking the wrong questions. "You gotta learn to keep yer mouth shut," he says. Lots of people say that to me — teachers and relatives, mostly. They all say I think too much and say all the wrong things — like questioning why the church needs money if all we have to do is pray, or why we have to confess our sins to a priest who's really only a man, no different than my father.

But I'm not very good at keeping quiet when I know something's wrong, and sometimes it makes me hate myself when I'm punished for speaking my mind. It's just that they say stuff that's not right and someone's got to tell them or else they'll go on thinking the wrong thing forever. And that's what gets me into trouble with my father.

Only when he's been drinking, though.

There was one night last October when he'd been drinking all day. He'd eaten supper as usual, and as far as I knew there were no upsets. He never got mad at no one and he didn't say a peep at suppertime, even though we were all laughing and carrying on.

That night he was extra quiet.

I remember Dad and I watched some TV show together and everyone else was gone out or gone to bed. Next thing I knew he was snoring on the couch like he often does and I left the television on so as not to disturb him. If I wake him up, I'm just asking for trouble. He might get it into his head that he needs a beer and a smoke, and if he doesn't have them he might send me out to bum one, or worse, he might go himself. And it'll be all my fault.

So I got out of the chair and started tiptoeing towards the bedroom. He snorted really loud and swiped at his face, and I figured he was going to wake up. I held my breath but then he rolled his whole body towards the back of the couch as if he were settling in for the night. Then I stepped into the hallway, careful not to step on the weak spots in the floor.

All of a sudden I stopped and looked at him. I mean, really stared at him. The way he just lay there made him look like he was dead. A long time had passed since he'd taken a breath — his chest wasn't moving up and down the way it should. He didn't even snore.

He'd been having some trouble lately with his circulation. The big toe of his left foot had turned blue, and then the whole foot turned that colour. The doctor told him to quit smoking and drinking, cut back on salty food. He was still drinking, but at least he was taking it easier on the other bad stuff. But I just had a bad feeling and the longer I looked at him, the sadder I felt.

I just stood there waiting for him to show some sign of life, wondering if I should wake him. But that would only lead to trouble so I didn't do anything, just watched.

A full two or three minutes passed before he finally let go a deep sigh, drew his left arm tight to his chest and started to snore.

Relieved but trembling inside, I released a breath of my own and went to bed. The three of us boys still living at home all shared the same room and everyone else seemed to be asleep. But I was awake and listening, expecting something bad to happen.

Later that night, about three in the morning, I was lying awake when I heard something going on in the living room. There were loud voices and quick stomping.

Something bad *was* happening.

* * *

Thinking about all this now I stroke the jagged edge of the rock in my pocket hard enough that I should be feeling pain. But I don't feel anything.

I stop in front of Green's Dry Goods' big picture window. I always play with words in my mind, and I like the idea of the big picture window — I imagine that if you peer into it, right up close, you can see the 'big picture'. Green's is at the centre of the shopping district. Anyone passing by, and the ones in their houses across the road, will wonder what I'm up to. But I don't care if they see me. They can look out through windshields or their white lace curtains as I take out that rock and wind back, draw a bead on the centre of the big picture window and fling the rock hard as I can. I imagine the crack of the glass, the clatter and chaos of the shattered shards as they fall to the ground.

The police will come and get me. They'll question me but I won't say anything. For the first time in my life I'll keep my mouth shut. They'll have to call my parents. But who cares? I mean *really*? Who the fuck cares?

* * *

A couple of hours after I stood and watched him, imagined him dead, my father had a stroke on the sofa. By the time I pulled on my pants and scrambled out to the living room his eyes were rolled back in his head and his body had gone rigid while my mother leaned over him, stroking his face and crying, "Please don't die. Please don't die." But he was the closest thing to dead I'd ever seen, barely breathing, his arms and legs straight and stiff. The strangest part — the part I know I'll never forget — was that he was talking on and on, but I couldn't understand a word. No one could. It was gibberish.

Awful things like this can never be unseen. Even as I look into big picture window, I can see them as if they're images on a big screen television.

The ambulance came and there were two attendants. They brought in a stretcher covered in a white sheet with a hard, white pillow. They talked to him. Asked him questions. "How are you?" and "Are you doing okay?" and "Do you know your name?"

He just stared through them like they weren't there. Every time they asked a question that he didn't answer I felt like lashing out at the attendants to make them stop. But I just kept it inside, locked in my mind.

They took him away with the red lights flashing and the siren wailing. Mom went with him in the back of the ambulance while the rest of us stayed behind. It only took a few minutes for the phone to ring.

One of my aunts was calling. "I saw the ambulance up at your place. Is everything all right?"

I felt numb. I didn't know how to answer the question, like I was having a stroke of my own.

I told her he was gone to the hospital and that was all I knew. The phone rang over and over, neighbours and family asking the same few questions. Bad news spread fast in my little hometown even though good news always seemed to get stuck in people's throats.

Next thing I knew a couple of weeks had gone by and I still didn't feel much like going to school or anywhere else. Didn't even want to get out of bed. My mother was shouting at me to hurry up or I'd miss the bus. But I didn't care because everything just seemed like a big waste of time. I'd rather spend the day in bed, hiding my head under the covers.

* * *

I dragged myself to the bathroom, where I looked in the mirror and sighed. I didn't mind what I looked like, even though I looked like something the cat had dragged in and chewed on for a couple of hours.

Ever since the stroke, Dad had been in St. Clare's hospital in St. John's — that's nearly two hours away, too far for me to visit. Thank God for small favours. The way Mom described him, I didn't want to see him at all. That's how I felt though I couldn't tell anyone else that. Mom spent the first week with him, waiting for him to stabilize. He still wasn't stable but she needed to come home and get some new clothes, make sure we were all eating regular meals and going to school, besides not killing each other. It wasn't just the boys that fought with each other — my sister and I could get into some doozies. We used to be really close, but not so much anymore. We argued a lot lately, and now and then she'd try and scrawb my eyes out with her fingernails just because she said I looked at her funny.

Miraculously, though, we were all getting along better than ever while Dad was in hospital — hardly ever fighting. My brother Patrick and I did almost all of the housework, along with going to school and making sure everyone else was up. I didn't mind, but most days I felt pretty dazed, like it was all just a bizarre dream where the adults had disappeared from our world. I wanted Mom to come home and cook the meals again and take care of the laundry and regular cleaning. But it didn't look like that was going to happen any time soon.

When she came home after the first week, she told us Dad was out of intensive care — whatever that meant — but the doctors were saying he'd never walk or talk again. At all. He was paralyzed on his left side and there was no hope he'd be anything other than bedridden for the rest of his life, assuming he lived much longer.

She asked if we wanted to go see him, and the older ones did — that is, the two who were left besides me. But I didn't want to. I could picture it all in my mind and the last thing I wanted was to see my big, strong father reduced to being a child. So when she left I stayed home.

* * *

Before long someone was pounding on the bathroom door and yelling for me to hurry up. "I'll be out when I'm ready!" I said, but I could hear him breathing out there, could practically see him — my next older brother, Patrick — already dressed, arms folded across his chest and tapping his foot while he looked at his watch.

That morning we had a substitute math teacher whose name was McArthur, and he'd already lost us. Most of my classmates were so out of control I thought McArthur might have to call in the army just to settle them down.

I minded my own business and sat tight until he could get a handle on the situation. I figured I still had a few minutes before he either got them under control or lost his temper, so I glanced through my geography book.

"What are you doing?" McArthur asked me, all red-faced and bug-eyed with that blonde, bushy beard that made him look like a Sasquatch. Of all the students he could've picked on. He was just on a power kick, trying to make an example of out of me, but he had no idea I was normally a good kid. He probably just figured I was trying to show him up. Yeah, right. Making a statement by reading my geography textbook. "Put it away now or you'll be marching to the principal's office."

"You're serious?" I asked. I mean, he was acting like such an arsehole. I couldn't believe it.

"One more word and you're gone, sir." He glowered at me, and instead of wilting I just got angry. But I also felt kind of sorry for him because I knew he needed to try to keep order or the rest of the class would just run all over him even more. I tossed the book under my desk and it clanked against one of the metal legs. He kept glaring and chewing his bottom lip like he was thinking about punishing me for making noise, but he let it go.

Lots of days were like that. One battle after another with people who didn't take the time to understand the situation.

* * *

While I'm still thinking about what to do with the rock, a police cruiser comes by and slows down. I see the headlights and bright reflection of the car in the window. The car pulls into the parking lot right behind me and I stuff the rock into my pocket, feeling like a criminal. I turn around and face the car. There are two cops in the cruiser, and the one on the passenger side rolls down his window and nods.

"Hey," he says, "come over here."

"Yeah?" My heart pounds as I walk over to the car, the headlights slightly blinding me. The engine rumbles, making me antsy. That rock feels like a boulder in my palm.

"What're you doin' out here by yourself?"

I shrug. "Nothin'. Just out for a walk."

He glances at the big picture window, then back at me. Looks me straight in the eyes and I look right back at him, though I'm nervous as a porcupine in a balloon factory.

"What's your name?"

"Gerard."

"Collins, right? You look like the rest of them."

I just nod. Don't want to give him too much information.

"Patrick's brother?"

Shit. Now I know I'm in trouble. "Yessir."

"Well," he says with one more glare, looking me up and down, "you shouldn't be out here like this. It don't look right."

"Okay, Officer."

"Need a ride home?"

"No, thanks. I'm fine."

"You sure?"

"Yeah. I'm sure."

It takes a while after they leave and the taillights fade from view before I can stop shaking.

* * *

Maybe being the last boy born gave me a complex, like they used everything up and by the time I came along there wasn't anything left. My teachers all had my brothers in their class in past years and they certainly had their fill of the Collins boys. Not that my brothers were troublemakers. But there were four of them. By the time I got to a class the teacher would take one look and ask, "Are you Cal's/Ian's/Jimmy's/Patrick's brother?"

"Yes, sir."

"Well..." And the teacher would make some remark of warning or endearment. "I hope you're as smart as your brother," or "God help me. Another one."

Either way, it's like my teachers have seen me and dealt with me already. So I've become invisible. Not just to them, but to my parents — and to everybody else.

I get teased now and then for my size. I'm not minuscule but I'm short and scrawny. Last year I actually worked up the nerve to try out for the varsity basketball team, but after two pretty good practices, just before final cuts, I broke my leg playing football against Cal. It probably wasn't his fault. He was defending the goal line and I was lunging for a spectacular catch. I cut laterally in front of him while he was charging forward. Anyway, that's my big bang theory as to how I wound up in a cast for nearly all term. Opportunity lost. Status unchanged.

Mostly, though, I'm too small to be much good at sports. All the boys who I play floor hockey, softball and football with are bigger and older than me. When the other team scores I get bawled out even when it's not my fault. Cal, my oldest brother and the best athlete, doesn't want to blame his friends or himself, so he blames me because I'm an easy target. "Get your head in the game," he snaps at me.

"It wasn't my fault!" I shout back. Then it just turns into a row. But I never learn. I'm always battling — don't have enough sense to stop arguing until someone gets hurt. Usually, it's me.

Maybe I get that from my old man. He's a brawler if there ever was one. If he doesn't have a job, he'll fight for one. If he needs a beer, he'll scrounge one. Out of smokes, he'll bum one. Supper cold? Well, let's just say I've seen him take a plate of cold beans and throw it with all his might against a wall. Mom was sitting across from him, and she ducked. The plate missed her, but she and I both got splattered.

I've never seen him punch her or kick her — nothing violent like that. But he'll push her, grab her sometimes and stand over her and say things that make me think he'd like nothing better than for her to fight back so he'd have an excuse to strike her. She taunts him, nags him like it's her job and belittles him until he's nothing. So he lashes out. That's her defence, though. She won't dare hit him. But the words hurt.

In fact, we all get bruised by the words they throw at each other.

One night after supper he pushed her against the wall and threatened to punch her. Another ugly moment I can't forget. She was covering up for something Cal did, and Dad wasn't having it. So he backed her up against the wall and threatened her. His chair went flying when he kicked it behind him.

"Leave her alone!" I yelled and stood between them. He grabbed me by the shoulders and pushed me back against the wall. "Don't think you're too big for me to beat the shit out of, ya little Christer," he said. Then he shook me hard and struck my head on the wall. But I didn't feel any pain. I just wanted to divert attention away from my mother. She's never had an easy life, and I knew she'd had a hard day.

"She never done nudding!" I said. "Just leave her alone."

Then my mother got mad at me for telling the truth and told me to go to my room. But it was enough to make Dad pause, and I could see the wildness in his eyes. He suddenly let go of me and marched out the door into the night. I knew where he was going. To the tavern where he could drink his worries away.

It's never easy with him.

* * *

I don't like school but I like home even less, so I go. I drag myself from home to school and from school to home, dreading my arrival at both places.

It's the last year for me. So you'd think I'd be happy about that much, right?

Everyone is making plans. They're going to be doctors, teachers, lawyers, fishermen, secretaries, nurses, business executives, world travellers, entrepreneurs, bankers and all kinds of great things.

Me? I'm just trying get through each day without killing somebody, including myself. I've got a bad temper. That's what my mother tells me when she gets afraid I might do some serious damage some day. But I'm too small to hurt anyone ... unless I use a weapon. I've been known to throw a butter knife at Ian's head so that it falls short or misses by a few inches. Or pelt rocks at the feet of someone bigger who's taunting me. I can only take so much from those lousy friggers before I got to take matters into my own hands. My brothers have never taken up for me. Not that I want them to. That would just be humiliating. But not as humiliating or frustrating as having them back some other kid who was laughing at me — that happens sometimes. Everyone in my family knows about my temper, so they torment me about girls and stuff, calling me names and saying how weird looking I am. They even make fun of my voice.

Still, no matter what they do to deserve it, I always get punished. Doesn't matter who started it. My temper always finishes it with no one getting hurt but me.

Smacked in the arse with a palm or a belt, sent to my room like a prisoner into a dungeon.

I can't wait to leave this shitty place. But where the hell do you go when you're like me?

I don't have any skills.

I get all A's but I couldn't care less. I don't care about math, and physics is boring. I've managed to avoid chemistry and biology like the plague. History's not so bad, but it's pretty useless. What can you do with it? Live in the past? Become a teacher? No thanks. School's just a big waste of time and the last thing I want is to spend the rest of my life correcting someone else's homework.

There's English, which I'm really good at. I can wield a sentence like a sword, especially in a battle of wits. Words are my best weapon. I can write an essay in under an hour that'll be the best thing my teacher's ever seen. I can use my imagination. Made-up stuff is the safest. No one gets in trouble if you pull the ideas from your brain.

I write stuff in a scribbler that I keep under my mattress but I never show it to anyone. Sometimes I think I'd like to do other stuff too — draw, paint, take really nice pictures, play guitar and start a band. But what point would there be in wanting to do any of it? I'm the youngest boy and there's no money. The committee at school is taking fees for yearbooks this week, and I didn't even bother to ask Mom for the money because I know she doesn't have it. So I'll do without the memories. More useless stuff anyway.

Like I said, even when Dad is working it's only part-time seasonal. So where's the money supposed to come from for paints or brushes or a guitar or even to attend school somewhere else besides the shitty-arsed trade school down the road where all you can be is a carpenter, mechanic or electrician?

It's cheaper not to try. Better not to dream.

*   *   *

I'd probably never kill myself but I wonder what it would be like to die. I lie on my bed sometimes and I think about it. Lying stock-still, I stop breathing — hold my breath until the pressure in my chest mounts and gets uncomfortable. My eyes shut and I relax. Dead people don't worry about anything. Arms crossed over my chest like they do with corpses. I can actually feel death creeping into my body, taking over my senses. Where a few moments earlier I was alive and angry now a warm, comforting darkness has taken over my entire body.

One time while I was doing that, the bedroom door opened and someone said, "Suppertime!" Pause. "What are ya at, lookin' like yer dead?" Another brief, pregnant pause. "Come on!" Patrick shook me and I didn't move or breathe. I could tell he was frightened because his own breathing was pretty fast.

Then he tickled me under the arm and I couldn't help but laugh out loud. He punched me in the shoulder. "Knock it off!" he said. "Supper's ready."

I told myself maybe it was a trial run.

*   *   *

I still didn't want to see my father, and for nearly six weeks I was able to put it off. I was hoping that by the time I worked myself up to it maybe he would've miraculously healed. In fact, right up until the last minute when I got in the car to travel to St. John's, I was convinced he'd meet us in the hospital lobby and say, "What the hell are you doin' here? I'm fine. Let's go home."

Mom told us he could barely talk, just mumble a few words that no one could understand, but even that was encouraging, she said. The doctors were actually a little bit optimistic because now he could wiggle the big toe of his left foot, which was supposedly pretty impressive. At the hospital she had to dress him, feed him, put on his socks and tie his shoes. He couldn't read because, according to the neurologist, the words on a page all appeared backwards to him. His whole left side was paralyzed, so his arm was just hanging like this big floppy thing that he couldn't control.

All the way to the hospital I couldn't help this feeling of doom, like something big was about to happen and it would change everything.

Taking the elevator to the sixth floor of St. Clare's hospital with my mother and Jimmy, I wasn't sure what to expect. The elevator was trembling. Or maybe it was my knees. I wanted to stop on an earlier floor and run away through the maze of corridors and go where no one could find me.

Mom was forcing me to go see him, and I knew this moment would change my life forever. "It's only been a few weeks," she'd said. "But he's lucky to be alive."

I figured I'd judge just how lucky he was for myself. I walked into the room, and he wasn't sitting up with a grin on his face. No smokes or beer. Nothing like I expected, even though I'd been warned.

There was no sign he recognized me. He just stared at the ceiling, eyes glazed over. "Hey, Pop." I'd never called him Pop before, but it seemed appropriate. He seemed older. His skin was the colour of cigarette ash and his hair had turned grey since I last saw him.

Hard to believe circulation problems caused all this. Maybe my parents and the doctor had seen it coming, but nobody told me.

He grunted what I took to be a hello as I stood by the bedside, trying not to stare too much. But it was fascinating to think he was in there somewhere, locked inside his own brain, not able to say much.

My mother sat on the far side of the bed and tucked him in. She held his left hand, which was limp in hers, and rubbed it like it was putty. "He's awful cold," she said.

"Should I get him a blanket?" I asked.

"No, no. That's all right."

"But if he's cold, he should have a blanket."

"I'm sure they would have given him a blanket if they thought he needed it."

"Obviously not," I said. "I'll go ask."

"No, Gerard." There was fear in her eyes. "I already asked for a blanket a couple of days ago and they said they didn't have any extra."

"That's bullshit," I said. "They have blankets and I'm getting one."

Again she told me not to, but I persisted and finally went out to the desk and asked. The nurse looked at me like I had twenty heads and said politely, "I'll see what I can do."

"My father's cold," I said. "To not give him an extra blanket is just cruel."

"I'll see what I can do," she said again. This time she looked at me like I was a real person and not just the hundredth angry relative of a patient she'd dealt with that day.

Ten minutes after I thanked her and went back to the room where Mom was still rubbing Dad's paralysed hand for warmth, a young nurse came in with a blanket, which my mother put over Dad and tucked it in on all sides.

She didn't acknowledge my effort to make him more comfortable, but I kind of wanted her to. All she said was, "You shouldn't be causing such a fuss. They're doing their best."

It was the last time I went to see him, but I imagine that, even though he had an extra blanket on his bed, he likely shivered for a lot of nights.

* * *

Two months go by and my father is finally out of the hospital and home again. To the surprise of everyone, including the doctor, he has taken some steps and, although they're being cautiously optimistic, the signs are encouraging. "He's as strong as on ox," the doctor said on the day they released him. "Maybe he can walk, after all." Still, it takes three of us to carry him into the house since we don't have a wheelchair ramp, and once he's inside he can sit in the wheelchair, but he can't manoeuvre too much because the space is so small. There are too many walls.

Within a couple of hours, though, things are as normal as they can get and for every day after that, my mother is doing most of the housework again — that is, when she isn't working part-time at the liquor store. As the youngest boy I'm the one who's at home the most, so it's natural that I help out the most. Plus Patrick and Cal are working and it's easier for me to take a day off from school once in a while if my mother writes me a note. Still, I wish the other two would do more. I understand why my younger sister is depressed and really not that much help; she's Dad's little princess and this whole thing must kill her inside.

At mealtimes I dish up his supper and lay it in front of him. I help him get dressed. He has a special left shoe with a metal brace on it that allows him to walk in short spurts with a hobble and a hop using a cane, and I have to help him get both shoes on. It's a pretty big job just to push it onto his foot, wiggle the shoe around, jam it home, twist it to make sure it's secure, lace it up and buckle it then, at last, help him stand up. Everyone's surprised that by March he can walk a little bit by himself even though it's only been five months since the stroke. He still depends on the cane and leans on my shoulder sometimes, and he can't leave the house because he might fall down. But he's making slow, steady progress.

He still can't talk, though. He mumbles a bit and gets frustrated when I can't understand him. His eyes are filled with rage and pain that I wish I could take away. Even more I wish I didn't have to see it every day. It's not the easiest thing to do — to watch your father become an infant. He's always had a lot of nervous energy. His dark blue eyes were always darting back and forth, looking around, taking it all in. He was never one for sitting still before, and no one could ever help him do anything.

Most times now he just sits in his wheelchair holding on to his dead left arm with his right hand, massaging it and trying to bring it back to life. I watch every day for some signs of improvement and I even pray for him — just in case God is listening even a little bit — but in my heart I don't think the arm is ever coming back. And neither is he.

Eventually Mom has to take full-time work at the liquor store because Dad is never going back to work. Not ever. He had to sign a legal contract that said he wasn't going to work anymore just so he'd get a monthly cheque from Canada Pension. We've never had much money, but now we've got next to none. There are no extras and the meals are pretty much the same every day: Kraft Dinner, frozen French fries, pea soup, baked beans, boiled potatoes or just homemade bread with ketchup on it. I can't stand any of it. I have a bad stomach — surprise! — and everything I eat makes me sick. Trust me, you don't know want to know the details. But everyone gets mad at me — especially when I can't go to Mass on Sundays or to school once in a while because I'm not feeling good. They think I'm faking it.

Meanwhile, I stay home with Dad and watch him like a hawk. I haven't told anyone, but I'm afraid he's going to kill himself. Not that he ever said he would. But I happened to see a news item on CBC that said people who get suddenly sick are prone to suicidal thoughts. So I wonder if he thinks about taking a full bottle of Aspirin in one big gulp when no one is watching. If it were me I probably would. The good thing is when he goes to the bathroom he can't lock the door. In fact I have to help him get settled in there, then wait outside in some other part of the house. But I'm always listening.

I heard him crying one night. He and Mom were in their bedroom and she was helping him get undressed and into bed. I caught a glimpse of him sitting on the bed trying to say something, but he couldn't get it out. Mom caught me looking and closed the door. But I could still hear them. He started to sob like a baby. Even though I didn't know what he was saying I felt sad for him, but I was also angry.

He hasn't been the best father, but he's still a good man. That's what people don't get. Just because he drinks a bit and gets mad at us doesn't mean he's not good. It's hard to explain, but one time, a year or so before he got sick, he sat with me on the front step and said, "You know I loves yer mother. She might have her ways but she takes care of ye and ye'll never do without anything. She does her best and don't you ever forget that."

It's easier to forgive him now that he's sick. And it's easier to be fair. He's not easy but he hasn't had it easy either.

Before he was always going out, drinking and having a good time. But now he's sitting home in a wheelchair or on the couch, barely able to walk or talk. As far as I can tell he's just waiting to die. Sometimes I watch him — I don't even know if he realizes I'm looking at him — wondering what's going through his mind. I wonder if he thinks about what he's lost or how it could have been different if he'd lived a better life.

It must be terrifying inside his head, trying to express himself when no one can understand a word he says. I can see the frustration in his eyes, so I know he's awake in there. More alive than dead, and that's got to be the scariest feeling of all. He's like the man in the iron mask from that book I once read — trapped inside his own head and no one can rescue him, not even himself.

Other days I wonder if he thinks about anything at all.

* * *

Molly Corrigan. I've known her since grade one. She's got long, dark hair and freckles, a cute, upturned nose and a faint sort of smile that makes you wonder if she's got a secret. I like girls with secrets — the kind that don't give you everything just by looking at them or exchanging a few words with them. Even though she's lived practically next door for years and I see her almost every day, I know hardly anything about her. I mean, we never talk to each other except for a few words here and there. Every time she gets off the school bus in front of her big, white house I find myself wondering what her life is like. I imagine she's very happy with her three older sisters and that they tease each other and love one another and share 'appalling secrets'. I read that in a book one time — *Little Women* — and I've always wanted to belong to a family like that, the kind that talks about everything, laughs a lot and cares for each other even more when times are hard. I think of myself as being like Laurie — the guy that pines for Jo March and winds up marrying her youngest sister. I could be happy with Molly's family.

She sits in front of me in English but it's the only class we share. She's going into office administration at the trade college in the fall and I'm not going anywhere. She often smiles at me in that mysterious way so that I can't tell what she really thinks of me. But sometimes I think that if I were to ask her out, she'd go with me. Most times I'm sure that I'm crazy just for thinking about it. Her boyfriend Rooster's part of the "in" crowd. One of the leaders, in fact. If there was an "out" crowd, I'd be the leader. Or so far outside of it that I couldn't be part of it either.

Second period is over now and I've got gym. She'll take a right turn and saunter towards history and I'll head down the corridor and turn left at the gymnasium. I'm just outside the classroom when she taps me on the shoulder and says, "How's your dad?"

All I can see is her beautiful face with the small freckles and upturned nose, the way her hair caresses the shoulders of her soft, grey sweater and the way her books are propping up her breasts. They're not the biggest but they're Molly's, and that's enough to make me stare without meaning to. I avert my eyes and realize she probably just thinks I'm shy.

"He's pretty bad," I say. "Can't talk much. But he's saying a few words."

"That's something," she says. "Well, see ya."

"See ya."

Then she walks away. Within seconds Rooster sidles up alongside her and she links her arm into his and smooches his cheek, shattering all my delusions about Molly and me going out and someday growing old together.

That thought haunts me as I saunter to the locker room and get undressed in front of half-naked strangers. I mean, I've gone to school with the same crowd for years, but lately I'm aware of how little I know about anyone and how little they know about me. Everybody and everything just looks weird to me, like one day I woke up in the same town filled with people who looked familiar but they were all just wearing masks. I pull on my shorts really fast and head out to the gym with thoughts of Molly Corrigan on my mind, how good she smelled, how pretty she looked in her grey sweater. How really, really nice it was of her to be concerned about my father and me.

* * *

There's not much doubt I'll be throwing the rock through the plate glass window of Green's Dry Goods. I stare at my reflection and grow angrier and angrier. I swipe at my runny nose and sniff, taking a close look at the boy in the glass. The handed-down jean jacket. The brown corduroys that I also inherited. The greasy black hair, the determined set of the thin lips and small chin — all copies of my father's features. The piercing hunger of my blazing blue eyes are also like his. A couple of girls at school have said they liked my eyes but I don't believe them. I don't know why, but whenever anyone says anything nice about my looks I think they're making fun of me — like if I take them serious, they'll laugh at me and say, "Just joking with you, b'y."

That happened to me one time in St. John's when I went to visit my brother Jimmy and his girlfriend for a couple of days. A gaggle of girls started following me around the mall and when I stopped and asked them what was so funny, their leader — a tall girl with big green eyes and blonde hair — said "You look like someone."

"Who's that?" I asked. There was a knot in my throat and my stomach was clenched for the worst that I knew was coming. I hated these kinds of moments, but I felt like a deer in headlights. Like when a teacher or one of my brothers made fun of me. I never felt I could just leave. I always figured I should stay and take it. Like it was penance.

"I dunno. Richard Gere," she said and they all laughed.

"No really," she said, but she was still smiling. "We all see it."

A smaller, dark-headed girl who reminded me of Mary Ann of *Gilligan's Island* because she was wearing a red hairband stepped towards me and said, "You remind me of a guy at school."

"Who's that?" I asked.

She said some name that I didn't know. They all agreed, still smiling.

"Is he good-looking?" I asked, fishing for a compliment. Anything to ease my embarrassment.

But all they did was laugh. Their own private joke.

"Well, I gotta go," I said and I strutted away, red-faced, through the doors of the mall and out onto the sidewalk, hoping they wouldn't follow.

* * *

I grip the rock tighter as I take it from my pocket. I stare at that face in the window looking back at me. It looks like the face of someone who cares about the world. And that's always been my biggest problem.

But it's also the face of someone desperate and lost. Alone in the world he cares too much about.

It's not that I don't love my family or that they don't love me. I don't know what it is, really. If I had to put a label on it I'd say I'm just so tired of caring so much that I don't give a shit anymore.

And that's about it.

Maybe if I throw the rock through the window someone will pay attention. I'm tired of being invisible, of having nothing I say matter to anyone. I'm sick of getting punished for speaking up when I think someone is wrong. I don't always have to be right. I just wish someone would listen.

I'm afraid my father will never talk again. I'm afraid I'll end up staying here for the rest of my life, putting his boots on for him, fixing his meals, washing his dirty dishes and staring into that frustrated old face, waiting for him to die.

When I look into the glass, I don't just see me. I see him too. And I don't like what I see.

I rear back and throw that rock. The glass shatters. Then a moment of silence.

I don't even think about running. I just stand there and wait for someone to notice what I've done.

But no one comes.

There's no siren. No police cars. No alarm.

The telephone wires keep humming.

I sit on the pavement and stare at the window. I see myself staring back, which is when I realize why no one has come to get me.

I didn't actually throw the rock. I only imagined it. Dreamed about it. Wished it. Life is still the same.

So I wonder: what if I really did it? Certainly someone would notice ... wouldn't they?

* * *

The last day of final exams. It was the twenty-fifth of June and the sun was shining.

Dad waited in the car on the passenger side. He never talked about what it was like not being allowed to drive. But he seemed to be taking some joy in the small things lately, so whenever Mom went anywhere he wanted to go too, which always meant a fifteen-minute delay while I or someone else helped him pull on his cardigan — very slowly, one arm at a time — then haul on his shoes. It was getting easier to jam his foot into the shoe with the brace, but it still took a while. He still didn't have much feeling in his left arm but I'd seen him hoist it almost up to the height of his shoulder, and when he did there'd be a twinkle in his eye. I could swear he looked momentarily like his old self but I hardly even remembered what that was. His mouth was crooked now, and when he smiled he looked impish and strange.

He seemed happier lately. He was able to speak again, and he talked a lot, even more than he used to. The doctors said it was because of the stroke — something got scrambled in his brain and it caused him to babble a lot. He told a lot of dirty jokes, too. He always used to, but now it was as if he couldn't help himself. It was embarrassing for him and everyone around him. His speech was slurred. He had trouble with "s" sounds especially and a few other consonants. But at least he was communicating.

He would never say anything about not being allowed to go back to work, but it was kinda obvious he couldn't do much except sit in his wheelchair or lie on the couch. Everything he did someone had to help him with it or do it for him.

My heart still ached for him but at least he was improving, learning to cope. My mom was always tired between work and helping him. She never gave up but I knew she depended on me — on all of us to different degrees — to help out as much as we could.

My grades were down a lot this year and they'd gotten worse since Dad's stroke. But I didn't talk about it to anyone.

I went to my prom back in May but I waited until the last minute to decide, and by that time all the girls had their dates lined up. Meanwhile Molly had broken up with Rooster so I wondered if she'd go with me. I mean, I doubted it. But it was the day before the prom and I decided that I actually wanted to go.

Just *wanting* to go was a breakthrough for me. So what if we couldn't afford to buy me a suit and boutonniere or a corsage for my date or to pay for a taxi there and back? So what if everyone else would be drinking and probably screwing at a party after the prom? Those kinds of things scared me because I was a good Catholic boy who wouldn't upset his mother for all the Communion wine in the world. I didn't want to make her feel poor by asking her for money to do stuff that didn't matter. I didn't want her to worry about me being out late at night consorting with bad people. I didn't want to get some girl pregnant and make my mother ashamed of me. Worse yet, that would mean I'd never leave this town. In spite of worrying about all of this I waited for my chance when no one was around and I picked up the phone and called Molly.

"Hi," she said.

"Hi," I said. "It's Gerard. Gerard Collins."

"Oh, hi." Pause. "How are you?"

I took a deep breath and leaped right in. "I know it's late and everything..."

Silence on the other end. Not even breathing.

"...but I was wondering if you'd like to go to the prom with me."

More silence.

"Don't take this wrong," she said finally. "But why are you asking *me*?"

"Because..." God, this was so hard. Why was she making it so hard? I wanted to hang up. "Because I've always liked you and I didn't think you were going out with anyone now and..."

"It's too late for me to find a dress," she said in a rush. "It's really sweet of you to ask, though."

"We could find you a dress," I said. "I'm sure you could borrow one." Dumb thing to say, but I was desperate.

"No," she said. "I'm sure it's too late." She thanked me again and I thanked her for some stupid reason (probably for not laughing at me — at least not right then and there) and then I hung up. I went to the prom with a girl from grade ten who was very pretty with long dark hair and had a dress of her own already. Mom bought me a brown polyester suit for twenty-five dollars at Dalfen's and I managed to get a discounted corsage for my date. It would have been nice to have Molly there but it's amazing how fast you can get over stuff like that. All of a sudden I was over Molly — mostly. But that phone call was pretty humiliating.

* * *

Dad was waiting in the car and Mom was finishing up the dishes. The horn was blowing, over and over, until Mom finally said, "Go out and see what he wants."

So I ran out to check. He was always doing stuff like that, always rushing us and ordering us around. But I tried to go easy on him because of the stroke. I often recited the line from Jesus on the cross: "Forgive him, father, for he knows not what he does."

As I approached the car I could see the passenger door was open and his legs were hanging out and jerking up and down. I ran to the car and peered in. He was stretched out, eyes rolled back in his head so that I couldn't even see the pupils, just the whites. His entire body was convulsing with foam coming from his mouth, bubbling like soapsuds.

I ran to the kitchen window and banged on it with my fist, yelling for Mom to come running. "Hurry!" I shouted. "He's having another stroke!"

She was there within seconds. "He's having a seizure," she said and together we somehow lifted him from the car and laid him gently on the grass. She told me to go get a spoon, and when I got to the kitchen and pulled open the drawer, the cutlery was all there. Soup spoons, tablespoons, teaspoons. All I could think was, "Which size spoon?" I grabbed the middle one and dashed out to where he was lying on the ground, turned onto his side. I gave the spoon to my mother, who was crying. "Pry his mouth open," she said. I placed my hands on his jaws and pried them open as if he were an animal. His jaw was so soft in my hands, I was afraid it would break. When his mouth was open enough, she placed the teaspoon under his tongue. "That way he won't bite his tongue off," she said.

I don't know who called the ambulance, but within ten or fifteen minutes there was one coming up the lane. Dad was mostly calmed down by then, with the spoon in his mouth, as he made little gagging noises and jerked occasionally. Mom was stroking his hair while I held his hand, thinking maybe he'd be all right.

But as they loaded him aboard the ambulance, I really doubted it.

Cal drove me to school, where, less than a half hour later, I sat in the gym and wrote my physics exam. Possibly the last exam I would ever write.

The worst exam I'd ever written.

I wasn't even sure I wrote my name on it. I'd never failed an exam before, but there was no doubt about the outcome of that one.

* * *

Early August came, and today I got a letter in the mail from the Federal Government. "Dear Mr. Collins: It is my pleasure to congratulate you on your excellent achievement in being awarded the Electoral Scholarship for your district." Apparently I'd won five hundred dollars by writing an exam that tested everything from history to math and science and contemporary topics. The letter went on to say that I should be proud, that the minister was proud, that my member of parliament, the Honourable John C. Crosbie, was proud. That last part probably even made my parents proud, and I was sure the money was important too.

Two months had passed since Dad's seizure, and even though he never had another one he was pretty depressed. As I read the letter out loud for the second time there was a gleam in his eye. "I voted for John Crosbie," he said and banged his right fist on the arm of the wheelchair. "Imagine that."

I felt kind of good about my "excellent achievement," but the award depended on whether I went to school in the fall. If I didn't attend post-secondary school, I wouldn't get the money. Considering I'd never even held that kind of money in my hands before, it was a lot of pressure. Sure, five hundred dollars was only a start but it meant they expected me to do something. Up until then no one had even asked what my plans were for the fall or even for my life, for that matter.

In a flash I realized that I'd floated all year, that I wasn't not going anywhere, that it was only a month until post-secondary school started again. People from my class would be leaving in droves for the city and far-off places or at least heading to trade school here in town.

I was staring at a wasted year.

Wasted years lead to wasted lives.

And it was too late to apply anywhere, even if I wanted to. I thought I would be okay with this, but I wasn't.

And I thought the scholarship would make me happy but it only made things worse. It emphasized what a failure I was.

I spent all day brooding, sitting on the front step listening to the chatter behind me — my mother on the phone bragging to people about my scholarship. I felt empty inside and wished I were dead.

By suppertime no one was talking about the scholarship. They were paying attention to Dad, who couldn't stop eating. I gave him supper — chicken and dough balls smothered in gravy. But when he finished his own he started picking at my plate. He did this at most meals, as if the stroke had done something to his brain that made him crave food constantly. He craved attention constantly, too.

This time, though, when he jabbed at my chicken leg with his fork, I told him, "No. You can't have mine."

He stopped, fork poised over my plate, and for a moment I thought he would cry. But instead he took another jab at my chicken.

"Stop it!" I said.

Someone said, "Gerard, just let him have it."

And I said, "He wants everything. But he can't always have it. Just once I'd like to eat a normal meal and have my own to myself. Is that too much to ask?"

I started towards the bedroom. Everyone was upset with me. When I glanced back at the table Dad was picking at my chicken, chewing my food. Everyone else was squawking and chattering about how impudent and out of control I was getting.

I stayed in my room with the curtains drawn until it was nearly dark outside. Finally I emerged and did something I'd rarely done. I pulled on my jean jacket and headed for the front door.

"Where are you going?" my mother asked.

"Out."

"When are you coming back?"

I didn't answer.

* * *

Still gazing into the big picture window with my back to the road, I stare for a long time at the rock in my hand. There's not a car in sight, only a scattered light beaming from a few of the houses. Now would be a good time.

With a deep sigh that threatens to become a sob, I flip my hand over and release the rock. It clatters to the pavement and I kick it hard. The stone rolls away, skips on the pavement and comes to rest in the middle of the road. I suddenly feel lighter, as if I've been released from a heavy weight on my shoulders and chest.

With one last glance at the face in the window — still brooding but looking less like my father and more like myself — I start the trek homeward along the same road. Wires hum. The lights are still on at the Esso station. The ghosts of the courthouse look out over the town. Flickering blue lights filter through white lace curtains.

Beyond the lighted section of town there's a long stretch of woods where there aren't many light poles. The way is dark, but I comfort myself by singing Beatles songs. "Yesterday," "Help" and "Let It Be."

When I get home my parents are watching a movie on TV. *One Flew Over the Cuckoo's Nest.* Dad manoeuvres himself to a sitting position on the couch and asks me where I've been.

"Just out for a walk," I say.

"Well, it's good that you're home," he says.

Mom eventually goes to bed early, leaving the two of us watching the movie, the lights from the TV washing over us both and keeping us mesmerized right up until Big Chief makes his escape from the asylum by smashing a window and climbing through it.

* * *

Two years later I'm standing in a line-up at the trade school in St. John's. The gymnasium is packed and the loudspeaker's blaring "Yesterday" as I register with my classmates for a one-year printing course.

"Sounds like an excuse to get away from here," my mother had said when I'd told her about my decision to leave. Standing in the registration line-up I remember her words in the kitchen that day, how certain they made me feel.

"Yes," I'd said. "That's exactly what it is." My mother was right. I didn't care about printing. I wasn't sure what I did care about, but doing something was better than doing nothing. And creating is always better than destroying.

So I'm here for now, until the right thing comes along, out where something is more likely to find me and I'm more likely to find something to love.

The main thing is not to impose limits on myself. I've wasted enough time. Two whole years. But for two whole years I've been waiting for this day when I'd fly away and start exploring the world.

It's amazing how fast the time goes, but once you get started, you never know where you'll go.

SOME OF MY PARTS

by Alison DeLory

Everybody has a soul, or is it that every soul has a body? Does our physical state define us more — or less — than the words that come from our mouths, the thoughts that form in our brains, the things we create with our hands, the love that comes from our hearts? If you agree that we are more than flesh, blood and bones, and value your body's utilitarianism without obsessing over its aesthetics, I commend you. For me, it's a work in progress. I'm getting there.

* * *

Once upon a time, in a land both far away and close by, a girl journeyed through the woods. As she walked, trees parted to expose a broad path. The dirt was dry and packed, and occasionally leaves crunched satisfyingly beneath her sneakers. She inhaled the intoxicating scents of pine, fir and dirt and picked a tall piece of grass to chew as she walked.

She was humming to herself, working out melodies she wanted to play later on her flute. This was typical of her day-to-day preoccupations, which mostly kept her mind unburdened by worries about things such as her changing body. Her aunt told her she'd grown a foot that summer, and she had furtively glanced down, wondering if she would see that extra appendage attached at the end of her legs.

Her feet were often so dirty at day's end that she scrubbed them with bathtub cleanser, yet they carried her capably through the forest. As she walked she kicked pinecones like they were soccer balls.

She'd heard rumours that a wolf lurked in these woods but she'd never felt threatened until that day when the wind picked up. Glancing around nervously, she stumbled on a tree root and fell, scraping her knee. No matter, her legs were already a connect-the-dots game of scabs, scrapes, bruises and mosquito bites she'd amassed from hours playing outdoors that summer.

Gray clouds pulled closer together until they formed a dull blanket, hovering over her head. A few drops of rain fell on her dirty blonde hair and red hoodie. She picked up her feet and ran. Her arms swung efficiently at her sides and she could feel her heart pumping in her bony chest. She was grateful that it was pushing blood through her veins and oxygenating her muscles.

The branches shook now as though the forest had been woken suddenly from a nap. The girl ran on, venturing faster and further into the woods than she'd ever been before. The trees no longer parted and she had to look closely to see the narrow and forked paths before her. She chose her course based on instinct and curiosity, but her certainty began to diminish as she pushed forward. Leaves slapped her face and thorns scraped her limbs.

* * *

I stood at the front of the sewing room. It was 1981 and I'd just started grade seven. Though my homeroom class was co-ed, the girls and the boys were separated on Monday afternoons. The boys would learn industrial arts — drafting, metalwork and woodwork — while the girls would learn home economics. That meant sewing in our first semester, and our compulsory assignment was to create a jumper. It was essentially a bibbed skirt with straps to be worn over a blouse, cut from a McCall's Misses' pattern. Before we went to the fabric store, we needed precise measurements so our mothers would know what size pattern and how much material to buy. One by one each girl took her place at the front of Mrs. Turnbull's classroom to be measured.

Mrs. Turnbull lassoed me with a tape measure around various parts of my torso, shouting her findings loudly for the rest of the class to hear. "Hips 30. Waist 26. Bust 30." She scowled as she did this. I stood very still, wondering what I was doing to displease her. My back was straight, my shoulders pushed back. I didn't speak. She pushed the tape measure higher on my chest. "Still 30, but I have a sneaking suspicion about you," she said, sucking her teeth. "I've seen this many times before. You're just starting to develop. By Christmas you'll be popping out all over the place." My classmates giggled. "Oh, it's true, girls. Just you wait and see." I stared ahead at the even rows of sage-green Singer sewing machines, avoiding eye contact with my friends. With a flick of her hand, Mrs. Turnbull dismissed me and called up the next student.

I clutched the sheet of paper that listed my measurements, self-conscious but also thrilled that in just three months I'd have a lovely new pair of breasts tucked under that jumper. It was going to happen, because Mrs. Turnbull had decreed it. She told the class we were all at an awkward age between being girls and women and would have to manage that transition carefully. I chose to announce this to my family at the dinner table. With no segue, I randomly blurted out: "I am no longer a child and none of you should treat me like one."

They all stopped chewing. My mother held a forkful of peas in mid-air. "What's this about?" she asked.

"It's true. I'm not a girl anymore but neither am I a grown-up. I'm sort of in between." I spoke with increasing speed, losing confidence. What seemed so true in Mrs. Turnbull's sewing room seemed ridiculous at my dinner table. I stared at the chicken breast on my plate. It was plumper than my own breasts.

My mother, brother and sister all began laughing. Loudly.

"Oh, give me a break," said my brother, rolling his eyes. He was all grown up at seventeen. I was eleven. I let the conversation drop. As the youngest child, my mother reminded me often that I would always be the baby in the family. It felt like I'd be treated accordingly.

Christmas came and went, and although I got the yellow vinyl Adidas gym bag I coveted, my new breasts never arrived. The ill-fitting jumper was finished, but buried in the back of my closet. I wore it only once. Many of the other girls in my grade were now wearing bras, the horizontal lines both faint yet obvious under the backs of their blouses. I waited patiently all that winter and through the next summer, certain my breasts would eventually appear. They didn't, but before I started grade eight I got a bra anyway, size 32A.

Eighteen years later and into my second trimester, I announced my pregnancy. A co-worker stopped by my office. "I guess you must be glad that you're finally going to grow breasts," she said. I laughed it off and wished I'd retorted, "Who knows? Let's wait and see if you're finally going to grow some sensitivity," but like all great comebacks, that line only came to me later. In the moment, I blushed and mumbled, "Who knows!"

To my co-worker's satisfaction and my own disappointment, even during pregnancy my breasts remained small. Why had every pregnancy book depicted and described women with voluptuous cleavage? Would I even be able to breastfeed? Five months later I was lactating like a champion. Those small breasts filled with so much milk I likely could have fed quintuplets from them. They were no longer tiny but they were leaky, sore and productive. They were doing their job.

* * *

She heard water splashing over rocks and soon came upon a stream. It wound its way through the woods to a small lake, beyond which was a meadow. She wasn't eager to explore the meadow just yet, so she stopped here. She searched for flat stones and when she'd collected a handful tossed them one by one the way she would throw a Frisbee — her best skipping a record seven times before sinking. Then she picked up a round, smooth stone and held it in her palm, rubbing it with her thumb. Her heartbeat was more regular now, and she breathed deeply.

She could see the reflection of the swaying trees and the sky in the water. She'd heard of Mirror Lake and rumours that if you stared into it too often or for too long, it sometimes showed you things you didn't want to see. The occasional raindrop plunked into the lake, and a black line cut through the picture. It was an owl flying silently overhead. Although the girl was technically alone, she felt the presence of the fish in the lake, the squirrels in the trees, and the birds in the sky.

Standing at the edge of the lake, she peered down at her own reflection. Her freckly face looked back at her. The skin on her nose was peeling. She pulled her red hood down and let her hair cascade in front of her face. She stuck out her tongue, sucked in her cheeks to make a fish face, and then practiced her smiles — closed mouth with a slight head tilt, open mouth with her head squared on her shoulders.

Then she lifted her hand, still holding the round, smooth stone, and threw it violently at her lake face. Her reflection fractured into pieces that spread in concentric circles toward the meadow.

* * *

My mother used to say I was the only person she knew who could emerge from a bath with a dirty face. I guess if I couldn't see the smudges and streaks, it didn't occur to me to wash them off. I'd be marched back to the bathroom with a bar of Ivory soap and a facecloth in my hand, to search in the mirror for whatever offences lay between my jaw and hairline, and rub them away.

I'd been told I had very small eyes. I wasn't yet aware that large eyes were better, so I didn't feel insulted when told my eyes were the opposite. I took it as mere observation, not judgment. Once again I went to the mirror to consider this possibility. I squinted to create the effect that my eyes were even smaller than they were. My vision was fine. I saw the words and pictures on the pages of my Archie comics and Trixie Belden books. I spotted the perfect climbing tree from a block away. I could even see underwater, diving for pennies and rocks at the local pool, although everything looked blurry there without goggles. Yes, my eyes could see, but they didn't look right.

Magazines later taught me that big eyes were beautiful. Articles like "Thirty-three ways to make your eyes look bigger" and "Ten-minute tips to turn you into a big-eyed beauty" promised solutions, but all involved makeup and grooming tools that I didn't have. I scoured the house for tweezers to pluck and sculpt my eyebrows, removing half an eyebrow in one overzealous attempt and then colouring it in with a brown eye pencil until it grew back. When I started babysitting and had a bit of my own money, I invested in the navy blue mascara that promised to make my eyes 'pop'. The result was less than I'd hoped for. By the time I was sixteen I knew with certainty that my eyes were unattractive, and that the French boy who asked me to dance and whispered to me in accented English that I had beautiful eyes was a liar.

I didn't know it when I started getting pimples, but I do remember the day in grade eight when Jimmy Fraser drew attention to one.

"Hey DeWhorey!" (His play on my last name. Though I was a virgin it was irrelevant, nicknames not having to reflect one's actual character.) "You got a big ripe zit on your chin," Jimmy said, just loudly enough so two rows of desks could hear him but our math teacher could not. I pretended to ignore him.

"DeWhorey! DeWhorey! You have a big zit that needs to be squeezed. Right on your chin. Right there. On your chin. A zit. A zit.

A big pussy zit. A big pussy zit that needs to be popped, DeWhorey. Pop it, would you. I can't look at it. I can't look at you. It's gross, DeWhorey. Fix that." Jimmy's mouth was barely open as he hissed the words. His dark blond hair hung lank around his pasty round moon face, and a jagged scar cut across his cheek. He wore a pink Lacoste golf shirt, collar flipped up.

The taunting continued while the math teacher droned on about integers. I'd never appeared more fascinated by a lesson on how to solve equations combining positive and negative whole numbers. I refused to look at Jimmy, instead trying to block him out by locking my eyes on the chalkboard. Nevertheless, 'DeWhorey' and 'zit' rang in my ears and tears hovered in the corners of my small brown eyes but miraculously stayed there.

I ran straight to the bathroom when I got home. Jimmy was of course right; the proof was there in that damned mirror. Now, along with my beady eyes I had the beginnings of my war with my skin, which I would pick, squeeze, scratch, medicate, cover up and otherwise battle for decades. Despite its overall tautness and functionality, I'd fret over my skin's unpleasant odours and textures, bemoan its itchy, rashy and eczematous nature, and try to darken my ghostly pallor with hours in the sun or self-tanning lotions. Clichés told me to "Love the skin you're in" or "be comfortable in your own skin," but the literal and metaphoric meaning of those phrases escaped me.

* * *

She cast her eyes ahead, spotting some mossy ground cover that was spongy and delightful. She trod on top of the moss with a renewed spring in her step until she spotted four hairy whitish pieces, about as long and fat as sausages. She'd seen a display in the museum titled "Whose Scat is That?" and remembered noting the unusual white colour due to the fact that wolves eat bones. They could swallow small animals like mice whole and used their strong jaws to open the bones of large prey to get at the marrow. So the rumours were true, she realized — a wolf did lurk in these parts. She felt a chill crawl up each vertebra.

It was getting dark. While the woods had seemed a peaceful and safe refuge early in the day, they were foreboding at dusk. The trees threw strange shadows and the temperature dropped sharply. She shivered and pulled up the hood on her beloved red sweatshirt, feeling the familiar soft cotton on her fingertips, but suddenly it was inappropriate. Yes, her hoodie was cozy but it was all at once ordinary, old and not a recognizable brand. Looking down, she realized her terrycloth navy shorts with white piping were also stupid and babyish.

She found a smooth rock to sit upon. The moon was glowing brighter by the moment.

"Hoo hoo, hoo hoo, hoo hoo," came from the tree above her. She glanced up. "Hoo hoo, hoo hoo, hoo hoo are you?" said the owl, peering down.

She must have misheard. A talking owl?

"I said, hoo hoo are you?" he asked again.

The girl looked around but there were no other humans nearby. She didn't want to embarrass herself but couldn't resist being drawn into conversation with the owl. Plus she needed help.

"I'm lost in the woods. I knew my way this afternoon. But then everything started changing and I no longer recognize my surroundings. Can you help me out of here?"

The owl swivelled its head back and forth. "You can't avoid the meadow any longer. That is your only way through."

"Can't I just return the way I came?"

"There are no round trips. You pass through but once, moving in only one direction: forward," the owl replied.

Dumb old owl. Weren't owls supposed to be wise? She'd just retrace her steps and return to where things were comfortable and certain. She stood up and turned back in the direction of the moss. She lifted her leg to take a step but couldn't lower her foot in that direction. It was as if an invisible wall prevented it. She scissor-kicked and threw a flurry of punches at the force field, but each kick and punch bounced back at her. She pushed sideways then tried to heave her whole body through it, but it was no use.

"What the?" she asked, but the owl was flying away, and she watched as his silhouette crossed the full moon.

* * *

In junior and later senior high school, everyone essentially wore uniforms. Not the prep school variety with blazers and kilts, but uniforms nonetheless. Jeans were part of this uniform. First it was designer jeans or pinstriped jeans, a trend I blinked and missed. As soon as that trend passed, kids buried them in their dressers and never wore them again. Ever. Next it was Levi's, but they had to be 501s with a red tab on the right back pocket. There were no exceptions to this, and I managed with great relief to get my own pair.

Kids wore sneakers, white canvas Nikes with the trademark Nike swish in royal blue. Later, after the *The Official Preppy Handbook* was published, it had to be tennis shoes, and these had to be Tretorns. The *Preppy Handbook* also ushered in the era of polo shirts made by Lacoste or Ralph Lauren. Those who could afford them wore these shirts with the collars flipped up. Button-down Oxford-style shirts from L.L. Bean were also acceptable, and so were socks and sweaters with an argyle pattern on them, or anything vaguely nautical. Many of these name-brand preppy clothes weren't sold locally, so kids lucky enough to own them generally came from families with money who went on shopping pilgrimages to the outlets in Maine, perhaps combining this with a ski trip to Sugarloaf Mountain. Those like me, who even when I got the trip to Maine didn't have $40 to spend on a shirt from Lacoste, wore knock-off versions by Daniel Hechter but never felt happy in them.

I'd figured out that there were sharks and there was bait at my school, and I was tired of being bait. I did my best to camouflage with the sharks during this period, assisted by my sister, who was four years older and holding down an after-school job to feed her addiction to fashion. Jo-Jo was in many ways my opposite — curvy to my flat, brunette to my blonde, effortlessly smart to my "needs to work hard," Veronica to my Betty — and inherently stylish. She still remembers what she wore to every major event in her life, including the outfit she had on the day she fell down the stairs at age two and chipped her front tooth. She understands that there is a difference between a coat that is camel-coloured and one that is merely beige.

Although she wouldn't lend me her clothes, she would let me flip through her fashion magazines and would glance over my outfits if I asked. She'd bestow her approval or disapproval and suggest modifications. Her closet was organized by category, brand and colour. I wasn't allowed in her room — the sign above her door read "Jo-Jo" but might as well have said "Keep The Fuck Out." I often snuck into her room anyway when she wasn't home just to gaze in admiration at her wardrobe and to learn from a master.

"You went into my room, didn't you?" Jo-Jo would ask me later.

"No, I didn't, I swear it," I'd lie, my face awash in a crimson tide.

"I know you did. I can tell you were in my room. Stay out, you annoying pest!" Jo-Jo never falsely accused me; she merely had a finely tuned sixth sense for trespassing when it came to airspace around her clothes.

Then along came Padma, who moved to Canada from India, disrupting the school's fashion status quo. She joined our class in grade nine. Padma wore brightly coloured saris from her home country in silky emerald green, ochre, dark yellow or sapphire blue. They were often adorned with beads or gold trim. She twisted her waist-length brown hair into a bun at the nape of her neck and painted a bright orange-red circular bindi just above the bridge on her nose between her bushy eyebrows. It would be a long time yet before *Slumdog Millionaire* or Bollywood were popular, or anyone was eating naan bread, or watching Mindy Kaling's TV show. Padma was not exotic; she was merely a petite Indian girl who smelled like she bathed in saffron and curry.

Padma shifted her head rhythmically left and right like windshield wipers when she talked. She was friendless at junior high school and often stood alone in the schoolyard at recess. One day she sought my advice.

"Ali-sewn, I was wondering if you could help me dress better, yes?" she asked, her head perched at a curious tilt. I tried not to inhale but couldn't escape her musky odour; she was a close talker. I wanted to back away. Turn away. Run away. I glanced at her sari.

"Uh, okay. How do you want to dress?" I asked.

"Like you and everyone else. What clothes should I buy?"

I'd never been cast in the role of fashion consultant, having always been the student rather than the teacher. I felt flattered and powerful. The words spilled out of my mouth. "Well, first get some jeans. Make sure they are Levi's 501s with a red tag. It has to be a red tag. Not a blue tag or an orange tag or a white tag. And maybe some shirts or sweaters," I offered.

Padma repeatedly nodded, thanked me and trailed off. A few days later she was wearing jeans. They were too-large Levi's, and the tag was blue. She wore a sari over top. My protégé had let me down. As always, I avoided her at recess.

"Ali-sewn, Ali-sewn, how did I do?" she asked after the bell rang and I found myself in line next to her.

"You look good Padma, nice job," I replied, avoiding her beseeching and bulgy brown eyes.

In the following months I kept my distance from Padma. She continued trying to incorporate Western-style clothing into her ensembles but always ended up wearing a hybrid of styles that depressed me. I hadn't helped her at all. She looked better when she wore traditional Indian clothes, I realized, but it felt too late to tell her this, so I said nothing.

Then it was school spirit week and the variety show was upon us. During announcements, the principal invited all students with special talents to showcase them. Students could sign up to sing, tells jokes, dance or perform skits.

Standing at my locker stuffing books into my knapsack, I overheard snatches of conversation and some giggling. The girl next to me whispered, "Did you hear that Padma signed up for the variety show? Apparently she's going to do a traditional Indian dance!"

"No way," I answered. "Not gonna happen." I couldn't believe it. She wouldn't dare do anything that outrageously uncool. I slammed my locker door shut and went to class, absolutely certain these were nothing but rumours.

The day of the variety show came, and my friends and I shuffled our canvas sneakers into a row and plunked our Levi's red tag-clad butts into the auditorium seats. There were a few warm-up acts before the student emcee introduced her. "All the way from India, performing a traditional dance, please give it up for Padma!"

A few people clapped unenthusiastically. The sounds of the sitar poured forth, and then there she was, centre stage. She wore a three-quarter length red sari and silk pants. Her feet were bare save for her bells that draped around her ankles. She wore yellow bangles from wrist to elbow on each arm. A pendant somehow affixed to her hair hung onto her forehead. She began her staccato moves, stomping from stage right to stage left and back again, her legs splayed open like an omega symbol, her arms raised at her sides and bent at the elbows like she was holding two invisible platters of food. Several times the music grew quiet and her moves slowed. *Please let it be over. Please let it be over*, I prayed. Then the notes rose again and she attacked her dance with renewed gusto. Her ten-minute performance was the longest thing I'd ever sat through in my life. I couldn't sort out my own feelings about the number, other than I was desperate for it to end and felt personally affronted. Had she learned nothing from me about fitting in, and dressing? Was she the fool, or was I?

My fifteen-year-old brain couldn't compute.

I wish I could write a happy ending for Padma, but this being creative non-fiction, the rules don't allow it. Truthfully, I don't know what became of her, and unsurprisingly she's not on Facebook or anywhere else I might easily locate her. I don't remember ever seeing Padma in school after that variety show. I heard she'd married young, and I hope the world showed her the acceptance and kindness that I did not. It shames me that I encouraged Padma to distance herself from her culture, and if I could watch her dance once again in her resplendent sari I'd clap the loudest of anyone in the auditorium.

* * *

She'd have to spend the night outside. She jerked each time she heard twigs snapping under feet that were not her own. The woods were dark and she worried about what was hiding behind tree trunks. She knew it was pointless to try to retrace her steps, so she followed the moon to where she thought the meadow lay. She walked down a slight hill until she saw an opening in the trees. The meadow was dimly lit by the moonlight. There were soft grasses and wildflowers there, and she found a knoll upon which she lay down to rest. Perhaps the meadow wouldn't be that bad after all, she tried to convince herself.

She couldn't get comfortable. She lay on her back and tried to find constellations in the stars, but was unsuccessful. Even the Big Dipper, which everyone said was obvious, eluded her. Growing frustrated, she lay on her side, but her neck cramped without a pillow. The ground was hard beneath her winged shoulder blades, and there was no give for the slight curve of her bum. She flipped onto her stomach, but her hip bones jutted out and dug into the ground. Giving up, she pulled herself to a sitting position and sighed. She crossed her legs and watched as gravity pulled the flesh on her thighs downward. She grabbed the skin on the sides of her buttocks and pinched it in places to watch it dimple. Disgusting. Her feet looked too big at the end of her legs. Size 9 already; she wondered if she'd be able to ski on them some day.

And then she heard it, a howl, clear and haunting, "A-roooooooooooo" in a surprisingly high pitch. "A-roooooooooooo, A-roooooooooooo." She froze. She felt in her hoodie's pockets but there was nothing there she could use to protect herself, just a balled-up Kleenex and a waxy bubblegum wrapper. She scrambled around the knoll looking for poking sticks or rocks she could at least pitch at the wolf if he got too close, but there were none.

"A-roooooooooooo, A-roooooooooooo." The sound got louder and louder, then

stopped. Glorious silence. Phew. She let out her breath, unaware she'd even been holding it in. And then she saw them. Yellow eyes, across the meadow, locked on hers.

* * *

I wasn't skinny, nor was I fat. I ate whatever I wanted, and if that was an evening snack consisting of a bowl of vanilla ice cream topped with maple syrup and peanuts then that's what I had. I was a physical kid, always active, and then I wasn't. I was an okay-but-not-great athlete, so when I reached an age at which those without the strongest skills sat mostly on the bench, I gave up team sports. I quit swimming once I got my period, and while I continued to walk a lot, I denied myself the joys of running, cycling, kicking balls, splashing, diving, bouncing, climbing and competing, not understanding that they are an essential part of me.

I heard that it was desirable to have a flat stomach, and the test for this was to lie on your back and place a ruler across your hips. If your stomach grazed the ruler then you had a paunch. I failed the ruler test and gazed down at my slightly rotund belly in frustration. A friend whose mother wanted her to become a model gave her a goal of working toward a 16-inch waist, and while I thought this was extreme, I admired her for pursuing it. It seemed a worthwhile ambition.

My weight went up and down throughout high school, as though my body couldn't decide where to settle. The first summer I moved out of my parent's house I had never cooked much more than noodles, so I stuck with either eating those or eating out. Unsurprisingly, I gained weight. Then I started university in Toronto with the phrase "freshman fifteen" ringing in my ears. Determined not to gain those fifteen pounds many first-year students apparently do, I deliberated every morsel of food I put into my mouth and asked myself if I really needed it. I learned to survive entire days eating only a muffin for lunch. I'd ride the subway lightheaded from hunger, later walking the five kilometres to and from campus each day so I'd burn off even the muffin calories. If I drank too much beer on the weekend I was glad when I threw up, relieved to get rid of the calories. A bout of diarrhea was even better to rapidly drop a few extra pounds.

I also began to run out of money. It was December and I could see my breath on my morning walk to campus, and my fingertips and toes would tingle walking home by myself in the dark. The end of my first semester approached and I only had to make it through two more weeks before I'd be back in my parent's house for the holidays, eating turkey and cookies. I had budgeted just enough so I could eat to fuel my brain through exams. And then the assignment came.

It was in a reporting class, and our instructor, Joan Fraser, told us we'd be taking a trip to the Atlantic Winter Fair, which was happening that week on the Canadian National Exhibition grounds. "Go, wander through the aisles," Ms. Fraser instructed. "Talk to some farmers. Look at some livestock. Discover something new and unusual, and write a feature story about it." She warned us that it cost $13 to get in. I had $16 to last me until the holidays.

I fretted. I didn't see any options so I walked to the fairgrounds and paid my $13. The cock-a-doodle-doo-ing of roosters drowned out the growling of my stomach. There were concession stands selling sausages, hot chocolate and salty, doughy pretzels. I walked past them quickly. I began feeling desperate. I wasn't inspired by anything I saw and had trouble focusing on anything other than my gnawing hunger. Then a solution presented itself.

A young woman my own age stood with a pageant sash cutting her torso into diagonal halves. It read, "Miss P.E.I. Potato Harvest." She had ruddy cheeks and shiny yellow hair, a smile on her face and best of all, bags of free potatoes in her hand. I approached nervously.

"Um, hi. Can I ask you some questions for a story I have to write?" I asked Miss P.E.I. Potato Harvest. "It's for a school assignment. I need to interview someone here at the fair." I whipped out my notepad and pen, counting on her to say yes and my scoring a free bag of potatoes.

She agreed and told me all about being crowned Miss P.E.I. Potato Harvest and her reign. She was travelling across Canada, promoting those wholesome tubers wherever she went. "How often do you eat potatoes?" I asked.

"Every day," she answered. "Every single day. Would you like a bag?"

I had to control myself from not snatching it out of her hands. If she could eat potatoes every day, then I could too. Unfortunately, that's all I would eat every day for the next two weeks, but no matter, if the Irish survived the potato famine (and some did ... right?) then I would too. They baked up nicely each night, and I topped them with a little butter I'd skim off my roommate's pat, hoping she wouldn't notice.

I wrote the story for Ms. Fraser. She gave me a B-. She felt it lacked balance; I didn't delve deeply enough into the pitfalls of potato eating, such as how fattening they can be.

When I returned home for the holidays I stepped on a scale for the first time since I'd left home and learned I'd dropped, rather than gained, the freshman fifteen. My clothes hung off me and my cheekbones had a new angularity. My small eyes looked bigger in my newly drawn face. My hipbones poked out in my pants and I finally passed the ruler test.

I knew I'd engaged in some unhealthy habits and had possibly teetered on the edge of an eating disorder. But I also learned that once you are thin, people come to see you that way and want you to stay as such. You get a lot of compliments when you are skinny. People ask you with envy in their eyes if you've lost weight. In the years that followed my weight crept back up to a healthier level. When I could no longer lay that ruler across my hips without my stomach bumping it, people — mostly family members a generation older than me who I hadn't seen in a while — would remark that I looked different, or would point out that I'd gained weight. I felt I was letting them down. I tried various diets for a month at a time such as cutting out all fats or going vegetarian, but I somehow always gained weight during these experiments. Slowly I learned how to cook and eat satisfying and healthy meals, and became increasingly more physically active. I settled into the weight I've been for most of the last twenty years. At least, I think I'm the same weight, because my clothes fit me the same way. I've quit stepping on the scale and hating myself every time I eat a bag of salt-and-vinegar chips. After all, it's okay, maybe even good, to eat potatoes, if not every day, then at least on occasion.

* * *

The wolf walked in measured zigzag paces left and right across the meadow, his eyes locked on hers the whole time. She willed herself to stay calm, not wanting him to smell her fear. As he advanced stealthily she could see the outline of his bristly grey/black fur. His ears were lifted upwards in sharp triangles and his damp black nose was pointed directly at her.

The girl trembled and looked around for a tree to climb, but the meadow afforded little protection. With nowhere to go and nowhere to hide, she realized a confrontation was unavoidable. Her only weapon was her tongue, and she knew how powerful words could be, so she planned to use them carefully.

"Hey wolf, come closer so we can talk." She beckoned to it. If the owl could talk, maybe the wolf could, too.

The wolf stopped pacing and let out a mighty howl. "A-rooooooo!"

She was unnerved but not ready to surrender.

"Impressive. Show me what else you got. Do you have sharp teeth behind those black lips of yours?"

The wolf came closer. With a spring from his strong hind legs, he could pin her down now if he wanted. "Of course I do. They're all the better to eat you with, my dear."

"Aw, wolf, now why would you want to go and do that? You can see I don't have much meat on my bones. Aren't there some dead rodents nearby that would make tastier snacks?" She kept her voice clear and calm.

"You insult me by suggesting I eat offal. But I do see your point. You look boyish and have barely any bosom at all." He snarled with apparent displeasure.

"A handsome wolf such as yourself deserves a more bountiful feast. With your hunting prowess you surely would be able to find something better than me." She'd bought herself another few seconds as he stopped and considered this.

"Yes, your skin is not clear either. A wolf as fine as myself shouldn't have to settle. Your eyes are too small within your face, while your feet are too big for your body. Your maker must have had trouble with proportions."

"I know, right?" she asked, smiling. She felt the conversation switching and saw something streak by overhead. It was the owl. While the girl and the wolf talked, the owl swooped down into the tall grass and swooped back up into the sky with a field mouse in his talons.

"How do you find yourself here, girl, in this meadow?" the wolf asked.

"I'm on a personal journey. A one-direction voyage from young me to older me. I didn't choose it but that's okay. It's quite a trip. I'm learning a lot." Despite herself, the girl was beginning to enjoy their conversation. She was buoyed by the possibility of not being chewed up. But she wasn't out of danger yet.

"Well, what if I decide there is to be no older you? I might choose to rip that red hoodie right off your back and eat you whole. Or maybe I'll just chew on you a bit and leave you scarred and broken, but alive. What then?" the wolf challenged.

"You can have the hoodie, it's unimportant, but I'm not going to let you have

me. If you come any closer, I'm going to thump my flat chest, and focus my small eyes, and pump my strong arms, and run on my big feet to get past you."

"You've got spunk, girl. A-roooooooo."

"All the better to outmanoeuvre you with, my dear wolf," she whispered while he continued to howl. She joined him, howling her very own A-roooooo and glancing at the moon as the owl flew past, flapping its broad wings as if it were clapping.

The wolf bid her goodbye, and she managed to sleep on the knoll for a few hours until the sun rose. Then she carried forward with more confidence. It would not be happily ever after, for there were many challenges she was yet to face, but she felt more assured now that she'd conquer them with her brain, her heart and her beautiful, perfectly imperfect body.

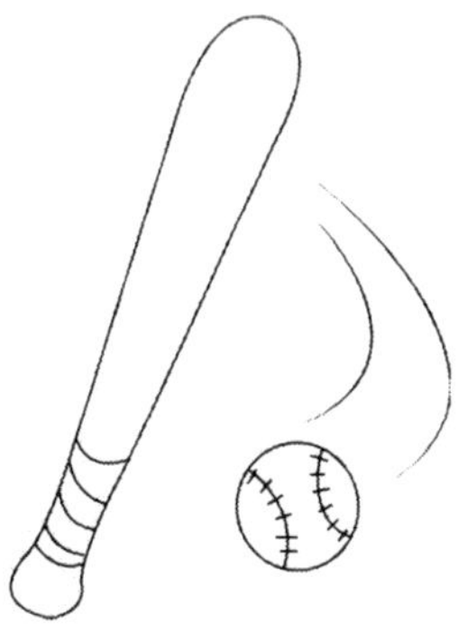

DIARY OF A FLUKY KID

by Lee D. Thompson

First

"Fluky kid is up," says the catcher as I take my place in the batter's box. He pounds his mitt, shuffles his feet and chuckles. In my first at-bat I had swung blindly at a fastball down the middle. It flew into right centre field and I flew into second base. Fluky? Was I expecting praise? The pitcher won't give in this time, I'm thinking; he'll only make perfect pitches. He and his brother, the catcher, they know what to do. So I really don't have a chance.

A fastball darts to the outside corner.

"Yeah. He can't hit that," says the catcher to the pitcher.

The next pitch is a curveball that bounces in front of the plate. I swing at it anyway. I don't know why; it's not anywhere near the plate.

I step out of the batter's box, tell myself to watch the ball, to be ready, but to wait. I tell myself not to swing at that curveball again, that 'drop ball' as my teammates call it. I tell myself this pitcher is fourteen, that's all. He's not Nolan Ryan. He's not in the big leagues. This is a night game at a small ballpark in Moncton. Ten people are watching. None of them are family. I readjust my batting gloves, step back in the batter's box and know it'll be a curveball, in the dirt, even nastier than the one before.

But it's a fastball right down the middle and I don't swing.

* * *

I bike to games on my orange ten-speed CCM. I have been biking to games since I started playing little league four years ago. Back then I had friends on the team, friends I had started with. I couldn't catch, and I could barely throw. I was much better at getting hit by the ball than actually hitting the ball. But at least I didn't run the bases the wrong way, like Lori did. She was pretty, though, with her long black ponytail and sunshine smile, so we never made fun of her. Well, not for long.

I bike in my uniform, which is powder blue this year and doesn't really match my black-and-white cleats. My glove, an outfielder's glove, is stuck in the handlebars. While biking I go over my best games, or my worst games, or I don't think of baseball at all, which is hard to believe, but my head is often in outer space; even in school it's often in outer space. Especially in school. My notebooks are full of drawings or doodles. I get to the end of classes realizing everything the teacher said simply bounced off me, maybe smacked a few other kids in the head, then bounded out the window.

"Thompson? Earth to Thompson? The largest continent on the planet is...?"

Fortunately, I read a lot at home.

"Asia," I say, like a satellite beaming down a weather report.

But if the teacher had started talking about baseball, if he had asked who knows the best grip for a slider or who can mimic Andre Dawson's batting stance, this useless information wouldn't have been able to hold itself in. I'd have leaped up, shouted *me* and then of course sat back down, embarrassed.

By the time I arrive at the ballpark, I've either convinced myself that I'll have a great game or that I should just stay on the bench.

* * *

The thing is, I hate baseball growing up. I hate softball too. I watch my father whip underhanded pitches to my older sister, Debbie, who somehow catches them. Light could be falling, yet the pitches get faster, faster, and the mitt snaps each time, and her hand must be hurting, and how can she not close her eyes, or scream that her glove is going to rip and smash her face? My father asks if I want to catch, and I shake my head. We play games in the vacant lot next to the house, the whole *fam damily*, all four hundred of us or so it seems. I don't know the rules. I can't hit the ball into the next driveway, which is a home run. I can hardly lift the bat.

And then, one day, I want to play.

I have a neighbour named Gino. He's even smaller than I am. He's new to the neighbourhood and I can't remember how it all gets started, but when you're kids sometimes all you need is to bump into each other at the corner store, both buying Orange Crush, or grab a ball rolling down the street, hand it to him and maybe he says, *Hey, want to play catch?* And maybe you shrug and say, *I don't have a glove*, and he says, *You can borrow my father's.*

However it happens, I fall in love with baseball.

We spend the fall — me, Gino, Diane and Murray — playing some variety of the game in Gino's backyard, with rules changed to accommodate so few players. For the bases we use newspapers (I have a paper route) and the home run fence is the end of the yard, where a field grows. About twenty feet into the field there are trees, shrubs really. If you hit a home run it spares you the trouble of being on base when you have to be at bat again.

I don't think we keep score, because there is no other team.

We just play.

And in the evening, just before dark, and on weekends, Gino's father plays. He is a powerful man, at least five foot four and one hundred and thirty pounds. Only Murray dares pitch to him. More often than not we end up scouring the shrubs for his home runs, some of which must have flown a hundred and twenty feet.

We play until our hands freeze and then take up street hockey. And when spring comes round we all sign up for little league.

Second

But winter, winter is long and hitting a balled-up sock with a wrapping-paper tube in Murray's basement, though fun, isn't quite the real thing. Murray has a mean streak too, throws brushback pitches telling me I'm crowding the plate (which really *is* a dinner plate), then fires the balled-up sports sock at my head.

"That hurts, you know," I shout, knowing he'll only throw the next one harder. "And you're breaking the bats too," I whine. In the corner of the basement rec room there's a pile of limp, bent tubes.

"Don't be such a wimp," says Murray.

"Don't be such a fascist," I say in return.

"Fascist? Like I throw the fasch-test pitches?"

"Fascist, like Mussolini, dummy."

"Who?"

"Like Lex Luther," I say to the Superman fanatic.

"Don't be," he says, gritting his teeth, "insulting," he adds, winding up for the next pitch. "Lex. Luther!"

But I'm ready and I duck. The pitched sock thumps against the drywall.

"So are you in love with Lex Luther?" I ask, tightening the sockball, making it reasonably round again.

"He's Superman's arts enemy, you know. So he's pretty cool," says Murray.

"*Arts* enemy?"

"Or harsh enemy, something like that. Go read more books, dimwad!"

"Maybe he's his farts enemy? Or how about his darts enemy? Spare-parts enemy? His shopping cart enemy! No, no, his K-Mart enema!"

Murray raises the tube bat over his head and tomahawks it toward me.

It clatters off my left arm. With my right hand I fire the sockball at his head, but he hits the floor and the sockball whacks the hanging, pull-string light bulb. There's a *pop* and all is black.

* * *

There's even less purpose to basement sockball than backyard four-man baseball. Yet I could play for hours. As a sockball pitcher I have impeccable command, can make the sock dart away, dive down, run up and in. I can throw a change-up that stops in mid-air, have Murray swinging at the mere thought of the pitch. This is what attracts me to baseball: the lines, the trajectories, the predictions versus the results. It's like math, like physics. It's rockets and orbits. It's numbers in your head, ideas becoming real.

It's like writing stories.

At the time, however, I suck at math and my stories always involve some hideous creature chasing and eating people. The monsters have variety: dinosaurs, aliens, mutants. I remember one story about a walrus that has a taste for blood. It starts eating seals, then polar bears (lots of ice blue and crimson in those drawings) and then uses its great mass to crush igloos. It eats so many people that its blubber is impenetrable to spears and bullets. When helicopters try to blast it with cannons, it uses its tusks to burrow underground. This new technique leads it to the cities, where it lives in the sewers, bursting through manholes at night to gobble up skinny businessmen and smelly garbagemen. The police go into the sewers with torches and their screams are heard for days. And then the scientists at the Sea Zoo decide to release all the sharks into the sewers, and the stingrays and the barracudas too. They corner the meat-crazed, insane-eyed walrus and feast.

The end.

* * *

To pass the winter we play street hockey. Or, more often, driveway hockey. Here again, Gino's father is king. We wonder if he could have played in the NHL, with his combination of finesse and smarts. While Murray will wind up his hockey stick and whack the ball with a golf-style swing, Gino's dad moves in slow, fakes, dekes, and I'm helpless. "I don't want to play goal, why am I always in goal?"

"Because you suck."

Secretly, I love it. It's not baseball but I'm wearing a catcher's mask and shin guards and a first baseman's trapper. I go down into a catcher's crouch and wait to snag the ball with my glove. Sometimes I succeed. More often I miss. Maybe I need glasses.

My older brothers all played hockey. Not this kind, but on ice, with real skates, not the black-painted figure skates I was made to believe were hockey skates. My ankles-splayed approach to skating brings me no offers to join teams. Photos hang in the house: brothers in red or yellow uniforms, stranding straight and not falling over (but put me in skates and it's drunk ballet). And my father, greying, developing a pot-belly, played every weekend. Black-and-white photos of his teams over the years line the stairway, the hallway.

But I'm the bookish boy, and no one even thinks of signing me up for hockey.

And the falling down is, in fact, a problem.

Third

One night, late that winter, while the world is sleeping, Murray and I take the keys to his father's company station wagon. We put it in neutral and push it down the street, then Murray jumps in, starts the car. I am twelve, Murray is thirteen. It's a quiet neighbourhood. No cars are seen at three in the morning and Murray is a slow, careful driver. He has done this before.

The white Cable 5 News station wagon rolls down Vista Drive, past Gino's house, then Glenwood Drive, past my house, past the Williams, Towers, Preston and Wallace houses. They are all sleeping.

"If we get caught, we'll go to jail," says Murray, more excited than worried. "They'll call my dad and your mom and we'll have a record."

"What if they don't answer the phone?"

"They'll knock on the door, dimwad," says Murray, now turning up busier Shediac Road, swearing and using his turn signal only after turning.

"But why would I have a record?"

"You're my accomplice, so we both do time."

"You're going too slow," I say, and Murray pumps the gas. I tell him to smarten up and drive like a grown-up but he says he forgot to adjust the seat and can hardly reach the pedal. "Watch out for the curb!" I shout, and Murray overcorrects, has us in the opposite lane. He's laughing and swearing, puts a hand to his mouth and bites off one of his mittens, then the other. Now we're going too fast. We pass the paper route houses of Martin, Gallant, D'Astous.

Then Murray swears again and turns sharply into the long, U-shaped driveway of the haunted Gaudet mansion.

"Pigs," he says.

"Where?" I say.

Murray hushes me. A cold yellow glow comes from an attic window in the haunted Gaudet mansion. Our hearts are racing, but we're only an empty wooded lot from Murray's home. He inches the car forward, sees no sign of police, and we crawl home.

"Shit," says Murray, parking. "Forgot to turn on the headlights."

* * *

"Do you think he'd let you drive us to our ball games this summer? You're a good driver for thirteen. You'll be almost fourteen by then."

Murray shakes his head. "You have to be sixteen."

"But what if your dad signs a note? Or maybe you could get a fake ID?"

Murray slashes his Pong paddle down and sends the digital ball (which is square on the TV screen) arcing high. I barely make the save, return the Pong ball. The blips and beeps bound round the living room.

"Biking is better," says Murray. "It builds up your muscles; it'll be our, like, superpower."

"Strong legs?"

"Super strong legs. And we should get some weights and work out. Especially if we're going to be pros."

"But this is good for our hand and eye coordination."

"Only if you're playing ping-pong. They need to make a baseball version."

"I think it's too complicated. You need NASA computers for that. The ball always goes straight, see? You can't throw curveballs in Pong."

"Hey. Do you like Mimi?" says Murray, throwing a curve of his own.

I hesitate.

"When she was here yesterday, we kissed," says Murray.

"Oh. On the lips?" It's dumb, but I'm not sure what else to say.

"Mostly," says Murray.

And I'm not sure where else he means, and most likely it was just bad aim, nose or chin or elbow, but more and more Murray is talking about Mimi, or Celine, or Monique, and that light bulb hasn't yet been switched on for me. None of them play baseball. But Murray's sister, Diane, does.

And she is good.

"Yeah, we were kissing," says Murray, face intent on the TV screen. "And then my father came home."

* * *

There are two fathers in my life, Murray's and Gino's. One tall, greying, square-chinned, yet unathletic, pale. He's loud, a talker, on TV introducing local news, hosting local events. A music jamboree. A talk show that usually features local hockey players or musicians. One show he interviewed a fly fisherman. Next show a candlepin bowling champion. After that a rhythmic gymnast in her leotard. These aren't sports, we agree. Neither is darts. Or croquet. Or curling, I say. But Murray tried it, says it was hard. "So what, knitting mittens looks hard," I say, "and no one's an Olympic knitting star."

Murray's father, we also discover, likes sleeping pills.

And the other father, Gino's, as I mentioned, is a small man, wiry. Easygoing. Kind.

Abandoned at the mall one night, I take the bus home. Gino's father is driving. We talk about baseball, only about baseball on the empty bus, and he laughs when I say if he would shave his moustache he could play on our team this spring. He says he might be a coach one day. He tells me I'm on the wrong bus, by the way, and not only that, it's the end of the line. I get to see the bus terminal, the garage. He drives me home in the family Volkswagen Rabbit.

He asks me what my father does, says he can't remember if I told him.

"Well," I say, "he used to work for EPA, fixing the planes."

"Oh, I used to fly on EPA all the time," Gino's father says. "Thank him for me because we never crashed once."

I just nod, wondering what Gino's father means. It's quiet in the car as we head back to Lewisville. It's dark out, but a few Christmas lights are still up. Gino's father swears under his breath, then says he's sorry, he'd completely forgotten, then asks if I had a good Christmas. Again he swears.

I tell him it was funny, with my oldest brother handing out the gifts for the first time, pretending he didn't know how to read. I tell him I got a radio, an electric alarm clock for school, a telescope.

"You like looking at the stars?" he asks, dropping me off.

"Yeah. The moon the most," I say.

Fourth

How I Spent My Christmas Holidays

By: Lee Thompson
For Mrs. Willowbend, 6C

This Christmas was the first Christmas for me since my dad died. He died from a heart attack in Nova Scotia because we were living there. The ambulance took a long time, over an hour and nobody knew CPR. I was sleeping and nobody told me until the morning that he had died. My brother Steve told me and when I woke up I saw that he was sad. He looked at me and he said, "Dad died." I didn't want to believe him but I heard noise in the living room all night and also the way he looked sitting on the bed and his arms hanging down and his head down, because of that I believed him.

So this Christmas was much better than last Christmas because no one died. And it was snowing and last year it was raining which is awful for Christmas. I always wake up first and this year I woke up so early that it was still dark out. I don't know why but I wanted to sit by the tree and also look out the window and watch the snow falling. There are a lot of people living in the house and I like it best when it is quiet. The falling snow was beautiful because of all the Christmas lights. The only noise in the house was the furnace coming on and sometimes a snowplough going by. And our cat Bobby because he has a short tail, he was purring and rubbing my legs. Bobby came with us from Nova Scotia when we moved back after the heart attack last Christmas.

I got lots of really great gifts for Christmas but I know we are not supposed to list all the gifts that we got for Christmas, so I will list some gifts that I did not get. I did not get a pet whale or a Corvette Stingray. I also did not get five tonnes of Swiss cheese. I also did not get a household flamethrower or a backyard bazooka. I did not get a pink dress. I did not want a pink dress. I also did not get a monkey that I could train to tidy up my room or even go to school for me. I did not get a free report card of all A+ from Mrs. Willowbend. There are always things we wish for but do not get at Christmas but the gifts we get are the best gifts because they are the gifts we are given.

PS: After opening my gifts I went sliding at the park with my friends and my nephew Cory.

PPS: My sister says I spelt plough wrong but just because she is in grade ten doesn't mean she is smarter than me.

Fifth

"You have to swing the bat," says Ray, coach of the beaver-level Flames. "Just watch the ball and try to hit it. You can't walk every time up." But for my first week of little league, I do. I walk or I'm hit by a pitch. Either way, I'm on first base. Baseball is easy.

But my second week of little league is spent striking out. The mop-haired pitchers with thick glasses have started to figure out my strategy of 'don't ever swing.'

"Swing the bat," my teammates say. Yet even fastballs thrown by twelve-year-olds sneak by me. I can't hit them in practice, no matter how slow the coach throws them. He tries underhanded tosses, but nothing.

"Just watch the ball," he says.

I watch it go into the catcher's mitt. I watch it thrown around the bases by smiling opponents after I strike out. I watch it humiliate me.

"You're not looking at the ball," he says.

By the third week I have managed to hit the ball twice, weakly, both times foul balls. And then I figure something out: you can watch the ball till your eyes bleed, but your eyes don't hit the ball (or they would *really* bleed); your bat does. This is obvious. Swinging the bat takes time, so if you start your swing early, right as the pitcher releases the ball...

It's such genius that I do not share it with my teammates.

In my first game with my new brain I hit a pop-up to second base. "See, see," says Ray. "Next time swing harder." In my next at-bat I hit the ball again, a grounder to shortstop. I run hard, because running is the one thing I can do better than my teammates. The shortstop rushes and throws the ball over the first baseman's head. I scoot into second base.

I finish the season with three base hits. More than the tiny Flanagan twins and pony-tailed Lori combined.

The Flames, named by me after my favourite hockey team, make it to the playoffs.

* * *

Diane, our star shortstop and Murray's stepsister, does not like losing. She does not like losing at card games, board games, tag, hide-and-seek, rock paper scissors and certainly not baseball. She's our best hitter, our best fielder, our leader. But if we lose, we hear it all the way home.

Our routine is to head to 7-Eleven after the game, buy a Big Gulp, get our sugar fix and bike home.

We're horrible. We suck. We have to practise more, practise harder. She's going to make us practise till midnight. She's going to make us run and catch and throw until we cry like babies. That's because we play like babies. She's going to leave the team if we keep losing. She's so damn embarrassed. *When are you guys going to start playing like men?* Next game, she says, she's going to pitch and strike everyone out.

It's a good thing we only lose four games all season.

It's a good thing we're old enough to realize what crazy is.

When I picture her mother, before and after she married Murray's father, all I see is tousled sleep-hair and a blue housecoat, and a woman always on a couch.

* * *

It's late August 1981. It's the Humphrey Zone Beaver Baseball Championship game. It's the Expos vs. the Flames. We are facing Ronnie, a chunky righty who has dominated us all year. But the Flames have an ace in the hole: Darren, a freckled, pot-smoking, raspy-voiced redhead who might (rumours have it) already be fourteen. He's too old for the league but no one asked for ID. He's a fireballing lefty.

Before the game, Gino's father has gifts: leather batting gloves. And Murray's father arrives in the Cable 5 station wagon. He has a speaker on the roof of the station wagon. He reads the lineups to the crowd. "And batting ninth ... Lee Thompson."

Murray is catcher, doing his best Gary Carter imitation. Diane is at her usual shortstop position (her pitching career was short, as she was skilled only at hitting batters, and the *more* batters the more furious she became at hitting batters). Gino is at third base, despite his trouble throwing to first base (he's desperately in need of a growth spurt). I'm in right field.

No one can touch Darren. From my vantage point all I see is the ball darting past the Expo hitters. No fancy stuff, just fastballs.

Earlier in the season Ronnie shut us out, striking out fourteen Flames. Ray was livid. "This guy will never strike out fourteen batters again in his life," he said, which made me think *I guess Ronnie isn't that great, won't make the pros*, which was a revelation. We are kids facing kids. No one all year had hit a ball over the fence, though Murray had come close. Errors were the rule. One kid tripped and fell over first base and wouldn't stop crying.

I can't identify what I feel when I step to the plate against Ronnie, with the largest crowd of the season watching, with the newspaper photographer there. It'll puzzle me for a few years before I realize it's a new feeling. I'm relaxed. I feel good. There's no panic in my brain.

In my first at-bat I shock myself and smash the ball to right centre. I run forever, hoping for an error too, but have to stop at third base. I had clobbered it.

What has happened?

And in my next at-bat, before I'm removed so Lori can prance out to right field, I loop a double over the first baseman's head and two runs score.

Last pitch and another Expos hitter strikes out. In celebration, Murray and Darren tackle each other on the mound.

Flames win.

Sixth

Things change over the next year. Gino's family moves away, not far but too far for easy biking. We can't understand why anyone would want to move from a house with a great baseball backyard to a basement apartment. Gino doesn't talk about it much and after a few months we stop visiting. No one bikes in winter anyway.

Murray moves from his huge bedroom in the basement to the rec room, where a cot is set up, a curtain used as a partition. Gone are the posters of Superman and *Star Wars*. Now there are posters of Cheech and Chong. He shrugs when I ask if he's angry about having to sleep there. His old room is rented to a lame bearded man who Murray likes to beat at arm-wrestling. Another boarder takes residence downstairs, a frizzy-haired woman, a secretary at Cable 5 who runs a bath every night. Her room is next to the rec room. We hear the water running and silently wonder what's on the other side of the wall.

Murray and Diane fight all the time, which upsets Zelda, the German shepherd, who then seeks someone 'not family' to bite.

Winter hockey involves shooting hard orange hockey balls against the side of Murray's house. After a while the siding starts to fall off.

And more and more often girls gather at the house, the junior high volleyball team. They talk, they dance, they sneak alcohol from their parents. One night Diane flirts with me, wants to dance close to "Babe" by Styx. This isn't right.

I think I run home.

Where I put on headphones, listen to Supertramp, Cheap Trick, Foreigner and Rush and read issues of *Baseball Digest*.

* * *

That winter, aged thirteen, trouble returns. Trouble is named David, who moved from the neighbourhood two years before. David's father and his older brother were bikers who rode Harleys (while his dad also owned a Jaguar). There was a rule at David's: Dad got off work at five and kids had to be out of the house. Kids, of course, don't have a great concept of time, and more than once we found ourselves frozen in fear as we heard the Harley or the Jag pull in. *Shit, shit, shit*, David would say. We'd scurry from the basement and out the back door, race across the lawn, climb the fence, run through the wooded lot, find sanctuary at Murray's and tell epic tales of how close it was this time.

David was always the biggest kid in school, the one no one dared to scrap with. He isn't so much tall as stocky, with short curly reddish brown hair. He rocks a jean jacket like no kid I've ever known.

We are on Murray's back deck one evening. We've just taken our Crazy Carpets from the roof, just taken the ladder from the eaves, just finished remarking how fun that was, house tobogganing into a mound of snow, more fun than biking on the roof last summer, when "Hi, guys" is heard. There are no hugs or handshakes, no "You look good, man," just a "What are you doing here?" and an explanation: Father in town, divorce court; *Can I sleep over, my dad doesn't care.* Murray's father is out with one of the volleyball moms while his stepmother is in hospital.

"So you're the man of the house?" asks David.

"I guess," says Murray.

"Have any booze?"

"No."

"Father have any stashed?"

"Yes."

That morning, many in the neighbourhood woke to find their cars turned sideways in their driveways. While David wanted to steal one or catch a cat and lock it in one or flip one upside down, I was the voice of reason and mostly sober. The plan was to turn all cars sideways, and David was the muscle, but halfway through our project we heard police sirens and fled in three directions.

* * *

I don't remember Christmas that year.

Perhaps there's nothing to recall.

Something has set in, two years after my father's death. A sense of gloom. I argue with my mother often, get into a couple of fights at school (fist, meet my mouth), see my grades drop. I miss two months of school, at home sick, yet somehow pass. A student named Fran — what kind of a name is that for a boy? — likes to tackle me into the snow. He's a boxer who can't get past grade eight. He runs at me, tackles me and says, with that brilliant mind of his, "Tackle."

Tackle, tackle, tackle.

Why? Because we have the same red-and-black winter jacket.

With Murray and Diane in different schools, I have more tenuous alliances — John, Mike, Geoff, neighbourhood pals, but I never see them outside of school. The lunchtime cafeteria, its smell of fries, its mean girls with feathered hair, is a bad dream played out daily.

I spend a lot of time in the art room.

And when warmer weather rolls round only Murray and I sign up for baseball, but we end up on different teams. And it's a new level, bantam, and everyone is bigger, stronger. I can't start my swing early enough. I'm thinking too much. I know no one on the team. After five games, I quit.

Seventh (Inning Stretch)

The Brothers Grottosen

A Short Story by Author L.D. Thompson

There were three brothers who lived in a cave outside of the village. Their names were Jeb, Theo and Heathrow Grottosen. They were lonely and always fighting and knew that they needed to find wives, as many as possible, even though for years getting even one wife was totally impossible. It was not because they lived in a cave, because it was a nice cave with bearskin rugs and fancy candles and running water from hoses connected to mountain streams. It was because terrible creatures lived in the forest between the brothers and the holy temple where the women lived and frolicked every day. At night they could hear the women splashing in the temple fountains, could hear their giggling and laughing.

"We need to capture some wives," Theo shouted. Jeb and Heathrow, who they called Heathy for short, roared in agreement and clanged their metal beer mugs together. Theo was the oldest and the strongest of the brothers. Heathrow was the ugliest and because of that he had no fear of anything. No bear or mountain dragon could mess up his already messed-up face. Jeb was the smartest of the three brothers, but he drank too much beer.

When they all were little boys their father Zachary was killed by a mysterious beast that some people called a Mist Tiger. Legends told about Mist Tigers creeping up on sleeping forest travellers and sucking their bones out. But when Heathrow found his father by the side of the road to the village, he still had all of his bones but his eyes and his hair and his skin were whiter than snow. His finger had scratched something in the dirt. MIST TI — and then it was a squiggle. The brothers cried and hid in the cave for many weeks but one day Theo took charge, and now years later they needed wives. They gathered round the fire in the cave and made plans. They talked in whispers so the creatures could not hear them. Their shadows almost looked like the monsters they would have to battle if they wanted wives.

The plan they agreed to was very simple. Theo and Heathy would run as fast as they could through the forest when the clock struck noon. Noon was when the forest was the quietest and the screams and hideous laughter of the beasts could barely be heard.

"They must sleep at noon," said Theo. "Before," he continued, "everyone tried to sneak through the forest at night, but they all died."

"We must get wives," shouted Heathy. "Little Jeb will slow us down and we will die too!" When Jeb moaned that he wanted a wife or two also, Theo said they would bring an extra sack. Jeb said he wanted a blonde or a brunette with wavy but not curly hair.

They drank beer and waited until noon.

When it was noon, the forest fell silent.

"Grab the sacks!" Theo whispered loudly. "And run!"

The two brothers, one very powerful and commanding with a beard like a forest fire, the other ugly and crouchy like a swamp rat, ran hooting and hollering into the forest before shushing each other. Jeb hid in the cave and waited and he could not even start to dream about opening his blonde in a sack before he heard the familiar but also hideous screams of his brothers. Heathy died first, he could tell, and Theo last after a lot of grunting and swearing.

I guess I am the only brother left, Jeb thought to himself.

Jeb was lonely without his brothers, but happy that he had more beer to himself now. There were barrels and barrels of good beer at the back of the cave, enough to last for years. For many weeks he lay on the bearskin rugs very drunk and totally numb. He did not eat, he only drank. He thought about his father, killed by the Mist Tiger, and about his brothers, killed by unknown things out there. He thought about the sound of their bones being crunched up and eaten. One night he woke from a nightmare and heard the singing and laughter of the women in the village. He even thought he heard one singing a song about wishing there were more men in the village.

I need to make a plan, Jeb thought desperately. *I need to be able to sneak past the beasts of the forest while they sleep at noon.* He thought long and hard and at first he thought he would build a giant slingshot and parachute, but who would pull the slingshot back? And anyway, he was scared of heights. Second, he thought be would dig a tunnel but he was scared of worms and who knew what the forest worms would be like? And third, he thought he would make himself invisible. He would cover himself in leaves and vines and moss and he would make shoes from the bearskins, big fluffy shoes that would make no sound when he walked in the forest.

The next day at noon he had a big swig of beer, belched, and put on his suit of leaves and moss and twigs. He had stayed up all night making it and was proud of it. Then he put on his bearskin slippers. He did not have a sack but he hoped the one who was singing about more men would be happy to come marry him in the cave. *I have come just for you*, he would say. Step by step he got deeper into the forest. The sun was hidden by the trees, but so far he was safe. He could hear breathing all around him, but he told himself not to be scared.

After a while he saw, in the trees, his brothers' clothing. He told himself not to look. He saw more and more clothing and shoes and sometimes bones and skulls. It was almost so black that he couldn't see. But he was careful. He walked slowly. He entered a clearing and then he heard giggling. It was all around him in the trees. He looked up hoping the women would be in tree houses, but they weren't women at all! They were giant hideous bats with faces like women except for the fangs. He had been fooled!

He waited to be eaten.

But the bat women didn't attack him.

Everything was silent. And then he saw it, entering the clearing. It looked like a cat but it was made of clouds. Its eyes sparkled like sapphires. The Mist Tiger crawled towards Jeb, who was shaking with fear. He thought it was growling but really it was purring. And then the bat women flew from their branches and circled Jeb and the Mist Tiger, giggling and laughing and singing.

"You are the first good man to enter the forest," the Mist Tiger purred. "We will be your friends."

Eighth

Usually, quitting is the worst thing to do. Everyone tells you this: don't be a quitter, quitting never got anyone anywhere. But maybe quitting isn't the right word. Maybe resetting or rebooting is the best way to describe what happens after I quit the team.

I quit the team, yes, but not baseball. In fact, I play more baseball that summer than I ever have. I play with my older brothers, play with Murray (who also quit) and others from the neighbourhood, sometimes forming teams, finding unused ballparks or open fields, playing until the sun sets. And all summer I work out at my sister's gym.

My throwing improves. I even start to pitch. At Murray's place we practise hitting with the house as a backstop. We can't use baseballs, so at first we use hockey balls, and once, unfortunately, one of those hard, heavy, grey-green Superballs.

Here's the scene:

Murray [with a devilish grin]: Hey, I wonder how far this Superball would go?

Lee [shaking head]: No.

Murray [still grinning]: I know, I know. Just toss it in, OK? I won't swing hard.

Lee [pointing]: *Don't swing hard.*

But it's a Superball, and even with a checked swing it rockets past my ear, goes bouncing across the street, skips over the neighbour's lawn and through a basement window. We watch and then swear. We run. We're hiding behind a tree in Murray's yard when a woman comes over, bouncing the ball in her hand. Murray waits then casually steps from behind the tree and says, "Hi, I see you found our ball."

* * *

"They're getting a divorce," says Murray one late-summer evening. We're on our bikes, taking a shortcut through the Lewisville Cemetery. His father, Murray says, wants to be with the mother of Lisette, one of the volleyball girls and Diane's closest friend.

"Wow, so she'll be your sister now?" I say, then add, "But what happens to Diane?" Murray stops, gets off his bike and asks me to help him put a tombstone back on its pedestal. It's heavier than we expect, but we manage. "Remember when we used to play hide-and-seek here?" I say.

"It's not facing the street," Murray says.

"What?"

"We put it on backwards."

I check the tombstone, look at the others and shrug. "I'd rather be looking at the trees than the street anyway," I say. Murray agrees, so we leave it as is. We walk our bikes the rest of the way since it's getting too dark to avoid the other tombstones, not to mention exposed tree roots. "So, Lisette's mom will be moving in and Diane's moving out?"

"He's selling the house and we're going to move into Lisette's," Murray says.

"But what happens to Diane?"

Murray gives me a strange look and says Diane is coming too. It all seems mangled to me. More and more my faith in adults knowing what they're doing is fading. They're more messed up than kids. I ask him when they're moving and he says they're not waiting for the house to sell. They're moving next week. "My dad says he'll come and get my friends or drive me out here. I can get my license next year...”

I go to their new place once, a birthday party for Lisette. It’s too far out of town, and soon Murray is hanging out with different friends. We both start high school that fall and are in the same school for the first time, but we only nod when passing in the halls. Eventually we don’t even do that.

* * *

High school. One of the first things I learn is that I’ve grown. I strut the halls of Moncton High proud of this, as if it hasn’t already been achieved by everyone else here. As if I willed myself to grow, or did it through long hours of study.

Which would never happen.

Eventually, toward the end of high school, I will be known as the art class guy, the guy who can draw so well. But in grade ten I’m quite anonymous. The misery of junior high is over. Kids everywhere are now a little less confused. I hang around with Paul, Roger, Mark and John, spending lunch hours at the video arcade. I hate the arcade and have nothing in common with these guys and will lose touch even before high school is over.

The fear of being alone makes you waste a hell of a lot of time.

The first day of high school, actually, I meet Rikky, who lives in my neighbourhood, but in a rough area. We say hi. We’ll be inseparable as seniors but for now we only talk in the halls. Had I been able to predict the future I would say, *Hey, so one day I’ll be best man at your wedding. Neat.* And he would say, *Hey, you’ll come stay with me in Germany. Cool.* And we’ll say, at the same time, *We’re getting guitars next year.*

All winter I keep working out at my sister’s gym.

I read books on science and keep writing stories.

I take down the baseball posters in my room and put up Duran Duran, U2 and Prince posters in their place. I take the old posters, my baseball glove and cleats, my batting gloves and bring them to the basement. There’s a box with other sports gear there, much of which belonged to my father: old-fashioned baseball gloves (tiny, strange, poufy things), catcher’s masks, chin guards. It all smells of old leather, years of sweat and summer. He’d be shocked by how much I love to play, I think. Instead of leaving my equipment in the box, I bring one of the old gloves up to my room.

Ninth

"It's fluky kid again," says the catcher. He's standing, looking down at me. He's at least a head taller. "Strike him out, Bobby," he says to his brother. He sounds like he's bored. Even before the season started, I'd heard about the brothers. Younger than everyone, but too good for the league, maybe future pros, they said. I wondered if this season would be a repeat of last season.

But so far, it's gone much better. I'm not a star, but I'm holding my own. No one's going to ask me to join the provincial team, but that's okay, I know my limits. I bat leadoff. I'm fast and I have a strong arm. My hitting is reliant on feeling confident, which seems to be reliant on not thinking too much. Just sit back, see the ball, hit the ball.

Don't try to predict what's coming.

Don't obsess about what's already happened.

I try to ignore the catcher. Even if I strike out again, I did hit that double. When I got back to the dugout after my first at-bat, everyone said, *Wow, someone hit Bobby's fastball. Man, you crushed it. Boy, is he going to be pissed.* After I struck out, they said, *Hey, join the club.*

The game is tied 3-3. The lights are on at Kelly Field but there's still some blue in the dusk sky. I dig in. Guy pounds his catcher's mitt. The first pitch is a fastball but I'm late on it, swing and hit a foul ball to right. *Damn. Throw that again, throw that again.* "Oh, he thinks he can hit your fastball, Bobby," says Guy. "I wonder if he can hit your curve."

Yeah, not falling for that again.

The next pitch is also a fastball, but I'm too eager, it's too high and I swing and miss.

"No chance, no chance," says Guy.

I step out. He *has* to throw the curveball now. But last time I thought that too. And got a fastball down the middle. No, it'll be a curve, I know. *No. Stop thinking so much!* I hear my teammates telling me to be patient, I hear someone say *Pitcher has a rubber arm*, I hear *Take him deep, Thompson, win this.* In the other dugout I see their father, who's their coach. I see the pride in his eyes.

* * *

I remember few things from my time with my father. You think I would remember more, but it was such a big family and he worked long hours at the airport. He comes home, sits in the La-Z-Boy, smokes a cigarillo and watches the Lawrence Welk Show. He has a glass of rum. He shushes me when I interrupt.

I remember him wrestling outside with one of my older brothers, clutching each other and rolling down a small hill.

I remember the coldness of the hockey rink, the chipped wooden bleachers, the boredom and waiting for him to come out of the locker room.

"Did you win?"

"No."

I remember running away for no reason other than thinking it's something to do and I won't be missed. I hide in an abandoned shack but in the evening I am found. I do not remember him searching for me.

I remember playing in the big maroon car, the Lincoln Continental, while it is parked in the driveway. This is forbidden. I remember my father getting in the car while I hide in the back seat. I remember that dilemma. We drive to the airport and, faced with staying in the car all day or telling him, I tell him. "Jesus," he says, startled. In the airport parking lot he turns the car around and takes me home.

* * *

When the ball comes out of the pitcher's hand, you have little more than a second to react. The next pitch is a fastball, high like the last one, but I don't swing.

"Good pitch," says the catcher.

"Strike him out so we can go home!"

"Blow it by him, Bobby!"

"Crush it again, Lee!"

There's nothing in my head when the pitch comes. I see the downward spin, the trajectory, know that it's not bouncing in the dirt this time, it's too high, it's a curveball and I wait, smack it up the middle under Bobby's glove, past the second baseman. My dugout goes crazy.

"Keep an eye on him," the first baseman says to the pitcher. "He thinks he's fast."

Whatever. I take a big lead. Bobby throws over a few times to keep me close.

"Try it, you'll get caught," says the first baseman.

But this is what I do best. On the first pitch I sprint for second, slide, see the second baseman lunge for the ball, which is rolling into centre field, so I jog into third base.

"Error, error, error," come the taunts from my dugout.

Their coach tells Bobby to forget about the runner (me!), to concentrate on the batter. I take a big lead off third base, watching the pitcher intently. He looks annoyed. I take a bigger lead. He winds up and throws a strike to our batter, who doesn't swing. It's strike two. Before the next pitch I take the biggest lead possible, too big, really. Bobby's eyes follow third baseman as he scoots to the bag — a pickoff — I'm dead — but the throw is terrible, bounces off the third baseman's outstretched glove and I race home.

My teammates rush from the dugout.

Score one for the fluky kid.

BEFORE I WAS ME

by Chad Pelley

I saw your mother in the grocery store the other day, looking lost in the bakery aisle. She had a loaf of bread in her hand, holding it by the twist tie end of the bag so it was swaying back and forth like a pendulum, the way you must have been swaying when she walked into the shed that day, looking for a gardening tool or whatever. Thinking you were at school, finding missing angles in triangles and passing notes to Jenny B. Living, happy. Okay.

You had this way of folding the notes you'd pass me in class so they were little self-sealed packages I had to unwrap like a gift. Remember that? You tried showing me how to do it, but I could never get my head around how to twist and turn and tuck the loose leaf into a perfect square. And I never had anything good to say anyway. *Have you heard the new Silverchair album yet?* It was you who had all the words and the way you worded your notes, the way I'd anticipate tearing them open to see your words — to know you just a little bit more, to learn one more thing about you, to be that much closer to solving the mystery of who you were — is probably why I'm a writer now. That one person could anticipate another's words so much. Look forward to them. Connect to them the way I connected with you back then. Before you broke that connection.

Half a lifetime later, everyone else's smile seems like a failed imitation of yours. No one laughs as recklessly as you did. The way you still should. The way you would if it weren't for that night at the bonfires. Your laugh was contagious. Even the teachers smiled when asking you to pay attention to algebra, to history, to French grammar, and all the things that didn't matter the way you and I did. At thirty-two I can't remember what I learned about in high school, besides you and how my reaction to you tainted and belittled all these silly things we waste our time on: degrees, day jobs, debt and waiting for those things to add up to something they'll never add up to. Something like you and me on a Ferris wheel, fingers sticky with cotton candy, making naive promises and plans that felt too big to ever break. And the way your eyes held mine like a handshake, a promise or a spell. Something I've never quite put a finger on. And you were gone before I could.

I was looking for a cooler in my attic the other night. I bought a house. I have an attic and a cooler: three more things you'll never own. The cooler was on top of an orange box full of stuff from high school. I took a peek inside and found it was mostly full of pieces of you. Proof you existed. Mixed tapes you made me, your funny handmade birthday cards. There was the little stone you gave me and told me to keep forever. It was the one you'd plucked from your shoe after a hike and you were amazed that it was such a perfect square. *More of a cube than a Rubik's Cube!* And you'd said, *Here, so you'll never forget this day happened.*

I put the stone on the tip of my thumb and flipped it the way you would a coin. I tossed it across the room, like parts of you needed to be spread out across the world, in places other than boxes and coffins and memory. I scattered that part of you like it could make you exist more. One day I'll move out of this house, take this box with me and leave a piece of you behind.

I found the first few notes you handed me in grade eleven. I can open those notes whenever, read the words, remember how you crossed your Ts with imperfect symmetry — the dash on the left of the T about three times longer than the one on the right. You did the same with your Ls, dragged the lower line out too long. I read the words like you were being intentionally emphatic: *LLLove. LLLife.* You left a mark on the world. You wrote on a piece of paper and folded that paper, and I can use these notes as a porthole back to the nineties, before I knew where my life was going. Not that I do know. Things change every year and I wish someone had told you that if you skip out on one year the way you did, you'd skip out on sixty more that would be both better and worse, but always different than the one you called your last.

That night in my attic, there were too many of your notes to read at once and I liked the idea of not reading them all in one night. I liked the idea of stumbling on these again in another sixteen years and re-remembering you. The last one I pulled out said, *Why are we here, learning about mitosis, when the world is full of much more interesting, socially relevant things? Isn't the world itself school? I feel like if we weren't so busy with schoolwork, maybe then we'd learn who we really are. What we really like. Life is happening right now, but not to us, stuck in this smelly classroom.*

I'd forgotten about that smelly classroom. It smelled like vinegar and eggs. Mostly vinegar. It was strong enough to wake you up in the morning, like someone actually squeezed a blast of the stuff up our noses as we walked through the door. Some days, somehow, the classroom smelled like 7UP too. That didn't make sense, the smell of 7UP, until our first kiss. The lip balm. Your 7UP lip balm.

It was quick kiss outside before the bus came. But the layers of balm on your lips had sealed mine to yours, making it harder to pull away before someone saw us. You softened my bones. The kiss promised me something. Not even something from you, but from life itself. Like there was more to being alive than what our teachers, parents and televisions were forcing on us as a formula for how to live: Good grades + good jobs = good lives. And if something was supposed to add more to that equation for me, Dani, I'm glad it was the taste of 7UP on your two lips.

I can't even picture the science teacher anymore in that smelly vinegary room, but I remember your punk rock eyeliner would get on the microscope we had to share and it always left black circles around my eyes. I'd take my face away from a slide of mitosis-in-action, and it looked like the wonder of science had punched me in the face and left a bruised ring around my eyes. First time it happened, your big goofy smile and laugh was worth a million bucks. I fell in love with you that day. In that high school sort of way. You hauling up your shirt to wipe the black off my eyes, me asking you about the belly button ring. *Thought you had to be eighteen to get a piercing?* It was the law, and the fact you'd gotten around the law was part of your allure.

See, if you hadn't died, you'd know what I mean about that *high school sort of way* two people can be in love. You'd know that even married couples don't love as urgently and absolutely as their kids in high school do. I let you carve a heart into my arm with a rusty nail and put your initials in it. That's disgusting and beautiful and the most romantic thing I can think of. *In that high school sort of way.*

It was you conquering me. The way you conquered everything you loved, like "Crazy Train" on guitar, flawlessly and better than I could play it. One day you made me go looking for a lost dog you saw on a telephone pole flyer as if we'd actually find the thing. It was like you were plugged into life and 1,000 volts of it ran through you every day, and anyone who touched you, anyone who held hands with you on the bus like I did could feel it there. Your fearless passion to be alive in the most immediate, desperate way. Sneaking into pools after hours like life owed you that pleasure, keeping a list of things to do the day you got yourself to Italy, reading up on the tattoo parlours you were so confident would hire you one day.

But one quick change, one bad four-month period stole that fire in your belly to live at a hundred miles per hour and crash into life head-on every day. And I could never wrap my head around that. How one pinprick could pop my big, overinflated image of you. Maybe we're all breakable, but you weren't supposed to be if I was drawn to you for the strength of your character. I liked you as the person who could shrug off what others thought. I liked you as the girl in weird knit sweaters and movie T-shirts no other girl in the school owned. It was four months, Dani. Four crappy months. You could have gotten through them. Because the other 780 months you were supposed to live would've come down like an avalanche on top of those four months and crushed them. Buried them.

And you were smart enough to know that. A *Jeopardy* nerd who played Trivial Pursuit with her nan in an old age home. A math whiz who hated math and didn't have to try. It's the math of your decision that haunts me. The average Canadian woman lives 972 months. Four divided by 972 was not even 1% of your life. But you let grade twelve matter more than the 99% of your life that had happened or didn't get to happen. Those ten kids in grade twelve: they loved you, then they didn't and then they would've loved you again.

You were one year from university. You would have loved it. I sat next to a redhead in an earth science class. She reminded me of you, minus her ginger hair and cookie-crumb freckles. She'd stare at people when they weren't looking, like she was just as interested in their lives as the facts on the board. She wore clothes that never came from the mall. She had Woody Allen T-shirts, like you, and I thought: *Dani would have loved university.* Because it's where you learn who you are. Not in the *What I Wanna Be When I Grow Up* sort of way, but more the opposite. What you don't want to be. University is where you get your heart truly broken for the first time and nothing builds character more than coming back from that. University is where your friends stop being limited to the kids in your high school and start being people with similar interests and personalities. You would've spent your week figuring out who you are and your weekends at parties with the music on ten, ringing through your bones as you danced with strangers and had life-affirming conversations with boys on backyard patio swings just like in the movies you made me watch. The girly ones with the epic parties where everything worked out okay.

The night it happened should have played out like one of those epic party movies you loved. Kids from four high schools partying in one big open field all weekend long, while our parents believed the watered-down version of what we were really up to.

There were boom boxes blaring in dewy grass, and the music separated the groups into cliques: jocks, keeners, grunge kids like us, drawn to the music that matched their personalities. Huge bonfires all over the field. When we got there we counted eleven fires before we stopped. Different cliques hung out around different fires and we couldn't tell how fun each separate party was until we went to its fire and joined the conversation there. Swapped names. More nods for another round of hellos. Turned out the field was mostly full of people who were in university. Drunk and high already.

It was easy to get separated that night the way we did. But in hindsight, it would have been just as easy *not* to have gotten separated. You stayed at the first bonfire with our friends, but the promise of something as utterly unimportant as a mixtape with some Pearl Jam B-sides lured me to another fire, then another, and I was running through a maze of fires and parties. And you were behind me or you were just ahead of me, or you were outside of the maze, or you were gone home. I didn't know. Until Jenny B found me at a fire and hauled me away.

"She's really drunk and I can't find her." She was petrified. Eyes so wide I could see their whiteness in the dark. She'd grabbed me by the arm, speed-walking and talking. "Dani probably drank two flasks of rum mixed with something super sweet before she knew how much those guys were giving her. She was falling over and they were helping her up with their hands all over her chest, copping feels."

I remember Jenny kept tripping over her own two feet, falling into me to catch herself as we stumbled through the big black field. The unmowed grass snared our feet every ten paces or so. There was no chance you weren't going to be there when we got there, but we jogged anyway. "She looked asleep, so they had to lay her in a chair." And when Jenny said, "They laughed that her skirt was pushed up," she looked like she'd done you wrong by not throwing you over her shoulder and carting you home.

You weren't where Jenny left you. You weren't where you were supposed to be. And the guys who were there were looking for a fight. They knocked my hat off and checked my pockets for booze or cigarettes. They lost interest when I didn't react because I was more concerned about looking around for you.

"Are you sure this is the fire you left her at?"

"I didn't *leave* her anywhere! *You* did!"

We checked the crowds at another other dozen fires and that took an hour, maybe two. I remember the stars shining like it was any other night and you weren't missing and everything was okay and the trees were swaying into the wind in the same way. Nonchalant, relaxed. I wanted the whole world panicking with us. But the music played on and everyone was partying like this was still a movie-worthy night — and we were the ones going through the part Hollywood never shows us. The part Hollywood lets happen in the background, where no cameras are pointed.

Jenny said, "She was kissing one of them, but I swear it was like she was only kissing back out of instinct. Like she thought it was you kissing her or something. She was that out of it."

There were too many tents to check but we checked them anyway. I pulled a hundred zippers up that night: saw people sleeping, saw empty tents, saw people going to second base, and further, saw every colour of sleeping bag you could imagine. I found everything but you: book bags, beer boxes, a girl crying alone because her boyfriend had just dumped her, seven people crammed into one tent playing Monopoly, four Goth kids having a seance, sitting around an expensive-looking Ouija board like it was a fire.

It was a time before cell phones to call you on, or Facebook photos to show people on iPhones. *Have you seen this girl?* We couldn't find you so we sat where you'd see us, now that the sun was coming up: there was one way out, one exit, and we'd find you there as you left. Jenny'd sit there and I'd take another walk around, calling your name, people telling me to shut up or people asking if they could help or people trying to find their own friends.

There were a few paths beaten into the woods. I checked them out and a stick caught me on the arm. There's still a scar there and that's fine, because it seems like that night should've left a mark on me the way it did you. I found Tim Carter pissing on a tree. I asked him if he'd seen you. He wasn't sure who you were.

"The hot chick in your homeroom with nice rack or the hot chick in our science class with all the wise cracks and the weird sweaters?"

"The latter."

"No, man. She probably had her choice of whose tent to sleep in, if you know what I mean."

Camp smoke. The musky sizzle of fir branches burning, or burning wood in general: the smell of it can still take me back to that night. The night I left you alone because of a mixtape I wanted to hear. Music mattered that much back then. Cassette tapes. Seems so long ago now. There are cassette tapes involved in the memory. You wouldn't know it but they're as out of date as typewriters and male perms. And it seems so weird that you wouldn't know what an MP3 is. An iPod. How easy it is now to have a jukebox in your pocket instead of a bag full of tapes and CDs the way yours was. Whatever you were looking for in your book bag, it was always buried so deep beneath cases it was like they were hiding whatever you were looking for on purpose.

When I started university without you, I got a locker. One day I shut the door and the girl beside me was a dead ringer for you. Eyes like quicksand in colour and pull. Shiny black hair the sun bounced off. But mainly in her mannerisms: she was constantly tucking hair behind an ear, laughing in a way that drew her stomach in. I looked away. I saw those three slots on my locker door — the ones near the top of every locker door. The ones Sally and the others used to slip notes into our locker, just for you, right off the bat in grade twelve. *Slut, whore, baby killer.* In late September, in English, a third of us had abortion as a debate topic and I thought the teacher could have come up with something different. I thought that she should have. You don't know this but I complained to my mother and she talked to the teacher, like, *C'mon, Dani has just had an abortion*, and the teacher didn't care. Instead she graded you harder on subjective things, like a Shakespeare paper, as if a pregnant teen couldn't possibly be bright. As if you all, all of you, make poor decisions. They didn't care that you were just a sixteen-year-old girl hanging out with friends in a field like every other sixteen-year-old girl in that classroom, distinguishable only by the fact you were the one fate served up to a pack of first-year university kids. You were the one who had to wake up in a dank blue tent with pine needles stuck to your face, pregnant.

Slut. Baby Killer. It's called a condom. The year before, in grade eleven, you were everyone's favourite person and I know that bothered the cheerleader types. That someone without lipstick and Gap sweaters and a crush on Tyler Rose could've been the kind of girl that all the boys were after. They were waiting for something to knock you off your pedestal, and it was easy to use the pregnancy as an excuse to do just that. To kick you while you were down. And how you'd gotten pregnant, it didn't matter. The shift in your reign as everyone's favourite did. No one, anywhere, maybe not even in war, is more capable of turning on someone than kids in high school. And the more people who do it to the same person, the more others join in against that person, and it's senseless, and it comes from nowhere, and even psychology textbooks say it's a phenomenon. It had nothing to do with you. In the grade eleven yearbook you were labelled *Most Likeable Classmate.* You were absent in the grade twelve yearbook. Dead before the day the photographer came.

The day you cracked it was mid-morning break. You cried and fell to the floor like a broken doll in five pieces. I didn't know how to pick you up. Because there was no picking you up at that point. It was just a moment you had to live through. And our lives are full of those. Kids' parents die in car accidents and they get raised by substitute parents. Children get cancer and their parents have to watch them suffer and cry in pain and be bloated and cough up blood. Soldiers step on landmines and lose limbs and come home to wives who can't look at them the same way anymore. None of it's fair but all of it is lived through, overcome.

You cried about the notes showing up in our locker, and the way the teachers were looking at you, and the way guys thought they could grab at you now that word was out you were a tramp. Someone slapped your ass the day you broke down to pin a Post-It note there. *Slut.* I found you at our locker with that Post-It note balled up in your hand, your punk rock eyeliner streaming down your cheeks. There was so much black on your cheeks it was like your pupils had burst. And there you were, breakable and broken and fragile and feeling buried under the weight of something. Just the two of us there and that son of a bitch walking away, laughing to himself.

I can say, from the day I met you two years earlier, that I had always thought you were invincible. That you were above being bullied and labelled by a bunch of brainless fools you only had to endure for another year. I can't say I know what you were going through. I've never been bullied and my parents were so ideal, everyone else's seemed subpar by comparison. Even before the pregnancy, your relationship with your mother had seemed so dry and formal to me. She wanted you to be more of a bore, like she was. And all I knew of your father was that he was a drunk working on and off in Alberta and didn't belong in the picture. A poor match for your regal mother and a poor father for anyone. And it shocked me she wouldn't tell your father about it. What happened in the tent. That you needed an abortion. *She's mortified*, you said, like you understood. Like it was excusable she was ashamed of what had happened, against your will. Like what had happened was affecting her as much as you.

Your mother wasn't much better than that clique of kids in high school, but in a different, probably more damaging way. Too ashamed in the abortion clinic to remember you were terrified and alone and wanted a hand held and an explanation of how the process would work. I picture her sitting there next to you or maybe one seat over, holding her own two hands, maybe even with a hood up so no one would recognize her or see the face they were judging. You had to walk past those vengeful, judgmental protestors outside the clinic, feeling like your mother was on their side. She was too busy getting herself through the shame of it to get you through the pain of it, and I guess I could have stepped in a little more. And you've left me to wonder about that.

But I saw your mother the other day in the grocery store buying a loaf of bread, and she looked lost in her own town, in a familiar store. Still. Sixteen years later. And it was hard to hold anything against her. How she was with you didn't mean she didn't care. We all handle things differently. I know that now. Ninety-nine out of a hundred women probably wouldn't have killed themselves had they been in your shoes that year, because ninety-nine out of one hundred women don't feel life as intensely as you did. Your heart was too big for this world, but that was all the more reason to stay. I believe in nothing but people like you.

And it was a strange thing to think, but when I saw your mother there clutching that bag of bread in the bakery, I thought about how much toast she's had to sit and eat, alone, since you died. I thought about how many years she had to hit your birthday like a speed bump as time rolled by without you. I thought about the throbbing silence in her home and how she'd probably hear things some nights and think it was you and then remember. And I thought about all the times one of her co-workers would mention a son's graduation or a daughter's wedding day, or Christmas shopping for the kids, and bam! More things she never got. Graduation photos, wedding planning, grandchildren. Simple things any mother deserves. Expects. Gets. Looks forward to. So much of her life was left empty and unfulfilled because of you.

I thought of maybe saying hello to her, but would she want that? All she has of you now are the people associated with you, like me, and I didn't know if she needed to be reminded that I grew up and you didn't — I write for the local papers, I'm not married, I did a science major ... there are answers to questions of what became of me. But not you. Never you. Because you killed yourself before you even knew who you were. I went to say hello to her, but three steps in I felt like the ghost of you galloping towards her, and I didn't want to spook her. She looked too fragile.

I'm not married because I spend all my time alone writing books about lonely people longing for love. So I can't find the time set up a date with one of the half-dozen women who remind me of you, who I'm interested in. You'd tell me that's stupid. That it's a stupid way to live. Five bucks says you'd be married by now with three kids. And they'd be lucky to be half the person you were. You'd have a garden, I bet, a greenhouse, weird hobbies, a book club. You could've been the person I trusted to read my first drafts and be honest. Because you were that: honest, helpful, supportive.

Someone might have asked you about high school along the way, but you would've only shrugged a shoulder and saw that time for what it was — a few fond memories from a place that granted you permission to attend university. Not the place that broke you.

Since I saw your mother in that grocery store, I've been missing who you might have been. I got home that night, threw some vegetables in a pan and thought about how that could have been you — not your mother — I bumped into sixteen years later. We could have caught up beside a stack of bananas and a shelf of buns and bagels. I could have heard all about the new you and seen in your eyes, or your electric body language, or the wedding ring on your finger, or the kid clinging to your leg, that you were alright now. Happy. Like the day we met in class, when everyone wanted to be you. Or at least the way you were. Brave and bold and easy to like.

I could have fallen in love with you all over again right there by the whole wheat breads — drawn in by your quicksand eyes or the kink in your hair or the life in your words — but instead you were the third suicide in high school for me. There was one every year. After the second we talked about Kurt Cobain. Watched Courtney Love reading his suicide note. His reasoning was, "It's better to burn out than fade away." At thirty-two, I'm older than he was when he died. Wise enough to know that you both got it wrong. You acted like we only get one wick in this life and it should never get windy.

What I know of life is this: Every cut lets a little more life in.

It's been sixteen years since we were sixteen. The teachers, the students who crucified you, I haven't seen a single one of them since. You wouldn't have either. You'd be here beside me now, laughing at how melodramatic we were in high school — you carving initials into your first boyfriend's arm and crying over notes put in lockers at mid-morning break.

You'd be a biochemist now, or a dog trainer, or you'd own your own tattoo parlour, and you'd love popcorn with M&Ms melted into them, or you'd love hotdogs — dirty as they are — and as I type this, you'd be eating one right now. The tang of mustard on your tongue warming your whole body. Or you'd be walking a dog named Rufus or Ruffles or Peter. Or you'd be keeled off on your blue or brown couch with a cat or a dog or a kid in your lap, watching a show or a movie. And I could cry for you, still, that you're none of those people I imagine you as.

I dunno who you'd be. That's my point. You don't get to kill yourself before you even know who you are. That sixteen-year-old kid with the punk rock eyeliner and the big red heart and the teen pregnancy. That wasn't you. Because you never happened. No one does, until they're older. I was twenty-eight before I was me.

PRINCE NAMELESS

by Patti Larsen

I was always an odd child, though I had no idea what odd was, really. Being raised by people just like me meant I had no clue I was different. My father was an avid reader, as was my mother, though it was Dad's passion for fantasy and science fiction that drew me in, far from Mom's love of romance novels.

I knew I wanted to be a writer by the age of twelve, having soaked up most of my father's extensive library. The few friends I maintained in my country-living neighbourhood didn't consider my bookish nature strange. And considering most of them gathered at my family home every Saturday and Sunday to play Dungeons and Dragons with Dad presiding as Dungeon Master, my life seemed to me absolutely ordinary.

I buried myself in books, horses and anything to do with make-believe, happily exploring worlds and people real only in the pages of novels and in my head. We never did have much money, but even that didn't seem strange, since no one I knew did, either. Besides, my life was rich and full of the imaginary.

Always very good in school, I found myself, in grades five and six, suddenly aware of the other children and how different their lives were to mine. Not everyone had a big red half-draft horse that waited at the fence for them every day, nor did they have made-up friends and adventures that sometimes seemed as authentic as the 'real' world.

*   *   *

The warrioress rides over the crest of the hill and pauses, her black horse snorting white puffs as he paws the dirt of the road. The shield strapped to her back has seen many battles; her well-used sword hangs from her hip as if part of her body.

It's been a long and empty road for her, and loneliness finally begs her to seek out others, a short break from her adventures and a chance to rest. The walled city below looks to be a likely place. She urges her weary mount forward again. His heavy hooves raise dust as he picks up speed.

The guards at the gate offer her no conversation, ignoring her as she rides inside. Just past the large iron barrier she sees it: a statue, perfectly shaped and painted, the image of the most beautiful man she has ever seen. Tall, dark-haired, with rugged good looks any maiden would swoon over, the placard at his feet proclaims he is Prince Nameless, the ruler of this city.

Her heart is lost, the road forgotten in a moment of absolute attraction. Fate has brought her to him. Surely here is the destiny she's been seeking her entire life. She has felt stirrings before, moments of affection toward the men she's met. But she has never known love. Until now.

Gazing up at him in adoration, she hears the sounds of horns. And to her utter delight, the object of her desire appears in a parade of pomp and circumstance.

Not thinking or considering her actions even for a moment, she spurs her horse forward, smiling, pulling her helmet free, extending her hand toward the prince and her future.

His shock at her approach is apparent as he pulls back from her in horror. His guards act instantly, roughly jerking her horse aside, clearing the way for the prince and his followers to continue on.

She watches him go, her heart yearning as it never has before.

He doesn't look back.

She was sure he would.

When she turns away, she looks down into the puddle of water at her horse's feet and understands. Her hair is a squashed mess, her face sweaty and filthy from her ride. No wonder he wanted nothing to do with her!

She must make him notice her, to see past the harsh leavings of the road. Something flutters in her peripheral vision and she dismounts to examine the sheet of parchment tacked to the side of a squat stone building.

A 'Wanted' poster. A giant threatens the peasants who raise crops for the prince. There is a monetary reward offered, but that's not the part that attracts her interest. The boon is to be personally granted by the man himself.

She's faced worse before. And she knows once she's proven herself, he'll love her for certain.

Settling her helmet in place, she remounts and wheels her steed back the way she came.

She has a giant to slay.

* * *

Thanks to one friend in particular, I found boys. I wonder still if I would have remained oblivious for a few years longer, so wrapped up was I in the happy places of my own making. But she drew me to her because she was so very different, just recently moved to Prince Edward Island from distant Ontario. She lived in a new house and possessed all the fancy clothes and makeup that baffled and fascinated me.

Because of her, for those two brief years, I found myself ensconced as one of the cool kids, with no clear perception of what it really meant. Lots of people wanted to hang out with me, boys wanted to kiss me. I had my first, second and third boyfriends in those years, and I still remember the time fondly. Not because they were really boyfriends in the technical sense, but because they were my friends at all.

It was a magical time. I had no idea being in the middle of such things was even possible for me. I became lost in my need to maintain what I had found and drifted away from my love of books and fantasy.

And then, out of the blue, it was over.

* * *

She finds the giant resting under a huge tree, hands folded over his rounded belly, eyes closed, humming a tune that makes the ground shake beneath her horse's hooves.

"Ho, Giant," she calls out, pulling her sword free. "I've come to save the peasants from your evil and receive the reward the prince has promised."

The giant sighs and opens his eyes, meeting hers as he sits forward to examine her more closely.

"You seem a smart girl," he rumbles, his breath ruffling her horse's mane and the folds of her cloak. "And yet you willingly believe the worst about a total stranger without seeking the truth."

His words make her hesitate. "You claim you are innocent of your crimes?"

"I am falsely accused," he says. "But there is a more important question to be pondered here. Ask your prince why he fears strength in others."

At the mention of the prince, his face comes to mind, and she finds her heart hardening against the giant.

"Do not try to deceive me," she says, sword swinging. "I will have the reward he promised from his own hands and shall save the innocent peasants, both with one stroke."

The giant bends his head to her, large muscles rippling as he kneels before her. "Kill me then," he says, "if he means so very much to you."

She pauses one more moment, not sure why guilt rises as she finally lets her sword fall to slay him.

Task complete, she ties the giant's head to her saddle and rides back to the city, a smile growing on her lips, all concern vanishing as she thinks about the prince and her reward.

* * *

The moment grade seven started, I was a nerd again, just like that. No longer were my hand-me-down clothes acceptable, or the fact I cared little for my appearance. What once mattered not at all turned suddenly into a gaping chasm, a divide I didn't have the money or the understanding to cross. And now I knew what a nerd was, and that I'd been one all along without understanding the terminology or the implications. The shock and hurt at my sudden ostracization hit me like a blow. Junior high was a wake-up call as I found myself mixing in with new kids from other schools, all brought together in a place far bigger than I was used to.

My confusion at my sudden loss of status forced me to retreat back into the imaginary worlds that had sustained me. Though now I used them as a hiding place, not a joy, and felt guilt every time I tapped into my creativity.

I felt as though I'd lost two precious things — my joyful, embracing make-believe worlds and all the incredible adventure they brought and the cool-kid status and experiences I'd only just begun to accept as my norm.

My nerdly nature was confirmed simply by my anxious and needy reaction to being rejected. Told I was weird and different and left out in the cold, I was taught by others my age that the passion I had for the creative was wrong and was to blame for my being outcast. It didn't take long for sensitive, expressive and creative me to back away from everyone, to hide in melancholy and growing hurt.

There were moments I raged against the injustice, watching the pretty girls in their beautiful clothes and their perfect hair while I wore the same jeans I used to ride in, the same clothes I'd worn only a year earlier, now completely out of style if they ever were to begin with. How did it happen? Where did my popularity go? How did the switch get flipped and who flipped it? My fleeting days of coolness were gone and I was driven, for reasons I was unable to comprehend, back into my world of weirdness, which ironically only encouraged my condition, as though it were a disease, to worsen.

* * *

She returns triumphant to the gates of the city. This time the guards take notice, but only to snicker at her, to point fingers and talk about her as if she has done something wrong. Not that it matters to her. She's acted as the prince commanded and now she is ready to accept her reward.

Odd how the nasty man at the front door to the palace doesn't want to let her in, looking down on her as if she's in the wrong place at the wrong instant and can't possibly expect to be allowed entry. But she isn't taking no for an answer, not with a giant's head preceding her past the spluttering guard. The horrible prize hanging from her hands, she drags the bloody mess down the main hall and to the prince's chambers.

She arrives breathless and full of excitement at the prospect of seeing him again. But he is busy.

"Yes, yes," he says, not looking at her, too enraptured by his reflection in the mirror as three tailors fit his shining new clothing. "Just leave it at the door."

"My reward, Your Highness?" Her voice cracks and warbles as her heart speeds up at the thought of receiving his adoration.

His sigh is long and deep and full of suffering. He alights at last with great grace from the small riser and comes to her side, though he seems more intent on stroking the soft fabric of his new clothing than paying any attention to her. The prince snaps his fingers, to which a young man leaps into action and hands him a small, worn leather bag.

Nameless's smile glitters, perfect white teeth shining in the light as he gestures to the boy, who drops the bag at her feet.

The prince turns away from her, already moving off. She has to stop him! This isn't at all what she'd dreamed, hoped, expected. Her bloody hands reach out before she can stop herself and latch onto the back of his perfect new tunic.

She's never been kicked out of anywhere before. Especially not by the man she loves. He is unable to speak from rage and so red-faced she is sure his head will explode.

Her heart sinks as she is ushered out of the palace and shoved into the street. The door slams shut behind her.

Her heart, still hurting, but more determined than ever, yearns for the prince and drives her to find another way.

There has to be another way!

* * *

I met him for the first time that initial fateful year of junior high, shortly after my lack of position made itself known, but too soon for me to realize just what my fall from grace actually meant when it came to possibilities. He shall remain, as always, nameless, but in my teenaged heart, he was Prince Charming. Tall, dark-haired, with the dashing good looks I'd come to expect from descriptions of heroes and knights, he was the epitome of everything I'd dreamed about.

He was as new as I was to the school, but seemed to arrive with his influence intact and even elevated. My instant love for him was shared by most of the girls, though I was absolutely sure none of them felt for him what I did.

At first I tried what I'd done in elementary school, rushing in to greet him, to know his name, only to crash and burn when my greeting was met with disdain and rejection. That was the moment I understood my place and put him, very firmly, on a pedestal I could never rise to no matter how hard I tried. In my imaginary world, there was no backing away from the object of affection. In every single book I'd read, the love affair worked out, no matter how rocky the beginning. In that way, the novels I'd read did me a great disservice, teaching me fantastic lies instead of the harsh truth of the real world.

I find it so sad now, in many ways, how I behaved. Both of my older sisters are outgoing and charismatic women, and always were, at ease with boys, friends, popular and always at the centre of things. But I learned in my first year of junior high my advances weren't welcome and it was better if I just watched from a distance and let the fantasy of what I needed fill in the holes.

Hello, weirdo. And yes, I was one; I know it, fair enough. But the reveal was the kicker, the painful unveiling that I wasn't good enough, didn't have enough, wasn't able to fit in even when I made feeble attempts at speaking up or injecting myself into cool kid conversations.

Crash and burn.

I was in the throes of first love. I followed him, a nerdy shadow, obsessed over him in my writing and imaginary creations and pined every day for one simple, single acknowledgment from him that he'd taken notice. I have no idea why I was so taken with him, outside of the mystery of him. I knew so little and had created so much, I think perhaps he grew past himself in my head to the point he could never have really existed.

The saddest part, really, was how painfully obvious it was to everyone else. I did my best to hide my attraction while trying to be noticed by him, but it was clear to the entire student body I was hopelessly in love.

* * *

The second 'Wanted' poster makes her shudder. A mighty gryphon has attacked the prince's cattle. Again a reward is offered, but this time the creature's pelt is to be brought back. Only then will she receive payment. And wonder of wonders, it includes dinner with the prince. Dinner! Even better than merely meeting him. She will have the chance to talk to him, to make a real impression.

Her horse sighs his long suffering but canters off with her on his armoured back. The gryphon is easy to locate, sunning himself on the banks of the river. She pauses to look upon him with a measure of awe, how shiny his fur, how polished his feathered wings. He is truly stunning to behold.

But she has a job to do and her prince to satisfy.

"Ho, Gryphon," she says. "I've come to slay you by order of the prince!"

The gryphon lifts his head. His eagle beak clacks together as he speaks, lion's tail twitching in the grass. "Warrioress," he says in the voice of a soaring bird of prey, "I have done nothing to inspire the prince's wrath."

This is the second time she's heard such. "He demands your death." It sounds weak to her. But dinner with her prince! How can she not act?

"I beg of you," the gryphon says, "ask yourself why it is the prince wishes my skin. What about his looks does he despise so much that he needs what I have to make himself pretty?"

She can't listen, though her soul weeps and pleads with her to stop. The gryphon is soon dispatched and his glorious golden hide drapes over her horse's withers.

This time when she rides through the gates, she is acutely aware of the stares and whispers and feels herself becoming self-conscious and uncomfortable with the attention. She reaches the palace gates quickly, though the servant at the door, not the prince, takes the hide from her.

"My dinner!" She's done things that have shamed her. She is not about to leave without her reward.

"Very well," the man says. "Return tonight. You shall have your dinner."

Feeling much better and now excited by the prospect, the warrioress leaves with plans to woo her prince by more radical means.

*   *   *

Grade seven ended and I pined away for him all summer, for my one true love, lost in the romantic fantasy I'd created. The story of *US* grew bigger and brighter and more elaborate with every sunny day that passed, though I spent my summer, totally unlike me, locked inside my house with thoughts of him. Gone were my childish playfulness, my daily jaunts to the local beach. I ignored the innocent pleasures of country living and exploring in favour of my total embrace of what I created around him.

*   *   *

The warrioress stares at herself in the mirror of the local beauty garden, shocked by what she sees. The dress she wears is a little threadbare, but she loves how it swings around her feet. Her hair is carefully arranged, though she frets it's too plain. Her eyes and lips are coated in cosmetics, and fake jewels sparkle on her hands and around her neck.

Here then is the woman who will sweep the prince off his feet!

She chooses to ignore the nasty giggling from the other women in the garden and the eye rolls and whispering about her appearance. She's done what she can, and it will be enough, she's sure of it.

She straps her trusty sword to her side, patting its familiar weight before she goes off, whistling and smiling, to meet her fate.

*   *   *

As the first day of grade eight grew close, I carefully prepared, now so deeply into him it was truly pathetic. I'd decided the only way I could attract him was to be one of the cool kids, to do what I could to shed my weirdness and act the way the popular crowd did.

With the carefully hoarded money I'd made working here and there all summer, I bought what I felt were trendy clothes, and my first makeup. I even had my sister's friend cut my hair, though she sheared it almost boy short.

I'm sure my few friends shook their heads at me, already bored to tears by my endless obsession. It was a wonder, really, that they were still my friends at all. Why didn't one of them take me and shake me? Although even if they had, I'm sure I wouldn't have listened.

My first day of grade eight, I walked into school with a fresh outlook and so much optimism. I was sure I'd done it the way I was supposed to, gotten it right at last. But I was only to understand, the moment I tried to fit in, I'd just made matters worse. I was now a weird girl trying too hard.

If anything, my attempts to be one of 'them' made me all the more pathetic.

He continued to ignore me. And my failure drove me deeper inside.

* * *

The man at the palace door stares at her, eyes huge, and she takes it as a good sign. She must look splendid if he's staring at her so. She is led down the long hall to a huge dining area. The walls are covered with beautiful tapestries; the heavy wooden table and chairs are carved with intricate designs. She spots the prince at the far end of the room and starts to head for him, only to be shown to her seat all the way down at the other end, between a snoring old man and a jittery little girl wearing thick-lensed glasses.

Despair rises in her heart. How will her prince notice her all the way down here? And there he sits, dressed in his lovely new clothes with the gryphon's pelt wrapped around him. She can hear some of what is said, how his hangers-on admire his appearance, how beautiful they tell him he is.

And he is. The warrioress sinks into her seat. She smoothes the faded fabric of her gown.

Dinner is ashes in her mouth, but she forces herself to chew, swallow, drink the slightly stale water she is served with the lumpy stew while she watches her prince and his followers eat the finest beef and drink the most sparkling of wines.

As she rises to go at last, not waiting for dessert, she notices two ladies she'd seen earlier at the gardens standing by the door. They had just been sitting with the prince, talking and laughing with him. And now they are smiling at her.

"Come," one says, taking her hand. "His Highness would like to speak to you."

"Yes," the other says, giggling. "But in private."

She laughs with them, hope soaring. Of course. He wants to thank her in person.

Excitement wins the day and she finds herself swept along by the song in her heart.

* * *

How? How could I make him notice me when I was obviously so ugly and he was so beautiful? I tried dressing provocatively a few times, but only had myself briefly labelled a slut for my efforts.

My heart broke every time I looked at him. I only wanted to be near him, to hear him say my name, laugh with me (not at me), gaze into my eyes and tell me he felt what I did but never had the courage to admit it.

My luck changed one glorious day when, miracle of miracles, I made some cool friends in Drama Club. Imagine! But they could do nothing to bring me closer to him, and finally my need and my weirdness drove them away as well. They didn't understand the fantasy world I'd built, slowly consuming me, the creations I'd made around him.

In this, my weirdness was cemented for the remainder of my school life. Cool kids had seen inside my private world and now I had nowhere to hide.

Let me be perfectly clear. I blame myself for all of this, or at least the hormone-laden girl I was who had no idea she practically stalked the poor boy — though I swear I never once went to his house.

Had his address, though. Just in case.

Because, who knew, right?

And then, one glorious lunch hour as I sat in the very public lobby of my school, directly across from him as I always did so I could watch him at all times, I was approached by two girls who were known as his hangers-on.

The girls who approached me that day were mean girls, though I had no idea at the time what the term meant and I'd certainly never, in my naiveté, thought of them in such a way. They were simply borderliners, the class between where I was and where the cool kids were, slipping back and forth over the invisible barrier. I envied them in a way. At least if I'd been one of the middle-ground kids I would have been closer to him.

Turned out their goal for me was the same. Or at least I thought so as they came to me, out there in the open, and asked if I wanted to be his girlfriend.

A silly question. Of course I did.

Only then did they drop their bomb of delight. He'd sent them, messengers of the god I worshiped with all my heart, to ask me. To include me, draw me in, bring me across the line and make me not only his but one of the cool kids, forevermore.

Amen.

I have no idea how I managed to play it so cool, to keep my exterior calm while my innards did back flips and excited gyrations. I calmly nodded to their proposal, accepting it with the aplomb of the Queen of School I was about to become. While my friends congratulated me on my coup, the cruel pair, giggling and whispering to themselves, left me there to plan my future while they crossed the seemingly endless expanse of the lobby to tell my true love his fair maiden had said yes.

And then.

The tragedy.

* * *

The prince sweeps into his chambers, instantly furious to find her there. She is shocked and hurt as he laughs in her face, tells her no matter what she does he will never love her. In fact, he says, "I think the very idea quite ridiculous."

She begs, she weeps, falls to her knees until she has to be pulled up by his guards as the prince sneers in her face and orders her out.

The guards carry her to her horse and the satchel with her old clothes strapped to his saddle. They wait for her to change, still sobbing, back into her warrior's apparel, force her to mount her weary steed and drive her out of the city while everyone laughs and points and makes a mockery of her.

And there, as she passes, her head down, sad face streaked with tears, are the two ladies who'd duped her. It is they who laugh the loudest.

*   *   *

They reached him as I watched, bent to whisper in his ear the answer I'd sent back. I felt myself smiling, half standing, ready to go to him even as he jerked away from them both, leaping to his feet, a huge scowl on his face as his horrified eyes met mine and he shouted for the entire school to hear:

"NO!"

The whole world stopped for a moment. And for a long time I wished it had remained that way because the instant time started up again, my utter humiliation was complete.

They'd all heard his rejection. Of course they had. How could anyone miss that single word of utter denial? I found myself running, retreating from the lobby and into the large area where the school lockers were housed, hiding in the maze of yellow tin doors while the sound of laughter, either real or imagined, chased after me.

*   *   *

She can barely see the road ahead of her for her falling tears. She does not pay attention at all as she replays the horrible scene over and over in her mind. Her horse, a smart old boy, knows enough to carry her safely while she mourns her broken heart.

The sound of pounding hooves approaching from behind barely breaks through her grief. But the young squire who pulls his horse up beside her, face panicked and out of breath, finally does the trick.

As does his string of words.

"His Highness!" the boy says, panting. "He begs you, Warrioress, to return and save him!"

Save him? "From what, pray tell?"

"The dragon." The boy shudders, eyes going to the sky. "Shortly after you left, it swooped down and kidnapped him, taking him away from us. His final words were to call for you!"

Her tears stop instantly. He needs her! His last command was to find her and have her save him. He does love her after all.

Heart renewed, she spins her faithful steed around and goes in search of the dragon.

*   *   *

I ran from my friends, from the realization of what had just happened, how I'd been used by those girls, duped for no other reason than their own amusement. Cruelty wasn't a common experience for me, relegated to antagonists in books and movies. The sting was sharp, the cut deep. All I could do was flee.

But he, he had nothing to do with it. I clung to my need to believe. He would come find me, talk to me. Apologize. Make those girls apologize. And everything would be okay.

It would. And he would finally see me for who I was.

* * *

The warrioress rides into the clearing ready for battle, only to find the prince alone, trapped inside a cage of bone and chain.

"Come!" he calls out, the gryphon's pelt in tatters from the dragon's claws, his perfect clothing torn and filthy. Weakness and fear bring him to his knees. "Save your prince and you may have whatever your heart desires."

"I want you to love me." All of her hope and need well up at the sight of him so badly done by. "To marry me and make me your princess."

What is the look on his face, in his eyes? No matter, it is gone as quickly as it appeared and he is smiling at her, though his perfect teeth aren't showing and he seems to be in some kind of discomfort. The dragon must have hurt him.

"Of course," he says, nervously gazing skyward. "Anything you wish. Just free me and slay that dragon!"

"I will save you, my love." She jumps down from her horse and strides toward the prince, her sword out, ready to attack the cage holding him.

A great wind buffets her and knocks her backward. The dragon has returned, the back sweep of his wings creating a powerful gale. Two sobbing women hang in his claws.

"Save us!" She knows the ladies, the very same two who engineered her humiliation. "Please, we beg you!"

"Well now," the dragon says to her in a voice like rolling thunder, "who are you really here to save?"

* * *

I found my locker and pretended to focus on the contents, not wanting anyone to look at me, wishing I was tiny enough to climb inside the tin can and close the door behind me.

All the while I hoped he'd followed, that he would find me and rescue me.

To my shock and growing amazement, he appeared at the end of the row. For the first time since we'd met, he was really looking at me, focused on me, not trying to ignore or avoid me.

This was it. He held my heart in his hands.

And with a handful of words, he shattered it into a million pieces. Words like 'never' and 'weirdo' and 'gross.' Hurtful, harmful, dangerous words to say to someone. Especially to someone like me, sensitive and with a massive imagination that could turn such terms into deadly weapons.

While my entire being rang with what he'd said, he stormed off like it was all my fault 'some girl' like me had the nerve to love him. The shards of what had been my adoration sharpened into razor edges.

* * *

"I must kill you," she says to the towering silver dragon, who tilts his great head to the side. Two thin columns of smoke drift from his nostrils. "The prince has said he will marry me, love me, if I free him and slay you."

The dragon nods slowly and settles on the ground, the two ladies still clutched in his claws. One golden eye comes level with the warrioress as he speaks.

"I have heard you killed the giant," he says, "and in doing so destroyed your own strength."

She flinches. What had the giant said about the prince's fear? Her love's eyes are full of it even as the dragon goes on.

"And the gryphon," the dragon says, "for his beautiful hide. But in that you have only shown your own loss of self-esteem and confidence. Where has the mighty warrioress gone?"

Again she twitches as though a blow has landed. Her gaze falls on the two handmaidens who had once embodied lady-like perfection.

How hideous they now seem.

"You are now conscious of what you perceive is your lack," the dragon says. "Things, beauty, love. Though until now you were perfect exactly as you were."

She can't listen. She has to finish the beast so she can have her true love. But the dragon isn't finished.

"If you slay me," he says, "— and I won't stop you if that is the choice you make — you destroy the last part of your spirit to remain yours and yours alone. The final fragment of your power, your hope, will be gone and you will have what you wish, in the end. You will be like him." He gestures with his muzzle at the prince. "And like these." He shakes the two weeping women in his grip. "So, if that is what you choose, then act. But be prepared for the consequences."

"Or?" She feels the sword in her hand, knows the dragon speaks the truth.

"Or," he chuffs out a little smoke, one eye winking, "go find the prince who loves you for who you are."

* * *

It still amazes me how quickly, to the sound of a young heart breaking, my obsessive love turned to hate. I despised him so much from that moment on I didn't look back. It was as if he'd never existed, the fantasies I'd created around him lost, gone forever without a trace they'd even lived.

So odd. I never thought of him again, not that way, and even the loathing I felt dissipated quickly, gone like smoke in a breeze. In fact, I found out years later he moved before we finished high school. I never noticed.

Or cared.

I suppose it helped that he never was like the prince of my dreams, the larger-than-life, charismatic and powerful person I imagined he was. No, just a teenager, like me, doing his best to fit in. Knowing what I do now, I wonder if he felt as out of place as I did, as pressured to do whatever he could to keep judging eyes from him.

Pretty likely.

Not that it mattered to me then. The feelings from that moment went on and on, defining me in my eyes and how I felt about myself. Not good enough, ugly, gross, always doing the wrong thing, saying the inappropriate, wearing the wrong clothes, too much makeup...

I was no longer a teen when I found out none of what I believed really mattered, that I actually was okay being me, and that the social awkwardness came from trying to fit in; when I stopped, it stopped — or became endearing to those who really loved me.

I don't blame Nameless for any of this. We were kids at the time, when empathy is not often a first choice. But because of his rejection I gave up on my need to be one of the cool kinds and accepted the fact that I could never be, cementing myself in the land of the nerdy. The silver lining? That choice allowed me to hone my creativity and lose myself in books and writing again.

It took a while, but I found my Prince Charming. And I love how my life turned out, knowing now that being me was the very best gift anyone could ever give me.

So thanks, Nameless. No hard feelings. No resentment. No turning you into a character in a book just to kill you off so I feel better.

Promise.

* * *

Her horse seems less tired to her, eager again to move on as she finds herself smiling at what the future might bring.

Behind her, screams fading in the distance, the dragon enjoys his very tasty meal.

I USED TO THINK I'D MAKE A GOOD BOY

by Cale Liom

If you want to get right down to it, I fucking hated my childhood. And I hate reflecting on it now. I don't want to remember that lost, messed up kid who was constantly beaten up. What I want is to forget she existed. I want to distance myself so far from that time in my life that I don't have to acknowledge I even *had* a childhood. I've spent a lot of time trying to block out my childhood, and I don't care if I lose the good memories in the process — I don't have that many good memories anyway. I want none of it. I don't want to remember any good times because then I'll remember the bad times too. I don't want to feel sorry for that kid — I want to erase her. I want to be a different person. Seriously, you can have all of the beach days and puppies, as long as you take all of the messages of worthlessness, all of the fists sinking into my organs and all of the fear with you. Fuck memories. Fuck pain. Take the goddamn trauma therapy and shove it somewhere painful, because really, I'm tired of suffering. I'm more interested in living and moving on than I am in reliving the bullshit I went through.

That said, I have agreed — maybe stupidly — to write about an aspect of my adolescence. Normally if someone asks me to talk or write about my adolescence I tell them to fuck off. For some masochistic reason, though, this project seemed like a valuable exercise. I thought I've already lived through it, so how hard could it be to write about it? Pretty fucking hard, as it turns out. I've got a lot of unresolved childhood shit. More than I'd thought. And writing this piece makes me want to get blitzed out of my mind. Don't expect me to reread it or cry over it or discuss my feelings with you, though. I'm not about to console anyone who feels they got a poor shake when it comes to my memory of things because, really, it's *my* memory of things. If you lived through some of it with me, maybe you have a different memory of it or a different opinion, but I'm the expert on my own life and experiences. I know what happened when the doors were closed and the lights went out. This isn't about you. If you think it is, write your own fucking story.

I grew up in Summerside, PEI. It's a small, isolated town. Top news stories often involve things like "Fisherman Discovers Blue Lobster!" or "Local Boy Opens a Business!" — seriously, take a look; a variation of one of these titles is likely in today's *Journal Pioneer*. There's a lot of generalized nervousness about cities, skateboarding teens and politics. Summerside is full of people who think of themselves and their neighbours as good, honest, hard-working folk. It's so damn wholesome that lots of people think nothing bad ever happens there — no physical abuse, no sexual abuse, no bullying, no hatred, no bigotry, no violence of any kind really. Just good old-fashioned people who work hard for a living and raise their families in a safe little town.

I've often been told that my childhood was idyllic because I grew up in a household with both of my parents in "the best town in the best province in the best country in the world." I think that saying something is idyllic when it isn't is a way of denying that shit happens, a tool to facilitate looking the other way. But, *of course*, all the same bad stuff happens in Summerside that happens in every other town or city in the world — the difference with an idyllic little place like this one is that often no one believes you when shit happens, or they gloss over it in a way that makes the victim feel worthless and unheard because those citizens want their hometown to stay as untainted as the fairy tale in their heads. I've met too many people in small towns who care more about maintaining a strong, happy and prosperous exterior than actually being truthful. These people have such pride in the image of their town that it overrides actual important issues and instead they fixate on mundane, benign things like the state of their lawn. It's unhealthy and it freaks me out. Plus, if you deal with your shit your precious town would be a hell of a lot nicer.

Any time I tried to speak up or reach out for help when I was a teen, I was shushed and told that I was very fortunate and not to say such awful things. But the awful things *happened.* My experiences have led me to believe that the most harmful secrets are hidden in families that are tight-lipped and present the most nonchalant exteriors. Show me a woman who anxiously tries to convince someone that her family is extremely tightly knit and her kids are all so *successful* and *happy*, and I'll bet money she's trying to hide something so horrendous that she can't bring herself to think about it, let alone talk about it.

Growing up in Summerside was a fucking nightmare. So much so that I still have a hard time reconciling my feelings with the town. I become highly anxious and agitated whenever I go there, whether it's for a family gathering, a doctor's appointment or I'm just driving through it — regardless of the reason for being there, I either feel worthless or angry when I'm in Summerside. I got an invitation to go to my high school reunion recently — even though the reunion isn't for another year. It's surprising how ill something like that can make me feel. Pretty sure I couldn't be paid enough to go.

"...even I can't stand you..."

So no, I was not a happy, carefree child. I lived in a constant state of fear and anxiety. I didn't feel there was a place where I could go and be *safe.* I think that's why I was forever building forts — like if I could just build the perfect tree house where I could hide from everyone and everything, and where I could largely be self-sufficient, everything would be okay. I know what it feels like to dread going to school every single day and yet to not want to go home either — to feel sick at the thought of facing the other kids again, to need to take antacid every day before and after school, to fear the taunts and jeers because of your appearance, to wonder if you'll be hit today, or worse.

It's hard to give a shit about yourself when you feel no one else does. It's not easy to transition from a constant feeling of being unsafe to a stable adulthood with trusting, healthy relationships.

There are, of course, reasons I never used to trust anyone. I didn't see people, relationships, even homes as reliable or stable. I didn't expect anyone to stick around. It became instinctive for me not to trust. And, honestly, I still see the negative, harmful potential in people — even the ones I like. I know what people can do, what they are capable of, so my friends and partners need to earn my trust and if they lose it, it's gone. Period. I can forgive, but it's unlikely for me to trust a second time. Sorry, but if I let you in, you knew the rules. So yeah, I hated childhood and adolescence, and the subsequent years of dealing with the fears and anxiety that were instilled in me from growing up surrounded by messages of homophobic hate from family, religion and kids at school — basically from everyone I knew. When I was a kid, I fantasized regularly about running away to a city where nobody knew me, about how my life would be if I'd been born a boy and about suicide. These three fantasies largely preoccupied my waking dreams.

My suicide fantasies involved less detail about the act and more detail about the finished product. I would dream of how nice it would be to feel nothing, to be rid of my overwhelming anger and sadness, to have a complete cessation of the deprecating words in my head that had been delivered to me over the years and pounded in with fists for good fucking measure. I still have these fantasies sometimes, though they aren't usually as consuming as they were then.

I would never have taken pills. It would have been violent and certain, with lots of blood. And crushing or crunching of bones. Something concrete that would leave no doubt or lingering. No heroic measures would be attempted. And my pain would be gone. Absolutely.

"...one day, you'll wake up and I'll be gone and you'll have no one..."

In grade five, I was beaten up by three girls in the schoolyard while a large group of kids gathered around and watched. I was told by one of the three who had pummelled me that it was because I didn't "look right." From then on, I've always been at least semi on guard. And rightfully so, it seems. Junior high was a blur of being knocked into walls, tripped, smashed in the head with math books, threatened and pushed into the boy's bathroom — while being barked at — because that's where I "belonged." High school continued in the same vein, but with increased homophobic jeers of "dyke," "homo," "lezzy," "ugly dyke" and "pervert." I also got a lot of "What the hell are you anyway?" "You're not a real boy," "Why don't you act like a girl?" and "No one's going to date you if you look like that/dress like that/walk like that/keep beating boys at sports," etc.

I believed all of it.

"...no one will believe you anyway ... everyone will think you're a liar..."

Throughout my childhood and adolescence, I dreamed of being a boy. I was sure it would fix everything. I already dressed like a boy, played sports like a boy, looked at girls like a boy, sat like a boy, swore like a boy, lied like a boy … I can't think of anything I did "like a girl."

I *yearned* to be a boy.

It was what was wrong, what was missing from my life. *It had to be.* Being a boy would make everything right. It would make everything the way it was supposed to be. I would no longer be mocked for my appearance, if I was a boy. I wouldn't be kept out of the 'boy' sports (that I was great at, by the way). I would be able to date girls.

But I wasn't a boy. I was a girl. A girl who hated being a girl. I was told I couldn't play hockey. I wasn't allowed on the baseball team either — despite the fact that I was better at baseball than most of the boys I knew. Instead, I had to watch the boys play and cheer them on. My brother — who hated sports — got to play hockey and baseball. Sometimes I wished he had been born a girl. I felt that then I would have been allowed to be more boyish.

I have spent hours staring at my face in the mirror — examining every detail — searching for something feminine, something that denoted 'girl.' Any clue to my purported gender. I couldn't find it — not a single feminine feature that would shout out "it's a girl!" to the people who scrutinized my face and body, clearly perplexed as to which gender category I fit into. I tried to picture myself as a boy and wondered if I would get mistaken for a girl the way I was constantly mistaken for a boy. I convinced myself that I was a boy being punished with a girl's body — that I must have done something horrible in a past life and that I was being punished for it with a vagina. It was the only answer.

I didn't believe there was anything about me that was decidedly female — not that the public could see, anyway. It felt insulting to be told to walk differently and dress differently so that I could attract boys. And it never worked anyway. Boys didn't like the boyish girl, and as I got older I ended up finding feminine men the most attractive since they fit the closest with my desires in the context of heterosexuality — which I was raised to believe was the only viable option for love and sex.

"...it's a sin ... there's really not much worse you could do in God's eyes..."

I started drinking heavily when I was fourteen or fifteen. Partly I was trying to cope with how unstable my home life was. Even now, I don't feel I have a 'home,' or that I ever did. Summerside certainly doesn't feel like what I imagine when I think of 'home' and I didn't grow up in just one or two houses. We moved a lot — every other year on average. My father was often out of work and my parents didn't exactly get along most of the time. My drinking started a little bit on weekend evenings and progressed to weekday evenings and then to daytime drinking. I wrote (and failed) all of my high school exams in my final semester while drunk. I don't think my parents knew — if they did, they didn't say anything, and you'd think that would be something your parents would talk to you about. I remember once my father questioned me about missing rum that had been replaced with water. I denied it was me, and he didn't question me further. It was easy to get older kids to buy liquor for me (usually rum) if I paid them a little extra, which was no problem because I had a job from the age of twelve. I don't know how I managed to avoid trying hard drugs as a teen, but I think I'm lucky I did. I was self-destructive enough on alcohol.

"...I'll give you something to really cry about this time..."

High school was a nightmare. But then so were junior high and elementary school. I can't actually remember a time, closeted or not, when I wasn't bullied in some way for my 'dykey' or 'masculine' appearance. It seems to make some people uncomfortable — it sometimes makes them feel afraid — if they don't understand why you dress the way you do or why you are attracted to certain people. I've spent my entire life having people try to change my appearance; partners trying to convince or force me to wear dresses, partners and relatives insisting that I have long hair because it's more 'feminine,' purchasing clothes for me of a style and colour that I never wear but that conform to societal expectations of femininity. I recognize these instances — sometimes subtle, other times very overt — as ways of trying to push me towards a more conventional and acceptable way of presenting myself to others.

I have never quite understood *why* anyone else would care about what I wear or what style I choose for my hair. It's fascinating that something as benign as one's appearance can elicit such strong reactions from others. I wear the clothes that I feel comfortable in. Clothes that make me feel confident and good about myself. Yet the clothes that I choose are often labelled as masculine — and I do get many of them from the 'men's' or 'boy's' section of stores. But why the hell should I wear something pink and frilly just because I have a vagina? I've even had family attempt (whether consciously or not) to make me feel as though there's something wrong with me for returning the feminine items of clothing that have been gifted to me that I *know* I will *never* wear and were clearly bought to help me fit in. Their statements usually sound something like "It would look lovely on you if only you'd give it a chance," "You never wear that shirt I bought you," "You don't want your aunt/mother/grandparent to think you're ungrateful" and "It's all the rage with girls your age." Statements like this are a way of "politely" asking "Why don't you dress like other normal girls?" or "Why don't you dress/behave/look like a heterosexual?" Well, maybe I don't dress like a 'typical' heterosexual because I'm not one? Maybe that's okay. And maybe not everybody has to understand that for it to be alright. I've even had boyfriends who lamented that I never wore dresses, despite the fact that I had never given them any indication that I would ever don one. My reply was always, "Maybe you should be dating a girl who likes to wear dresses." Because, really, I am a girl who doesn't wear dresses — I don't like them on me, I don't feel comfortable in them and I won't wear them to please someone else.

Around my sixteenth birthday one of my uncles pulled me aside and demonstrated the way a girl is 'supposed' to walk. He told me the way I walked wasn't feminine enough, that I would never get a boyfriend unless I learned to walk properly and shake my ass a bit more — you know, to entice the slow-witted boys in my town. This moment really stands out in my memory for two reasons. Firstly, because it was so fucking offensive — I mean, how hard would it be to change the way you walk? We walk the way we do rather unconsciously and the way we move becomes so habitual, trained and natural that it is an outward expression of who we are. I felt my uncle was telling me (like so many people have told me, and still do) that there was something wrong with me — something so innately wrong that it made other people uncomfortable. Secondly, I wasn't sure I even *wanted* to attract boys. My confusion about my sexuality made my uncle's words even more poignant, because what if I didn't *want* to attract boys? What if I didn't *want* to have a boyfriend? Everyone else wanted me to have a boyfriend, but I wasn't sure it was what I wanted. I can remember wishing I had a boyfriend because I thought it would fix things. I hoped that if I had a boyfriend, if I proved I was a 'normal' girl, I could engage in the boyish activities I wanted to without all of the passive-aggressive disapproval. My uncle's statement still haunts me. It's a reflection of how I feel North American society largely looked at mannish or boyish women in the 1980s.

"...they're all perverts ... they disgust me..."

North American society is littered with examples of people endeavouring to force others into neatly ordered gender categories. Just try to go into any public washroom with someone who doesn't dress 'appropriately' for their gender. I, like many other 'masculine' women, have had problems simply trying to use the 'women's' washroom. For whatever reason, in North America we have our washrooms separated so that you use one if you have a vagina and another if you have a penis. But how does one police this strange type of arrangement when the evidence for whether or not you fit into either category is hidden under your clothes? Well, people patrol it by judging a person's exterior — the clothes they wear, their haircuts, their shoes and whether or not they are wearing makeup. People who look 'gender appropriate' don't always realize how difficult it can be to go to a public washroom when your gender isn't blatantly obvious. I was in a washroom at an amusement park once when a young girl said to her mother "There's a boy in here!" as she was pointing at me.

The girl added, "What's a *boy* doing in the *girl's* washroom?"

The mother's response was to say in a hushed voice, "Don't look, just leave," and she then very quickly ushered the child out of the washroom without even washing the girl's hands. Now, I don't know if the woman felt threatened by my presence, was homophobic, or simply embarrassed, but it was pretty fucking upsetting to be made to feel as though I didn't belong somewhere because I didn't look *right*. And, I'm not that easily mistaken for a man. But still, I don't have all of the typical female signifiers either. My partner tells me I should "flash my tits" in instances such as this one, but as gratifying as that might be, it also seems ridiculous that I should have to *prove* that I actually *belong* in the 'women's' washroom.

"...if someone was really thinking, they'd round up all the homos and leave them on an island to die ... better yet, shoot every last one of them..."

I didn't always know I was gay. It wasn't an option in my small town. No one I knew in my community was gay — at least no one was 'out.' It wasn't safe to be out there. More than once I had witnessed a group of guys driving around town, shouting "faggot" from their truck at a guy with long hair. Plus, I was regularly getting the shit kicked out of me for "looking like a dyke," so it sure as hell wasn't an option to *be* a dyke. Growing up, my family was Catholic and homophobic. Really, considering the way my family talked about gay people when I was growing up, I'm not sure I can ever completely let go of it, even when they act today as though they have no issue with me being gay — how do I know that they aren't judging and gossiping behind my back? I grew up with no positive imagery of gay people, no real knowledge of gay people, nothing to indicate that this was an option, nothing to show me it wasn't perverted, wrong, disgusting or sinful.

"...they're all sick, the whole lot of them..."

Looking back, it's obvious that the crushes I had on boys as a kid weren't about me wanting to date them. These were boys I wanted to be like. I wanted to have what they had. It was always about the advantages, never about sexual attraction. The boys I wanted to date when I was a teen, for the most part, exemplified the life I wanted — they were strong, they drove fast cars with manual transmissions or large trucks, they excelled at sports, they were confident and the pretty girls wanted to be with them.

I tried to ignore the crushes I had on girls. They started when I was very young, though — the first strong crushes I remember were in grade seven — and they were frequent. Much more frequent than any feelings for boys were. And more emotional. The crushes I had on girls simply had a different quality. As a teenager, girls captivated me. They fascinated and entranced me. They made me feel dizzy, giddy and tongue-tied. They made my mouth water. With boys, I just wanted to punch their bicep and play sports with them. I wanted to impress boys so that they would like me. I was confused that they rarely seemed attracted to me, but I don't think I really cared — at least I wouldn't have cared if I had known it was okay to be attracted to girls.

I had no outlet for my feelings for girls, so I kept them to myself. I didn't even *know* a person could *be* gay for a long time — really, I had only heard about it in the context of it being wrong, so I wasn't about to nurture my feelings, question them or pursue them.

I buried my feelings. And I wished I was a boy.

I wanted — *more than anything* — to be a boy so I could ask a girl to dance, feel a girl's hand in mine, kiss a girl's lips. I *needed* that feeling. When I was young and kissed a boy, I didn't pay attention to how it felt to kiss him. I studied how he seemed to feel. I wanted to know how *he* felt kissing *me*. I wanted to experience it vicariously, because I couldn't have it in reality. It's not like that at all with women — women have this way of taking me over physically and emotionally. They make me weak in a good way … I've never had the same feeling with men. The first time I kissed a woman it felt natural, comfortable and right. It didn't feel like kissing a man at all. Kissing a woman brings me the closest I've ever felt to being safe and having a sense of belonging.

"...just shut your mouth ... snot-nosed crybaby..."

I started growing my hair in 1992. I didn't grow it because I wanted long hair; I grew it because I was so fucking sick of being mistaken for a boy. I thought that if I had long hair, maybe I could at least fit in a bit more on the outside even if I still felt out of place on the inside. It largely worked, too. For everyone else, that is. I grew to hate how unlike me my hair felt — it didn't feel as though it belonged with my self-image. And yet I was terrified of having it cut too short. I took comfort from the perceived fitting in, even though I often felt like I was wearing some kind of disguise. I gained the confidence to break away from this image when I started to question my sexuality. I found through coming out that not only was it okay to be myself but that there were thousands of other women like me. When I was a teenager I grew my hair to fit in so that I wouldn't be bullied as much. I kept it long until two years ago, and cutting it off then was symbolic of me moving away from caring about impressing others and conforming to their notions and ideals of femininity. I can't imagine growing it long again.

I don't experience overt homophobia in my life nearly as often as I experience difficulty because of my nonconformity to a rigid gender binary and the definitions within this that dictate that boys will look a certain way and girls will look another way. I experience way more discrimination on a regular basis because of my supposed "masculine" exterior than I do because I date women. There's such a narrow viewpoint in PEI of what a woman or a man should look like. And I'm not just talking about the 1980s — I'm talking about today, too. It absolutely astounds me how often I am mistaken for a man.

Once I was at a walk-in medical clinic because I was having asthma-related difficulties. I spoke with the receptionist and found out that there were a lot of people ahead of me. I stood near the receptionist and texted my partner — the clinic was only open for three hours that evening, so I was weighing whether I should stay at the clinic or go to the hospital. The receptionist seemed put out that I hadn't sat down, even though I was a full metre away from her window and was in no way blocking anyone who might want to approach her. I had been standing there, quietly using my phone, for maybe one to two minutes when she leaned out of the window she sat behind and curtly said, "Sir?"

I looked around the room at the other twenty or so people, unsure who she was addressing. She then repeated "Sir?" much louder, and most of the people in the room looked up. I looked toward her as well and was rather surprised to find that it was me she was addressing.

I said, "Me?"

She responded, sounding rather annoyed, "Yes, you, sir. Why are you standing?"

I said, "I was trying to decide if I should stay here or go to the hospital." I was so embarrassed that I handed the form she had given me upon my entry into the clinic back to her and said, "You just made my mind up for me."

Now, I totally get that I don't fit perfectly into the female gender mould … but I also certainly don't fit perfectly into the male gender mould, so why do people constantly try to pigeonhole me into one or the other? I left the medical clinic with my head down, unable to make eye contact with any of the people in the room who I felt knew I was not a "sir." I was mortified and angry. Why did she have to call me by a term that denotes a specific gender? Why couldn't she have just said "Excuse me?" I ended up going home, rather than to the hospital, even though I clearly needed medical attention. I was admitted to the hospital the following day — the doctor in the ER told me I should have come in a week ago.

"...you better run FAST..."

When I was in high school there was a girl who used to hit on me a lot. It was clear that she wanted me. Really, I probably could have gone for it and saved myself years of confusion. I didn't, though; I was very insecure, unsure about my sexuality and not at all into her. But somehow it got out around school that I had slept with her. The screwed up thing about it is that the girl and I experienced completely different reactions from our classmates. She was seen as this ultra-hip bi girl (experimental and cool), whereas I was ostracized and picked on even more. I was the perverted dyke, not cool and sexually adventurous like she was. I'm sure this incident kept me in the closet a number of years longer than I would have been if I hadn't experienced it. It cemented for me, once again, that it wasn't okay to be gay in my town and that I would experience even more social problems if I decided to pursue my feelings for women. And really, who wants to be socially rejected and beaten up more? I sure didn't. I wanted to be liked and accepted, even if that meant burying my feelings for women and trying to be with men.

"...worthless ... no one will ever love you ... how could they..."

It felt so natural for me to be attracted to women that I assumed there must be other women who felt as I did. I had no idea how to find them, though. I felt I had no one to talk to, confide in or turn to. There were no available resources for LGBTQ people that I knew of when I was a teenager. Most people were so vocally homophobic that I would never have felt safe enough to ask for help. Because I had no outlet as a teen, it has become very important to me to help support gay-straight alliances in schools and other youth-focused support programs today.

Today, when I think of my adolescence, especially ages fifteen to nineteen, I still wonder how I got through it — how I didn't end up killing myself, intentionally or unintentionally, through risky behaviour due to my own lack of concern about my well-being; how I didn't end up in an addictions facility; how I managed to not run away permanently. I did run away a few times — I just didn't go far enough. I somehow always remained on the island I grew up on. I think I knew that a lot of what I was dealing with had been ingrained in me, so it didn't matter where I went … all of the shit would still follow me. I could never get away from the hatred and harsh words in my head.

"...just wait ... you won't see it coming..."

One of the best tools I had to help me cope was the ability to easily reach an emotional numbness. I can shut down like it's an Olympic sport I've trained my whole life to be the best at. It's a survival tool I developed as a child. When you're being beaten and you pass the point where you are able to tolerate it physically or mentally, something changes — you either freak out or you go numb. You either viciously begin to fight back or you shut down and take it. My body automatically goes into "play dead" mode in these situations. I think this is my ingrained response because as a child you can't really fight back if the person attacking you is an adult — it would be futile — but to act as though their actions no longer affect you does work. Sometimes it even makes them stop.

"...you haven't felt pain yet..."

I have dated men. It was not an attempt to fit in or conform to societal expectations. It was not a game. It was not a lie. It was all I knew.

I was attracted to women, but it hadn't even entered my mind until my late twenties that I could have a sexual relationship, let alone a *life*, with a woman. I just thought this was part of who I was, that I was more attracted to women than men. It never occurred to me that I was *lying* or that anyone else might think I was until I came out and people started calling me a liar and telling me that I was deceitful and cruel. I had actually been as honest and open as I could with the few people to whom my sexuality was any of their business. Plus, as far as I knew there weren't even any women to date in Summerside when I was a teen in the nineties. Really, I don't know of that many women who are openly gay there *now.*

So, like every other girl in my town, in my teens I dated guys. I won't say there weren't times when I felt I would have liked to try being with a woman, because there were, but it didn't seem like a realistic step. I got married when I was twenty-seven because it felt like the right thing to do — we got along well and we wanted kids. When I ended my marriage, I did so with the conviction that it was the absolutely right decision for all parties involved. I ended it with the same conviction that I entered it with. I stand by the fact that the only decision I made was to live openly and to accept my sexuality — thereby giving my ex the chance to find a more suitable partner, allowing myself to find happiness and setting a positive example for my children by showing them that they should never stay in a relationship they're not happy in simply to please other people. Still, though, an incredible number of 'friends' and 'family' felt wildly betrayed by my decision. I felt as though they were lining up to tell me how horrible they thought I was. They still periodically come out of the woodwork to tell me how much of a bitch I am.

I think the best thing about coming out was that I could be myself — my real self — for the first time in my life. I could be a woman who played sports, was strong, dated women and didn't wear dresses. Talk about liberating! I'm not sure exactly when I recognized that I didn't actually want to be a boy, but my outlook changed drastically when I did. I may have only fully recognized and accepted that I didn't want to be a boy when I came out at thirty-one and found that I could be all of the things I wanted to *and* have a girlfriend. That's when I understood that what I wanted wasn't to be a boy. What I wanted was access to the privileges that our society gives to boys. It's even more than that, though; it's also about wanting the same freedoms that heterosexual couples have. I'm talking about simple privileges like walking down the street with a woman's hand in mine (without the jeers) and not having my sporting and intellectual abilities negatively judged on sight, to the (unfortunately) complex ones like raising my children with my partner and having the freedom to marry the person I love and having the same legal rights as heterosexual couples.

"...you'll never be able to take care of yourself..."

Someone told me recently that my past is still a part of me. My initial reaction to this statement was anger — extreme anger, like, why would you say such fucking bullshit to me when we're supposed to be friends, livid kind of anger. I want to deny any connection to my past, fight it and distance myself from the rage, isolation, shame and separateness that my childhood instilled in me. I don't want to be that kid who feels worthless anymore and I haven't yet learned to empathize with and care about that version of me. All I want to do is detach myself from that kid. Even *I* didn't want to look at the awkward ugly kid with the bad hair who was trapped somewhere horrible in the middle of the male-female spectrum.

Yet there is truth in the statement that my past is a part of me, and as much as I (successfully or not) try to distance myself from the things and the people who hurt me, I also recognize that a great deal of my strength comes from surviving my youth. As I move from the rawness of the pain, I see that it also shaped me, my values and my morality, along with my fear and distrust. A lot of the stuff I experienced taught me how I don't want to be, how I don't want to raise my kids, and what qualities I appreciate most in others and in myself.

I guess the trick is not to let your past become your present. *Way easier said than done!* Puppies help me. If I could live my adolescence over again I don't think I would. In fact I don't think anyone could pay me enough to go back to those years. The trials of those days were among the hardest of my life and keeping my head above water was challenge enough. I'm lucky to be here, breathing, today.

I'd love to know how to have less hatred and anger. I'd love to say that I'm totally adjusted and that I no longer feel difficulties because of my childhood, but that would be a lie. I walk around with so much anger sometimes that I feel I could explode and kick the shit out of anyone who crosses me. Half of the time I'm fine and the other half I have no idea what to do with my emotions, how to keep them under control or how to accept the terms of my life — like that I only get to see my children half of the week and that the other half they spend with my ex and his partner, and I have no idea what they're doing or how they're feeling during that time. Any parent would likely find this difficult, but for someone like me who hasn't figured out how to emotionally navigate the world, it's a nightmare. I've taken up boxing to try to release some of my aggression. It helps, but it's a temporary fix.

I still have a hard time believing that anyone will love me at all, let alone forever or unconditionally. I don't know that I'm capable of complete trust. Is anyone really, though? It's probably not normal that I expect the people I care about to break my heart, if I even ever let them in, and betray me to the fullest while they're at it. That said, though, I am trying. I have a fantastic partner who I adore and plan to marry. She helps me raise my kids and she's a great mom to them, too. I think I try to undo some of the difficulties of my teen years by striving to be a good parent and partner. One thing my kids definitely have is a ton of love and support in both their homes.

"...can you even imagine the shame? ... I'd rather have a murderer for a son than a fag..."

So, I keep writing, studying, kicking the shit out of a heavy bag, running until my asthmatic lungs want to give out and trying, every now and then, to love, even though I'm afraid. It's like when the bathwater is too fucking hot, but I know that if I ease my way in, I may never want to get out again, so I keep testing it a little bit more in case the right time is now.

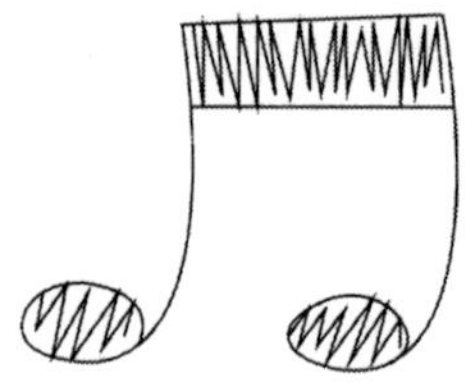

THESE MEMORIES CAN'T WAIT

by Jamie Fitzpatrick

Picture a twelve-year-old boy running as fast as he can.

His brown hair lifts in the breeze. His unzipped windbreaker flaps back around his arms. If you run with him, and if the street is quiet, you'll hear him singing under his breath to the *slap-slap* rhythm of his sneakers.

The boy has to run because lunch period is almost over and he can't be late for history. It would be the second time this week. Nearing the school he leaps a ditch and cuts through the tall grass behind the parking lot. The rhythm changes to *swish-swish*. Kids linger outside the school, kicking at pebbles and enjoying the spring sun. Mr. Philpott smokes in his car. The boy slows to a walk and takes a soggy ham-lettuce-and-mayonnaise sandwich from his pocket. Downs it in four bites.

He's at his desk in time for history, shirt collar damp and sweat rolling down his sides, the sandwich hard in his chest like he swallowed a marble.

"Alright there, Fitz?" Mr. Philpott eyes him, arms folded across his green blazer.

"Yes, sir," the boy croaks, still catching his breath. Everyone laughs.

It's all worth it. By racing home at lunchtime he got to hear his favourite song *three times.*

Why run? What's he chasing? The song isn't going anywhere. It won't expire. It's always waiting. Side one, cut two. A slice of black vinyl. Its magical grooves gleaming when held to the light. Needle ready to drop on his older brother's turntable.

The boy doesn't consider these questions. He doesn't have time. He's twelve and life is moving fast. The questions that concern him are more urgent and probably don't have answers. Like the question of a girl named Marilyn. She's been in his class since kindergarten with Miss Greening. But kindergarten was a lifetime ago. Everything before right now feels like a lifetime ago.

The song talks about a girl but that's not why it's his favourite. It's his favourite because it's amazing. It contains some kind of private message. Not in the words exactly. In the *feel* of it. It's full of wonder and dread and pain. It feels hot and cold. It's ecstatic and a bit stomach sick. The song loves and hates itself.

Thankfully the word *love* never appears in the lyrics.

He can't separate the song from Marilyn. He can't control how he feels and the loss of control excites him. He's running just to keep up.

* * *

For a long time you've been imagining a very particular scene. It's not even a scene. It's a moment. In this imagined moment you arrive somewhere, a strange empty place without colours or dimensions. Marilyn arrives at the same time. She looks up and sees you. Looks right at you. That's it. Nothing else happens.

You feel like you've been watching her half your life. There was summer vacation when you didn't see her at all, but that didn't help. Now it's a new school year and you really are alone with her. Because you won't act in the school play.

You were in last year's play. Had a small part as a foolish old priest so you put on a shaky voice and walked like you just shit yourself. Everyone laughed and Mrs. Cochrane said they were supposed to laugh. She said you were very authentic. But for reasons you can't explain, you refuse to act again. Mrs. Cochrane can't change your mind so she assigns you to the stage crew.

It's you and Marilyn staying after school to paint the big canvas flats that will be the backdrop for this year's production of *Our Town.* You arrive at the auditorium as she and Mrs. Cochrane are spreading drop sheets over the stage floor. Marilyn has a smooth shell of yellow hair and a floppy red T-shirt that hangs past her butt. Probably got it from her dad.

Sometimes the other boys talk about girls. You've never heard Marilyn mentioned so maybe she isn't pretty. *Pretty* is another suspect notion. Not as bad as *love* but you're not ready to trust it. You say the word out loud to yourself. *Pretty.* Roll it around in your mouth, testing it like a jawbreaker.

Mrs. Cochrane shows you paint and brushes, turpentine and rags, then disappears down the hall to the staff room. Then you're watching Marilyn pour paint, thick ripples of blue folding into the tray before her. She won't look up or chat any more than necessary. You'd be disappointed if she did. Marilyn isn't one of those smiley, sunny girls.

This isn't the imagined scene because it's happening in a real place with paint and brushes and a paint smell and Marilyn stopping to blow her nose because there's a cold going around. This scene can't stop. It has to move forward. From songs and TV shows you know that everything changes when a boy and girl are together. They ought to end up kissing unless there's a very good reason not to.

You don't know what to do with this information. But as you watch Marilyn apply herself to the job, back straight and eyes serious, barely a glance your way, a plan takes shape.

The plan originates with stories told by your brother. He says kids in big cities go to huge concerts held in giant arenas and football fields. A type of mass hysteria erupts at these events, with boys and girls helpless to resist the music's hypnotic grip. It sounds like something from *Boris Karloff Tales of Mystery*, your favourite comic. Your brother says some concerts go on for days at a time with kids dancing and rolling in the mud. Boys kiss girls they don't even know. Some even take off their clothes.

Your brother can talk a lot of crap. But you've seen pictures on album covers that back up these stories. A typical picture shows a band playing and a mob of hairy kids pressing towards the stage. There are always hands reaching from the mob, as if in desperation. A need to make contact with the music.

Your plan also involves Bobby Morrow. Bobby is in grade ten. He knows music and has the near-sacred task of assembling tunes for Friday's junior high dance.

Bobby spends most of his free time alone at a cafeteria table making art. He decorates textbooks and notebooks with demons and wizards at play, knights and knaves waving broadswords, handmaidens and noblewomen cradling goblets in bejewelled hands, horses, unicorns, birds of prey and the like. He caught shit when a teacher saw the inside cover of his math book with its long-lashed mermaid rendered in precise detail, gloriously topless.

"Bobby?"

"Hey." He doesn't look up from his work, which is hidden by a curtain of black hair that brushes the table.

"You're doing the dance, right? So I guess you're all ready with the music and stuff?"

"Pretty ready, yeah."

"Do you need a song? I mean, there's this song…"

"You wanna hear something?"

"Yeah. There's a song. I mean, not too early 'cause it's best if it's at the right time, you know?" This is hopeless. You're not making any sense.

Bobby's pen stops. He looks up and pushes the curtain across his spotted forehead. His eyes are obscured by the glare from his John Lennon glasses.

"Who's the girl?"

On Friday night you wear your jean jacket. You're still thrilled to have a jean jacket, a major victory in the clothing wars with Mom and Dad. Your very first school dance was last year but that was before you had a jean jacket. The most astonishing thing about that night was how they turned the lights down low. The world is a different place with the lights down low.

Marilyn is in a blue checked shirt. This is perfect because almost everyone is wearing a checked shirt, a jean jacket, or both. As long as you blend into the crowd you can work up the nerve to follow your plan. You arrived alone and you've scouted out the other guys from your class. Most of them are clustered at the canteen like moths seeking light.

Suddenly the song begins. Louder than you've ever heard it, a deep rumble from huge speakers at the front of the gym. *No, Bobby! Not yet!* This is *not* the plan. Bobby didn't listen. You haven't had time to size up Marilyn's position. You haven't seen her dance, haven't seen if she wants to or if other boys want to ask her.

The first verse is already over. The song is melting away. You rush to the table where girls are sitting in a closed circle, drinking pop.

"Wanna dance?"

A moment's confusion. They can't hear you. *What did he say? He wants to dance? Who with?* By the mercy of dumb luck Marilyn is directly in front of you across the table. You extend a hand and immediately feel like a complete knob. Your stomach drops so fast you might have to run for a bathroom stall.

Marilyn does the only thing she can do, which is climb over the tangle of chairs and legs — it takes forever — and head for the dance floor.

The chorus is coming around again by the time you get there. There's still the bridge, another verse and the chorus twice. You believe — some part of you *knows* — that Marilyn has never heard the song before. You'll be able to watch her as she takes it in for the first time.

You're recovering. Your insides are still liquid but the song is good for dancing. You and Marilyn ease into its slipstream.

She shakes this way and that and you step forward and back. She looks around a bit but not at you. She turns all the way around. Does she have a nice ass? You've heard other boys talk about nice asses, but would you know one if you saw it?

You're alone with Marilyn and the song. Surrounded by other kids, of course. But dancing has shut out the rest of the world. That's the idea, isn't it? The thought of shutting out the rest of the world is thrilling and terrifying. Marilyn looks neither thrilled nor terrified. But maybe she's like you, with all kinds of emotional chambers waiting to be filled.

Then it's the chorus twice and the third one that fades out. And somehow you've missed it all. You wanted to see her face during the last verse, the part where the singer is nearly shouting and you always get goosebumps. But you missed it somehow. Everything happened so fast.

Marilyn smiles and almost looks straight at you. Gives a little wave. Then she's back with her group. Two of her friends are laughing, probably at you, and in that moment you hate girls. All of them.

A new songs starts before you can escape the dance floor. It has a relentless, lumbering rhythm. Everyone else is gone and you're standing there alone like an idiot. As casually as you can, you back up, turn around and jog to the front of the room as if urgently needed. That's where Bobby Morrow commands his stereo array, a speaker on either side of him. The speakers have a polished wood finish but it's fake. It's a vinyl covering like wallpaper. You can see it peeling away at the corners.

Nobody can dance to the new song and nobody tries. Bobby doesn't care. He thrusts his head forward, black hair tossing with every emphatic nod of his chin. He's oblivious to the room. As if to prove it, he performs an almost feminine wiggle with his hips and hands. Flexes his long artist's fingers.

The song warns that females must be approached with caution. They're fickle. They like diamonds and pearls. They can be fun — they can go *wild* — but this is also when they're most dangerous.

Eddie Skinner is at Marilyn's table and the girls seem to be talking to him. It looks awkward because the music is so loud.

Could you go over there and talk to Marilyn? Look her in the eye and say *Hey* or *Whaddayat* without the refuge of the dance floor? Without a song to back you up? No way. Talking to a girl is like going to a strange country where they speak the same language and the words are supposed to have the same meanings, but the more you talk the worse it gets, until you don't understand anything.

You could go get a Coke and talk to the guys. But you can't face the harsh light of the canteen. You remind yourself that you're wearing the jean jacket and absently lift a hand to brush the denim.

Bobby Morrow sees you and shouts, "Great pick, man!" A few minutes later your song comes ringing from the big speakers again. It's hammering in your chest and stomach, even in your balls when the bass hits a low note. But it's not the same. You know every drum roll and jangling guitar chord, every swinging dip in the singer's voice. But you don't ask Marilyn to dance, don't share Bobby's urge to close your eyes and jerk your head.

The euphoria of the last few weeks has lifted. The song is over. It won't make you run anymore.

* * *

The boy reclines on the basement couch, drops his hands over his head and gazes at the ceiling. He's finding patterns in the stucco. He's not sure if the patterns are there or if he's imagining them. The glare from his glasses doesn't help. He polishes them on a shirtsleeve, stripping the lenses of their oily film. That makes the glare worse.

The music is wild. The stereo bristles with it. Speaker cones whirr and honk and shake inside their pressboard cabinets. Last week one of the speakers went for a walk and tumbled off its cinderblock stand.

A crackling interlude as the record pauses between tracks. It resumes with towering chords of church organ followed by squiggling synthesizers. The boy doesn't know what synthesizers are. But sci-fi sounds that can't be identified are usually attributed to them.

The basement room was finished to his brother's specifications, the stucco roughly applied so little icicles of it hang down and cast shadows. The floor is a sea of blue shag and white walls are flecked with blue and silver sparkles. The boy had his friend Terry over and they agreed that being in the room is probably like being on drugs. With his brother gone away to work all summer the boy has full use of the room with its stereo and record box. The furnace cuts in and out behind the far wall, leaving the room musty and tropical. That corner is dotted with the husks of long-dead carpenter beetles.

This music is insane. He pulled it from the box because there's a skinny flaxen-haired guy on the cover looking dead serious. There's no singing but the band is going crazy with drums slapping and the bass all fuzzy and shrieking guitar. It's all about the flaxen-haired guy and his keyboards. Synthesizers squiggling up and down and around like you're on a carnival ride. Then a quiet piano bit and it could be classical music with guys in tuxedos until the squiggles cut in again and ringing bells and a plaintive lilt that reminds the boy of a Robin Hood movie.

Terry called it "bumblebee music" and said the synthesizers sounded like "spaceman farts." He wanted to go out and play catch, but the boy wouldn't go, so Terry went home. He's just scared. Scared of the cool basement air and the druggy feeling in the room. Scared of the patterns in the stucco because maybe they aren't really there. Scared of all the stuff that's bigger than both of them.

* * *

Michael Grimes is the first guy in your grade with long hair. Not just unkempt, should-have-been-cut-a-week-ago hair. The real thing. Blond ringlets tumbling over his shoulders and trailing in his wake as he strides the school corridors in his weathered cowboy boots.

It's the late 1970s. Long hair is critical. You're through with the barbershop, with its respectable grandfather smells and ancient oils and powders. The predatory hiss of the hydraulic chair. Electric clippers crawling around the ears and up the back of the neck. Barbershops are for little boys. From now on shags and fringes will go unchecked, looping off in all directions. Everyone wants Michael's billowing, freshly washed rock 'n' roll curls. A look both primitive and hyper-modern, hostile and beatific.

Michael is new. Just arrived from Ontario. There are rumours of an absent parent. Maybe his father is gone, replaced by an unshaven, liquor-swilling interloper. You have been raised to honour the conventional mom-and-dad unit. A label like 'stepfather' or 'stepmother' evokes the shadowy world of a Bogart movie. Wolfish men and hysterical women. Tear-stained hankies, stolen kisses and murderous glances. Desire unleashed and respectability squandered. Very cool stuff.

Michael doesn't talk about his family but his stories command an audience from the first day: the band he used to sing in back home, the two girls fighting over him, a neighbour's car borrowed for a late-night joyride. He works his outlaw status. Works the hair, too, setting it in motion with a toss of his head. A knowing grin splits his lean face.

All you guys are looking leaner these days. Faces once smooth with baby fat have grown long. Eyes are hollowing and shaping. Chins and cheekbones emerge and show tufts of fuzz. Limbs sprout and it's a struggle to keep spaghetti arms and oversized feet under control. You squint hard through smudged horn-rimmed glasses and carry your head like a pigeon, poked out, trying to get a read on the path before you.

Slouching and sprawling, you try on various attitudes of contempt. You quit Boy Scouts and minor hockey. Skip church. Smoke cigarettes. Frown with deep seriousness. Tell dirty jokes and practice a new laugh, guttural and manly. Refuse to zip your jacket.

The private changes are even more acute. Your fantasies are astonishing, a delirium of substitute French teachers, sitcom starlets and other unattainables. There have been orgasms, not all of them involuntary. The shock of the new is everywhere.

You grope about seeking the end of childhood. Surely it must be around here somewhere.

With so few resources at hand you have claimed music as a guide and sought out like-minded compatriots. Together you pursue the next song, the next album, the next band like your lives depend on it. When the music plays you aren't lost. You are pioneers, ready for the vastness before you and the vastness beyond.

The arguments are endless. Beatles or Stones? The Who or Led Zeppelin? Black Sabbath or Deep Purple? Eric Clapton or Jimmy Page? Mick or Keith? John or Paul? Arguments so fierce it feels like civilization itself might hang in the balance.

The same debate threads through high schools the world over. That's fine with you guys. You don't want to distinguish yourselves from the rest of the world. You want to *join* the world. The records you covet are made in London, New York and Los Angeles or exotic, rustic locales like Texas and Georgia. That's the world. Newfoundland is nowhere, boring and backwards. Embarrassing, with its comical accents, toothless baymen and dumbass Newfie music. Michael Grimes says he's blowing this dump as soon as he's allowed to quit school. Not going back to Ontario, though. Setting out for parts unknown. Probably start another band. He reclines as he says this, tilting a chair back and propping a boot on the teacher's desk. Michael's jeans are skin tight, mashing his crotch into lumps. Sort of like Robert Plant in that Zeppelin concert film.

Radio is hopeless, full of squealing teenybopper hits, and country and western hurtin' songs. The supply of real music is limited to a few department store shelves. You haunt these shelves after school, mentally cataloguing new releases. Funds are scarce so you can only linger over the sacred objects, fondling them in their shrink-wrap. Anxiously you await Christmas or your birthday, maybe an unexpected windfall from a generous grandparent.

The purchase of a new record is an event. *Paul bought the latest Clapton! Doug got* Blood on the Tracks *for his birthday!* The names and titles alone can set imaginations on fire.

All hands gather in a bedroom or split-level basement where

juvenile relics are still on display. The board games and model airplanes. The comic books that once consumed entire Sunday afternoons.

The record cover is closely examined. How do the artists present themselves? Do they glower with grave purpose, or grin maniacally, or bash their guitars under brilliant coloured lights? You compare your hair to theirs. Or perhaps there are no cover photos at all. Just cryptic, loopy artwork suggesting great depths of meaning. It all seems to come from a mystical land of youth, glamour and urgency.

The room is close with the funk of excitable boys, their wrinkled shirt-tails hanging out and zit-clogged foreheads furrowed. Winter afternoon fades to twilight. The opening chords rattle the "hi-fi" — a cabinet the size of a small casket — or snake from a pair of Radio Shack speakers.

There are moments of air guitar and occasional grunts of approval — *wicked, man!* — but mostly you listen. Ears open up to vast, undiscovered lands of the imagination. Lands rich with enlightenment and liberation. At its most sublime — maybe when a voice takes an ominous turn or a guitar solo climbs up an octave — the music finds a deep unknown headspace. You give yourself to it. Go with it.

"Okay, dear. I think it's time those boys went home for their dinner."

"But Mom! It's the new album! We gotta hear side two!"

"Has someone been smoking in here? I better not catch you with cigarettes, young man."

"No. But—"

"Those sneakers! How many times do I have to tell you? I just had those carpets done!"

"But Mom, we were just—"

"And turn off that music right now, please. You father will be home any minute."

"Okay. Sorry, guys."

Out the door to greet the end of the day. Streetlights glowing. Cheeks stinging and wind freezing in your nostrils. Icy sidewalks take you home to a steamy kitchen with its boring dinner and homework. But your confidence isn't shaken. Music is an interior journey. It will deliver you beyond Mom. Beyond dinner and muddy sneakers and your-father-will-be-home-any-minute to a place where authority is deflected with a knowing smirk and a toss of blond curls. You will live in a different world, the one you hear when the records play. You can't explain how or what it will look like. But you know you'll get there.

On the first school day after Christmas you're all gathered in the hallway between classes, brandishing your latest treasures. The new year is rich with new music for after-school listening.

Michael Grimes slumps against the wall, his legs extended to obstruct traffic until Mr. Nolan arrives with his "Break up the party, boys." Michael's anecdotes have grown richer and more finely detailed. Mythic Ontario tales of parties and beer and blowjobs and petty crime sprees that foil the cops and scandalize the parents. You wonder what it's like to have that hair, to sing in a band, to be pursued by *two* girls. It hardly seems possible. Ontario is far away, across the water and in the middle of the real world. Maybe girls are different there.

"Lemme see," says Michael. He grabs one of the fresh records. Runs his fingers over the creamy white facade — the cardboard is of a smoother, more substantial stock than most record covers — and squints at the embossed logo in the centre.

"Bunch of fruits," he says. "English faggots. Fag music."

He laughs and you all laugh along, knowing you are meant to. The prejudices of a small white town are supposed to be invisible. Left unspoken so they never have to be challenged. Michael doesn't know this or doesn't care.

"Real music," says Michael, "*honest* music is made by real dudes rocking out on real guitars." He flicks a dismissive hand across the album cover. "Not fruits prancing around in silk jumpsuits."

Real music is Pink Floyd because they were "so totally smoked up, totally wrecked when they made that album." Real music is Zeppelin because they get "down and dirty with the nigger music." The most real music of all is heavy metal because it's for guys only. Girls hate it. "It keeps the bitches at bay," Michael says.

He laughs and you all laugh along. As long as you're laughing you don't have to think.

The regimented confines of high school keep the Michael myth intact. Elsewhere he falters. He bums cigarettes, pocket change and snacks. *Leech* is the whispered verdict. He claims to have an inside track on black hash from Toronto but nothing comes of it. He trashes Jane Kennedy's house party, swinging a hockey stick around the kitchen. After that he's excluded from weekend plans. He barely makes it through grade ten, then he's gone. Blowing this dump, striking out for parts unknown.

He's back within a year, passing through town with his new best buddy, a tattooed pothead named Frank. They scrounge and steal, sleep on basement floors and gnaw on a giant ham from the grocery store. Frank just grabbed it and walked out in broad daylight. It's a good story. But nobody wants Michael's stories anymore.

Their final showing is a midsummer party at Jeff and Howie Buchan's house. Frank carries the remains of the ham in a knapsack. He shows off ten grimy pockmarks on his arm, a self-inflicted cigarette burn for each day he spent in jail last year. Passes out in a patio chair. Michael is shirtless and stoned, babbling non-stop to anyone who can't dodge him. He pushes through a crowd on the front step and out to the lawn where he performs an inebriated jig. The Stones blast full volume from the house. Michael leaves a trail in the dewy grass. His jeans are soaked up to the knees. He shuffles and jerks like a marionette, beer held high and foaming over. "Come on," he shouts. But it's just Michael out there. Pale chest thrust forward. Hair still angelic, wisps of it fluttering in the streetlight's glow.

* * *

The boy is running again. But it's treacherous. He skids and slips and churns through the slush with his parka flung open and boots half-zipped. Around the square where grinding snowploughs are freeing the town from last night's storm. He climbs the drift blocking the alleyway next to Moonlight Restaurant. Gets through the alley, crosses a street, staggers over a final slick lump of snow and finds the modern world.

Opening day at the new record store. Sam the Record Man. Just like Toronto! It's a tiny place. Smaller than McGrath's Convenience where the boy plays pinball. But it's all music. Walls and racks and shelves of it. Boxes of it not even opened yet. The sound and smell of *new.* Fresh plastic and carpet and paint. Opening his mouth to let it in, the boy feels new music on his tongue. He can almost chew it. There's a guy behind the counter with tinted glasses and a gold chain nestled in the hairy open neck of his denim shirt. It's just Chris

Sooley who worked in his dad's furniture store. But he's not just Chris anymore.

The sudden heat of the store presses on the boy, making him aware of the damp winter breeze that has been blowing through him since he left home. He sweats and his teeth chatter. Snow melts in his half-zipped boots. A young woman is climbing a stepladder to fuss with the window display. She holds a record with a bright cover, its title announced in sugary Christmas hues of brilliant green on candy red: *Talking Heads 77*. The boy is seventeen years old and a dutiful reader of music magazines. He's never heard Talking Heads but knows them to be a "critical sensation" on "New York's burgeoning punk scene." The young woman is skinny and short and has to stretch up high to clip the album to a wire. The butt creases of her jeans are worn white and the stretch exposes a sliver of pink flesh. The boy knows he will spend his precious savings on *Talking Heads 77*.

His bedroom fills with the glare of untouched snow. Outside his window it's deep enough to bury fences, merging backyards up and down the street. It's perfect for snowballs. Wet and sticky and thick as snot. The boy pulls the curtain, reducing the glare to a muted glow. He peels off wet socks and shoves them under the bed out of his mom's sight. Sits in his dead grandmother's rocking chair. He likes to rock while he listens, facing the speakers and the posters on the wall above. Peter Frampton, Linda Ronstadt, Freddie Mercury. The faint outline where Bobby Orr used to be.

He listens. Feels a crawling disappointment begin in his legs and move north. By the third song it's lodged in his throat. How *small* this band sounds. The dinky plinky guitars. Drums doing the pitter-patter of a child's music box. And that singer. The nasally squeak of a kid destined to get the crap kicked out of him after school.

What the hell? Where's the affirmation? The defiance? The drama? The soaring chorus that makes the boy close his eyes and shout along even when he knows his brother can hear and will tease him mercilessly? (*Hey Bruce! Working on "Born to Run" today, Bruce? Where's your leather jacket, Bruce?*)

The boy's mind is wandering back to the store and the girl on the stepladder. Which means this absurd candy-coloured album is a failure. It delivers none of the euphoria he expects from a song. There's no immediate rush. No grandiose pronouncements of youthful vigour and hope and triumph. Maybe the dorky singer is trying to be funny. This possibility makes the boy flinch with embarrassment.

He wishes he had opted for the Sex Pistols. Punks who look the part, sticking to familiar motifs and poses. The girl was hanging that cover in the store window too and when she reached for it a hipbone escaped her jeans. The boy looks straight at the speakers and tries to hear Talking Heads again. It's four or five songs in and the singer is whining about indecisive people. It sounds creepy. At least it chases away the image of the girl with her hipbone and relieves the boy of a miserable erection. He stands and parts the curtains. The Vardy kids from next door are out in the winter sun, half-submerged in the snow. Struggling and flopping and falling and pelting each other with clumps of the stuff.

* * *

You're more than ready.

Classes are done early because you skipped psychology. Who gives a shit about second-year psych when the sun is summer-hot on the first Friday in October? When the girls are in T-shirts, stretched out half-asleep on the common, their Lopi sweaters rolled into pillows.

Back to the Rathole on Highland Street. Dennis and Moaner are already there. Already into the last of the beer. You are secretly proud to have a roommate named Moaner, to call him that. You were there when he earned that nickname. First night after you moved in. Moaner got Dirty Red back to his room. He was the one who called her Dirty Red. That's what everyone called her back in school, he said. Back in Halifax. Sitting in the living room that night, listening, you knew you had made the right decision. The debauched life you longed for was finally at hand.

Books are discarded in a sloppy pile behind the door where the cat peed. They've saved you the last Alpine. Not your favourite beer. But still. They're your buddies, Dennis and Moaner. Your mates.

"Cat piss." You say it just to acknowledge it. The smell is different on a hot day after it's had a few weeks to settle in and you sprayed it with all those cleaners. Turns kind of bittersweet. You thought Dennis would kill that cat, grabbing it by the tail. Then the landlord showed up. "Sorry, boys. Sorry." His cat.

You open the beer and thumb through the albums. The music picks are yours. That's understood. Every pick is critical on a Friday afternoon, with the weekend stretched out before you like an open plain. You choose The Police, a new favourite band. You tell the boys — assure them — that no record has ever sounded like this one. In your short life, no record ever has.

The first song is the hit single. The one about horny schoolgirls. Dennis calls them hard-bellies. Talks about where he would stick his fingers and how many would fit. He's disgusting when he goes on about it, which is the point. If Dennis really heard this song he'd love it. But he's not a listener. Neither of them are.

You take turns mocking professors. Foreskin Forsey with his poems and his penguin waddle. Gracie the Mole in sociology. Rasputin, scaring people away from philosophy.

"Can you believe he's married to Lisa in athletics?" says Moaner, stretching out in the greasy rocking chair.

"There's a porn flick you wouldn't pay to see."

"How about Maggie Maclean? I'd pay to see her."

"Who's she?" You're always behind on this stuff.

"Phys ed prof. Runs the ass show."

"The ass show?"

"Volleyball," says Moaner. "She coaches the volleyball team." He stands. "Beer run now, boys."

"Oh my god," says Dennis. "You haven't been to a game? It's worth it to go. Seriously." He makes a throaty noise that could be pain or ecstasy.

You pool crumpled bills and run practiced undergrad lines, the three of you settling in your roles. Talking crude and dumb to keep the world boxed in and manageable. *The arse on that one and did you see what's-her-name in that little blouse when she bent over, it was all hanging out buddy I guarantee you. Some wasted tonight, man. Some wasted.*

Second-year university and some days you still feel like a stranger here. But Dennis and Moaner needed a third to make the apartment happen and you didn't give it much thought. You know them a little and they don't seem like assholes. Dennis proposed a nickname for the three of you: the Epicureans. According to his philosophy class the Epicureans were a crowd of ancients "devoted to their appetites." He's got the right idea but it doesn't catch on. Sounds too smart, like you've been thinking about it. You're not here to think.

You never planned to end up in Nova Scotia. Never heard of this school until grade eleven, but any escape will do. Get out of Newfoundland where the girls wouldn't give you a second look. Where your brother died and the house is still sick with grief. Middle of nowhere. You escaped and your favourite albums came with you. The albums have got your back. You can always turn to them to confirm what you believe in. Experience is more important than meaning. Ambiguity trumps clarity. Decadence is a route to authenticity. Music doesn't just speak to you. It speaks for you.

Sting is singing about waking up in his clothes and trying to figure out where he is.

"Freaky song," says Dennis.

There's a dinner plan if you ever get around to it. A pack of wieners and a brick of cheese. You chop the wieners and fry them up good and greasy. The cheese slices go on top and you keep frying till it's all glued together. Slice like a pizza or hand out forks and eat straight from the skillet for the authentic Rathole experience. Dennis is in the Chevette and off to the liquor store while he's still fit to drive. You get the shower first, then Moaner. He turns up the stereo and dances in a towel. Spots a big brown spider perched on the empty toilet paper roll and nails it with a bar of soap. Perfect shot from across the bathroom.

"Under mah thumb…" Moaner is up on the couch, shouting along with the Stones. He doesn't know the words but that doesn't stop him. He grunts and sputters and makes nonsense Jagger noises until it's time to bark the chorus again. The threadbare towel is patterned with sailboats and foamy ocean waves. His thick belly shakes and his boobs bounce. How does he do it? Is it the way he talks to them? You're always watching for clues but he's elusive. He's at the party. Then he's gone. You get home and there's a girl's jacket on the floor. Maybe her sneakers too.

The skillet is warming on the stove when dinner goes awry. A perfect strip of green runs along one of the wieners like a racing stripe. Dennis squeezes the package, raising bubbles of milky-looking fat.

"Maybe they're okay," you say.

"Want to try one?" Dennis holds the package to your nose. "We'll watch."

"Time to step up to the plate, Fitz," says Moaner. "Time to do

The Heave. We need food."

"I don't know." You're working three shifts a week at The Heave and you get the staff discount on meals. But Mrs. G doesn't like running tabs. "Depends on who's working," you say.

"Gotta try, man. We need every penny for tonight."

Dennis is at the kitchen window throwing rancid wieners into the street. Aiming at parked cars, the fire hydrant, an old lady smoking outside the laundromat, until Moaner grabs the pack and drops it in the garbage.

You've matured together. You and Dennis and Moaner. A year ago you all would have been at it, ducking and giggling when the old lady looked up. A year ago you would have turned on each other, jamming wieners down the other guys' sweat pants. A year ago everyone needed fake IDs. Now it's just you, still seven months short of nineteen.

You're in the street, which is a great idea because you need something to quicken your pulse. Striding the middle of the road, dodging cars, in and out of the sharp autumn sun. Friday turning into Friday night. By the time you get to The Heave somebody across the street will be blaring music from a residence window. Probably AC/DC. Which you love for its big, chunky, dumbass guitar riffs. That's what weekends are like. Big and chunky. Stupid and amazing. You're humming "Back in Black" under your breath.

No sign of Mrs. G. It's Friday after all. No customers either. Just her brother Rollie, perched on a stool outside the kitchen. Raising a cigarette to his red lips with a thin, fine-boned hand. Staring at nothing.

"Jesus!" he says, giving a start as the door squeaks. Rollie is small and nervous with a strip of wet black hair combed over an eggshell scalp. He lives in a little one-room apartment above The Heave. Tonight he'll close up and get drunk in his room. Tomorrow he'll work the morning shift with you, then get drunk down at the Legion.

You join him in the kitchen while he cooks. Rollie drops three patties on the grill, watches them and smokes, spatula in hand. He perches the cigarette on the edge of the grill and grabs three handfuls of fries, tossing them in the deep fry basket. Gobs of fat shoot back at him.

"Jesus!" Rollie shakes his hand. "Put some music on, will ya?"

There's not much on the jukebox. But you pop in a quarter and do the best you can.

"Who's this then?" asks Rollie, scraping and flipping a bundle of blackened onions.

"Seriously?

"Must be The Beatles, is it?"

"Yes, Rollie." You shake you head in disbelief.

He sticks his smoke in his lips and tilts his head back to balance the ash while he turns burgers. A strip of black hair releases from the top and bends over his ear like a weeping willow.

"Had a girl once," says Rollie, who begins many stories with that line. "We'd go to her house and put on her parents' old records. Benny Goodman and Louis Armstrong. Stuff like that."

Her parents' records. That's funny. You imagine Rollie and his girl decked out in their Sunday best. Waltzing around the room like they've got poles up their butts. You can only picture Louis Armstrong as a musical clown in black-and-white film clips. Benny Goodman is just a name. How could anything that old matter anymore?

"Don't tell Mrs. G," says Rollie, handing you bags of food.

"Not a word. I'll cover it tomorrow."

"She counts the patties on Monday. We got to account for every one."

"We'll cover it."

* * *

The Rathole fills with people and beer cases and bottles of screw top wine. Bodies just started walking in while you were eating. A girl you've never seen opens the wine and says, "No corkscrews for us. Why pull it when you can screw it?" You had to leave home to hear girls talk like that.

Then everyone's out in the street kicking through the dead leaves gathered ankle deep along the curb. Back to campus. Residence was okay for a year. But too many disco boys in their disco shirts, playing their shitty disco music at parties. This is better. Dennis and Moaner are both from Halifax and they know lots of girls. Maybe a few will fall your way. Rejects or leftovers. Back home Mom and Dad are suspicious. The three of you out on your own. *Better keep your marks up*, they said.

The campus pub is woozy with body heat. The air is thick on skin, dulling the knife-edge of early evening. The band stinks. They do a really bad Rush cover, a couple of Doors songs. They crucify The Police. You're at the side of the stage, offended and pleased with yourself for identifying the fraud. "These guys suck," you say. Nobody seems to care, but they know you as someone who takes music seriously. You'll take that reputation, though it has yet to impress the girls. The only girl you got anywhere with last year was Patty what's-her-name from Oromocto. She wouldn't kiss you until you shut off the stereo.

"Oh man," you say. "That drummer is just butchering the tempo. Putrid."

This may or may not be true. Your ear isn't attuned to the finer points of drumming and tempo. You don't even know what tempo is, really. But it feels good to display expertise and authority. Everyone needs a calling card. Yours is music and you're sticking with it even if you don't always know what you're talking about. Sometimes you might be faking it. But it's all in the name of a true authentic experience. Only music can deliver that.

You join a breakaway group to a res party, pulled along by a cold wind whipping across the football field. The field is rotten, its grass uprooted and churned to muck. Behind the dining hall a couple makes out and a girl stands alone, waiting for someone or something.

The party has a tropical theme. It's the basement of a girls' residence with cinderblock walls and fat water pipes snaking around overhead. Everyone's skin turns alien green under the lights. You smash your head off a low-hanging water pipe. Girls are handing out plastic cups of sweet reddish-pink stuff. Some of the girls wear bikini tops, exposing belly buttons and chest freckles.

At some point there are joints on the fire escape, where rain drips from the eave and down your neck.

At some point an alien bikini girl uses a water pistol to squirt a stream of something down your throat.

At some point they're handing everyone shots of God knows what. You smash your head again.

They keep playing that day-oh banana boat song. Everyone green and sticking to the floor because the reddish-pink stuff spilled everywhere. Swaying and singing. Screaming.

Sunlight fills the Rathole. Your nose is pressed into the couch inhaling its ancient woolly smell and whatever a thousand bums left behind. Lifting your head you see through to the kitchen and a new hole in the wall, a hole the size of a basketball.

Who's the girl? She slumps at the other end of the couch, one foot on the floor, the other laid across your legs. Not a bikini alien. A blue checked shirt under a blue cardigan. Nobody wears cardigans. Her hair is a mass of brown curls draped behind her. You turn and examine the leg in your lap, a thick strip of ankle exposed between her black sock and the cuff of her jeans.

A network of empty beer bottles on the living room floor, unmoved since the last mouthful was taken. The last thing you recall is convulsive music making plastic cups dance on a table in front of you. Was that here? The party? Maybe you were somewhere else?

"You have no idea who I am, do you?" The girl has her hands over her face and opens them, flashing a peek-a-boo smile. She might be a head case. "I'm Elaine. We're in Poli sci together. With Harris."

She sits up and shrugs out of her cardigan, draws a fistful of hair back from a fully rounded baby face. Her eyes are brown like her hair, her nose long and straight and acne-scarred. It doesn't fit the face. She pulls off her scruffy sneakers and rubs her feet.

"Oh my God," she says, hanging her head.

Floorboards shift, a door squeaks and a redhead exits Moaner's room. Half-smiles at you and heads to the bathroom. You and Elaine listen to her pee and then she calls out, asking if there's any toilet paper. You bring her napkins from The Heave. She opens the door a crack and takes them. The toilet flushes. She's out then, straight for the door without a jacket. You had never considered Dirty Red as a person. In daylight. Peeing and needing paper.

Elaine waits until the door closes.

"Does she live here?"

"No."

"Do you?"

"Yeah. You know Dennis from Halifax? Or Malcolm? Moaner we call him."

"I don't know anyone from Halifax."

Elaine stands and gives each leg of her jeans a tug. She's a big girl. Biggish. Dennis and Moaner would have good sport with that. Still. She's here. She walks to the kitchen, shirt tail flapping. Lots of brown curls. Unexpected girls in unexpected places. There are songs that told you to expect this. Though none of those songs mention acne scars or a strange new hole in the wall or vicious morning sun that makes you feel like throwing up.

"Are there any clean glasses? Wait. Never mind."

The tap runs and she gulps, sighing heavily into a glass.

There's music from Moaner's room. Probably the radio. The Doobie Brothers or some shit. He's cranking it up, the arsehole. The bass notes pound like they're trying to escape.

Elaine is back, kicking beer bottles aside.

"Dance," she says. The bottles roll to the walls as she dips a shoulder and claps twice, shuffling her feet to turn a 360. She's got substance. A thick, rubbery torso, just like Moaner's.

"Come on. Dance."

"I gotta work." But Rollie won't be on time. You'll be standing there waiting when he limps down the steps to open. Wet black hair sticking up everywhere. Sucking his breath mints. Clutching his stomach to squeeze out belches as you prep the burgers and fries and bacon for the Saturday rush.

"This stuff is shit," you say.

"Shit, how?"

"Shitty music."

"So what?" Elaine twirls again, breaks into a little smile. A tangled strand of hair across her mouth. If she were alone in her room, she would probably dance just like this.

"Everyone here likes shitty music," you say.

"Everyone where?"

"Here. The whole campus." That's not entirely true. Randy back in res knows the right stuff. He understands. But Randy's an odd little guy. A loner.

"So," says Elaine. She licks her lips and works her jaw, stretching it out. "What's good music?"

"Something you'd know?"

"Something I'd know."

"Well. Springsteen, I guess. You know Springsteen."

"Sure. We dance to Springsteen." Shoulders rolling up and down. Knees buckling in and out.

"It's not about dancing." You wave in the direction of Moaner's door. "This stuff is commercial shit. Springsteen is so completely … it's real."

"Okay." Elaine stops dancing, which is good. "There's that one Springsteen song. The one where he sings about working in a factory and getting laid off. You know?"

"Sure." Whichever song she's referring to, you don't doubt that you know it.

"Well, he doesn't work in a factory. He's not laid off. He plays guitar and he's a millionaire." The dancing starts again. Shuffling, doing the shoulder thing. "What's so real about that?"

"It's poetic instinct." A phrase you picked up in Currie's English course.

"Is it, now?"

The shoulder thing is nice. Up, down and squeeze. Pushes her breasts together. Her black socks are half off, flapping from her toes.

"Springsteen is a writer. It's a character."

"Well, I'm a character, too," says Elaine, changing her rhythm as the next tune comes thumping from behind Moaner's door. "Love Will Keep Us Together." Another stinker.

Who the hell is this girl? Dancing in a strange house in front of a strange guy on a woozy Saturday morning. Not caring what she looks like or checking for bad breath. Breaking through the hard shell of a girl's inhibitions is a rare feat, one you've been finding nearly impossible.

"What are you doing tonight?" you ask.

"Dancing," she says. "Come on."

She reaches a hand and lets you take it just long enough to raise you from the couch. There's a big smile on her face now. She sticks her tongue out at you. Your head feels swollen to bursting.

You're moving. Lifting your heels and throwing your arms around. But you won't lose yourself to it. Dancing is suspicious. Foolish.

You're so close to Elaine you could reach out and grab her.

She needs a nickname. A nickname will make her more believable and turn her into a story to tell the guys. If you could coax her up on the coffee table you could call her Table Dancer. A label like that gives you control. You can hide your fear behind it. It makes the urge to touch her less terrifying.

Your head is pounding and the room is rank with stale beer and cat pee. You need a shower and you're parched. The song is worse than awful. It's absolutely shameful, a lumpy rhythm fighting through a door. Elaine's cheeks are red and she tosses her feet up to kick off her dirty socks. The socks turn flips and her toenails are blue. You love the toenails. But you're faking the dance, moving just enough to keep her in front of you. Just enough to keep her right there. Maybe until she's up on the table and has her nickname. Until you invent a breezy anecdote that starts with *Girl wakes up next to me* and ends with *Of course I nailed her, right there on the couch.* Though you've never nailed anyone on the couch. Or anywhere else. If this is what it takes you'll dance all morning. No matter what the song. The two of you will dance to the shittiest music in the world.

*   *   *

Tuesday afternoon and the rain is pounding, streams of it racing in the streets and shooting from eaves. It thaws the frozen mud and a winter's worth of dog shit. The boy dashes from the car to the front door and plants a new shoe in a puddle in the porch. Strange plodding music comes from the living room. Richard dozes in the recliner, which is set within reach of the turntable. He's half-naked, wearing cut-off jeans that would barely pass as a loincloth. The recliner is old and doesn't recline anymore. Its yellow vinyl is full of splits and the stuffing inside smells funny, like bug spray or something. Especially on rainy days. The boy will buy a new one if the guys don't beat the crap out of it. He can afford it.

He's hardly a boy anymore. Or so he would argue. Finished grad school. Making good money. Got a car that usually starts and a suit for weddings and meetings. The boy is experienced now. On his second girlfriend. The first one hinted around about moving in and then she dumped him while he was in Ontario finishing his degree. She flew up there to say, "I'm not breaking up with you," and then she flew home and phoned him and said, "Yeah, I am." That was a kick in the stones but at least he had his records. That was a couple of years ago. Now she's pregnant and he's got more records than ever. He'll take his end of that deal any day.

The boy is old enough to have a musical history. He's pretty much done with most of that stuff. The Beatles songs that coloured his every move for about three years. The Neil Young song he used to sing to himself playing street hockey. The hateful Bob Seger record he listened to when his brother died. The Dire Straits album from the first girlfriend. A deep, unhealthy crush on The Rolling Stones has run its course. Springsteen is starting to sound faintly ridiculous. He only liked the Blondie record because his room smelled of sex the first time he heard it.

He's sharing a house. That's not so different from his student days. All the guys have records too, so the stereo is going all day and half the night, stoned or straight, drunk or sober.

He should mop the puddle in the porch or get a bucket under the picture window. But the boy is unnerved by the song, how its droning voice and stubborn rhythm fill the space around him. He drops his wet jacket to the floor and extends a foot to give the yellow recliner a shove.

"What's this?"

"Huh?" Richard blinks.

"What's this album?"

Richard sits up. His bare back peels from the vinyl like tape from a roll.

"It's Talking Heads, you stupid git."

"Really?"

"Of course it is." Richard yawns and strokes the rattail at the end of his goatee.

The boy finds the record cover under an ashtray. It's not *Talking Heads 77*. This one has a plain black façade. The cardboard is flabby with humidity and when the boy sets it down his fingers leave misty prints in the black. The house is always clammy and on a wet day like this he imagines mould blooming in its hidden spaces. Climbing up and around them.

"I don't know it," he says.

"You do so know it."

"I don't."

"Wanker."

"I'm gonna play that song again."

"Flip it over," says Richard. "Side two's better actually."

"No," says the boy. He lifts the needle from the record and pulls it back to repeat the song just ended. He listens and it settles in him like the damp settling into the bent timber and crumbling Gyprock. The band has changed. But not nearly as much as the boy. The hapless seventeen-year-old who couldn't come to grips with *Talking Heads 77* is long discarded, sloughed off like an old skin. It's almost laughable to picture him now, shutting his curtain and hiding his dirty socks from his mom. Alarmed by his strange new record. Miserably erect.

"Not too loud," says Richard, tilting his head back and closing his eyes again. "Nora's asleep."

"Isn't she always," says the boy. "Just gonna play this one more time."

The song is called "Memories Can't Wait" and from that day the boy carries it with him. It's silly and serious, as if the band is playing a gloomy deadpan joke on the listener. He's never had a favourite song like that before. He hardly ever sings it to himself. Almost never thinks about it. It hasn't hooked him. It's more like a burden, one he can't quite get out from under. Sometimes he avoids the song in the same way he occasionally avoids the girlfriend.

Of course it wears itself out. The fine edges of any favourite song are rubbed smooth by repeated listening.

Then it disintegrates.

A creeping atrophy overtakes the boy as years pass. His musical memory hardens and falls away in increments. He lets it fall. He forgets the track listing on *Sgt. Pepper's*. He has no recollection of the Peter Gabriel concert, only the T-shirt insisting he was there. The first REM album is as cold and distant as a betrayed lover. And "Memories Can't Wait" is lost altogether. He can almost summon a relentless groove. An echoing, industrial texture that suggests anxiety. A black record cover. But he can't hum the tune or recall the words.

Without a turntable in the house his original LP is an artefact, tucked in a box, awaiting its inevitable trip to the dump. So the boy Googles the song and dons a headset. He glances over his shoulder, faintly ashamed. It's as if he's looking up an old girlfriend. Excited by the nostalgic tug. Anxious to see what she looks like and recall what it was like to have his hands on her. Flustered by the prospect of an email. Maybe a flirty email.

When the song is over, the final bit lingers with him. It's the only part that doesn't feel rinsed clean of meaning. The part where the band releases the groove for the last time and the singer drifts back in. He sings about being wide awake. The memories are doing it, keeping him awake. He repeats the title over and over, voice climbing until the band grinds to a halt. These memories can't wait.

In those final seconds a remembered scenario takes shape. It's a false memory, but brilliant. A twelve-year-old boy runs fast with "Memories Can't Wait" turning in his mind like a mantra. He's a child playing with nonsense sounds, chanting them over and over as he sprints through the schoolyard. He hears it when he meets Marilyn in a featureless place and she looks up at him. The song stays with him as he watches her pour paint. When he strokes the denim of his new jean jacket. It thunders from the speakers at the school dance, Bobby Morrow jerking his head in time.

"Memories Can't Wait" didn't exist back then. But the vision is alive and brimming with clarity. It will crumble and dissolve at any moment. A kind of musical dementia has set in. The years are collapsing in on each other. The circuitry of memory has broken down, leaving an agitated scattering of thoughts and senses and feelings and moments.

If there's anything credible in this fumbled tangle of image and emotion, it's the twelve-year-old boy at the core. The boy when he was just old enough to have memories and construct a past from them. Why shouldn't he sing a song he can't possibly know? Why should he wait until the band is formed and the record is made and he's old enough to know it? He's absolutely wide awake right now, anticipating all the memories yet to come. He's chasing them down. Memories that can't wait.

BIOGRAPHIES

As a retired blogger of mild renown, **Ben Boudreau** has shared more with the Internet than any sane person should. After being the first cast out of the inaugural CBC Canada Writes top five, he went on to earn three Canadian Weblog Awards and a single tweet from Kelly Clarkson. Recent projects include spending far too much time writing this short bio.

Jo Treggiari was born in London, England, and raised in Canada. She spent many years in San Francisco and New York, where she trained as a boxer, wrote for a punk magazine, and owned her own gangster rap/indie rock record label. Somehow she found herself on Nova Scotia's beautiful, inspiring south shore with her kids and two dogs. Her most recent book, *Ashes, Ashes*, a YA post-apocalyptic adventure, was published by Scholastic Press in 2011.

Chris Benjamin is the author of *Eco-Innovators: Sustainability in Atlantic Canada*, winner of the Best Atlantic-Published Book Award and finalist for the Richardson Non-Fiction Prize, and the novel *Drive-by Saviours*, which was longlisted for Canada Reads and a ReLit Prize. Chris's creative work has been published by VoicePrint Canada, *Descant*, *Arts East*, Third Person Press, Nashwaak Review, Pottersfield Press, Rattling Books, *The Society* and *The Coast*. He owes a debt to St. Lucia for changing his life for the better.

Gerard Collins' first book, the short story collection *Moonlight Sketches*, won the 2012 NL Book Award, and his first novel, *Finton Moon*, has already won the Percy Janes First Novel Award. He's won several arts and letters awards, been shortlisted for the Cuffer Prize and published in *Hard Ol' Spot*, *Zeugma* and various other anthologies. He has been a guest speaker at numerous literary festivals and taught workshops in writing for youth. He has a Ph.D. in English and teaches at Memorial University.

Alison DeLory is a freelance journalist, editor and part-time writing instructor at Mount Saint Vincent University. She enjoys all forms of creative and nonfiction writing. Her children's novel, *Lunar Lifter*, was published in 2012.

Born and raised in Moncton, New Brunswick, **Lee D. Thompson**'s fiction has been published in four anthologies, such as Random House's *Victory Meat, New Fiction from Atlantic Canada* and Vagrant Press's *The Vagrant Revue of New Fiction*, and in more than a dozen literary journals across Canada and the U.S. Lee's first novel, *S. a novel in [xxx] dreams*, was published in 2008 by Fredericton's Broken Jaw Press.

Chad Pelley is an award-winning author, songwriter and photographer from St. John's. His debut novel, *Away from Everywhere*, was a Coles bestseller, won or was shortlisted for several awards, has been adopted by university courses. A film adaptation is underway. His short fiction has been published in journals, textbooks, anthologies, and recognized by several awards. Chad is the founder of Salty Ink, President of the Writers Alliance of Newfoundland & Labrador, and has written for variety of publications, such as *Quill & Quire*, *The National Post* and *Atlantic Books Today*. As a result, he rarely sees more of the world than his computer screen, and his hottest one-night stands happen in his own bed, with books of Canadian fiction.

Patti Larsen is an award-winning middle grade and young adult author with a passion for the paranormal. She is a full-time writer and a part-time teacher of her *Get Your Book Done* program. Patti lives on the East Coast of Canada with her very patient husband and four massive cats.

Cale Liom is a novelist and poet currently living in Prince Edward Island. Her first novel, *Hide Your Life Away*, was nominated for the 2009 Montaigne Medal, was a winner in the General Fiction category of the 2009 Eric Hoffer Book Awards, and a finalist in the 2009 Indie Book Awards. Her first collection of poetry, *A Study in Love*, was published in 2010 and was nominated for a 2011 Golden Crown Literary Society Award, and was shortlisted for a 2012 Island Book Award. Liom is currently working as a paramedic while writing new poems and fiction, and raising children.

Jamie Fitzpatrick's first novel, *You Could Believe in Nothing* (Vagrant Press), has been called "a fast-moving, unsentimental look at amateur hockey, masculinity, mid-life crisis, drink, drugs and family secrets … brisk, engaging and, in the end, very moving." (*Globe and Mail*). His writing has also appeared in *The New Quarterly*, St. John's *Telegram*, Newfoundland Quarterly and the 2013 Cuffer Anthology (forthcoming). He lives in St. John's.

CPSIA information can be obtained at www.ICGtesting.com
Printed in the USA
LVOW11s1705250914

405879LV00006B/920/P